AMERICAN EXPLORATION AND TRAVEL

THOMAS JEFFERSON, AMERICAN TOURIST

THOMAS JEFFERSON
AMERICAN TOURIST

Being an Account of
His Journeys in the United States of America,
England, France, Italy, the Low
Countries, and Germany

by

EDWARD DUMBAULD

NORMAN
UNIVERSITY OF OKLAHOMA PRESS
1946

10508

To the memory of my parents

H. S. D. (1869–1945)

and

L. G. D. (1870–1936)

In te speraverunt patres nostri;
speraverunt, et liberasti eos.

Ideo non confunditur Deus
vocari Deus eorum,
paravit enim illis civitatem.

Preface

❀

ABOOK about Thomas Jefferson's travels has long been
needed. The lack of a complete volume on this subject
became painfully evident to me when, during my student
years in Europe, I sought to follow Jefferson's footsteps as a
sightseer.

Although unfortunately I did not then have at hand a sub-
stantially complete account of Jefferson's journeys such as is now
made available to my readers, I did recapture the delight which
Jefferson had experienced when I visited some of the fascinating
places which had pleased him. The memorable charm of Nîmes
and the Pont du Gard I recall with particular rapture. I found
there the same enchantment which had captivated Jefferson.

Afterwards, when preparation of the present volume had
been undertaken, I enjoyed similar pleasures in those parts of
our own country having associations with Jefferson. Of many
striking scenes I remember these especially: the parking lot and
"hot-dog" stand which I beheld with some dismay on the site in
Philadelphia where the Declaration of Independence was written by Jefferson; the ruins of the house where Jefferson's wedding took place, accessible after a long trudge through mud and
weeds in the seclusion of the Virginia countryside; the first view
of Poplar Forest, at sunset, from a bend in the road; and the
towering majesty of Natural Bridge through morning fogs and
mist.

In addition to information obtained while thus visiting the
places themselves which were connected with Jefferson, the task

of writing this book required gathering data from a multitude of unpublished manuscripts, scattered in many collections, as well as from a vast mass of printed material. Jefferson's voluminous correspondence and account books, in his distinctive and legible handwriting, seemed to reveal the workings of his mind and personality, as well as the details of his daily life.

My interest in public affairs, especially international relations, made me aware, also, of the extent to which Jefferson's experience as a traveler had influenced the development of his political philosophy, and thus affected profoundly the growth of democratic institutions and the history of the American people.

The vital truths which Jefferson enunciated regarding the basic characteristics of American life and government are especially timely and valuable today, for the course of events in recent years has produced conditions resembling in many respects those with which Jefferson was confronted. Liberty has again been menaced by tyranny and the United States endangered by the hostile might of alien despotisms. His fellow countrymen today may well find inspiration and example in Jefferson's undaunted faith in the future of America and his unwavering devotion to the cause of human freedom.

I trust that this book will prove particularly useful to other American tourists abroad and at home who are desirous of visiting the scenes where Jefferson spent his life; and that it will also be of value to devotees of Jeffersonian lore, to students of government and politics, and to readers interested in American history and biography.

I hope, too, that by arousing the zeal of local historians and antiquarians my book will serve to stimulate the preparation and publication of localized studies (such as my "Thomas Jefferson and Pennsylvania," Joseph Jackson's "Jefferson in Philadelphia," and Thomas Donaldson's "The House Where Jefferson Wrote the Declaration of Independence") treating, with greater minuteness than has been possible here, the details of Jefferson's movements in particular localities. In New England and Virginia, especially, investigations of that sort should bring to light much interesting information regarding the towns and taverns as well as the homes and persons visited by Jefferson in the course of his travels.

Edward Dumbauld

Washington, D.C.
   March 20, 1946

Contents

❖

Illustrations

THOMAS JEFFERSON : AMERICAN TOURIST

Jefferson as a Traveler

❁

PERHAPS no genius America has produced—not even the venerable Benjamin Franklin—united such diversified gifts or displayed such versatility of talent as Thomas Jefferson. Accordingly, there has been no lack of literature treating various phases of Jefferson's activity. Many pages have been written of Jefferson as a statesman, as a political philosopher, as a party leader, as a diplomat, as a legislator, as a lawyer, as a man of letters, as a student of languages and natural science, as an architect and designer of landscapes and gardens, as a family man, as a friend of the French, as a citizen of the world, and as a patron of education and religion. But no one has seen fit to present a comprehensive picture of Jefferson as a traveler. Yet this interesting aspect of Jefferson's life is well worthy of attention.

To be sure, many a modern globe-trotter would find nothing extraordinary in the voyages of Jefferson. It has been computed that the time he spent en route amounted to a year of his life. He visited no remote regions of the earth. Though one of the first to preach Pan-Americanism and the Monroe Doctrine, he was never in South America. Nor did he ever set foot in Spain, although by the purchase of Louisiana, formerly belonging to that country, he acquired for the United States a vast "empire for liberty."[1] While in Italy he did not visit Rome, Florence, Venice, or Naples; Berlin, Vienna, and Budapest he never saw. Scarcely

---

[1] To James Madison, Monticello, April 27, 1809 (Andrew A. Lipscomb and A. Ellery Bergh [eds.], *The Writings of Thomas Jefferson*, XII, 277).

half a dozen European countries and twice as many states along the Atlantic seaboard comprised the territory Thomas Jefferson surveyed as a tourist.

George Washington traveled more extensively in America than Jefferson. Only the Eastern states were familiar ground to the master of Monticello, and late in life he advised a prospective pioneer: "You could not have applied for counsel to one less personally acquainted with the Western country than myself, having never been 50 miles westward of my own house."[2] But for that matter few of Washington's contemporaries could equal his wide knowledge of America. Undoubtedly his travels played a significant part in the development of that comprehensive patriotism which so eminently qualified him for national leadership. Benefits of the same kind came to Jefferson. The long, slow journeys by coach and on horseback gave him an intimate knowledge of his country and the needs of its people.

Indeed, curiosity and pleasure were not the motives impelling Jefferson to travel. The illustrious Virginian boasted of having devoted three score years and one of his life, uninterruptedly, to the service of his country, and his journeys were usually undertaken for the purpose of transacting public business.

Born on April 13, 1743, at Shadwell, in what is now Albemarle County, Virginia, Jefferson attended college at Williamsburg. "When Jefferson started for William and Mary College in 1760, on horseback, a five days' ride, he had never been farther than twenty miles from home, had never seen a town of more than twenty houses, and his acquaintance was limited to his schoolfellows and the families of farmers around Shadwell. Yet within a few months we find this awkward youth of seventeen the fa-

---

[2] To D. A. Leonard, Monticello, January 20, 1814 (Missouri Historical Society, "Correspondence of Thomas Jefferson, 1788–1826," *Glimpses of the Past*, Vol. III, Nos. 4–6 [April–June, 1936], 120). Yet Jefferson's desire to travel persisted. "I have never ceased to wish to descend the Ohio & Mississippi to New Orleans, and when I shall have put my home in order, I shall have the leisure, and so far I have health also, to amuse myself in seeing what I have not yet seen."—To Lucy Lewis, Washington, April 19, 1808 (*ibid.*, 104).

vored and frequent companion of Francis Fauquier, the most elegant and accomplished gentleman Virginia had ever seen, Doctor William Small, the most learned man in the Colony, and George Wythe, the leader of its bar."[3] Studying law under Wythe's mentorship, Jefferson came to the bar in 1767.

In May of the previous year he had obtained his first glimpse of the world beyond Virginia. In order to be inoculated for small-pox by the celebrated Dr. Shippen of Philadelphia, he had visited that city and then had gone on to New York.[4]

In 1769 Jefferson was elected for his first term as a legislator, but had served only five days when the royal governor dissolved the House of Burgesses. However, he remained a member of that body until 1775, when it ceased to function. He attended the second Virginia Convention at Richmond in 1775; the preceding year he had set out for the first Virginia Convention at Williamsburg, but was taken ill of dysentery on the road and forced to be absent. However, he forwarded his *Summary View of the Rights of British America* for perusal by the members.

This clear and forceful statement, shortly afterwards published as a pamphlet, was a prelude to the Declaration of Independence. It enumerated in striking fashion the unlawful acts chargeable to the British monarch, and inquired: "But can his majesty thus put down all law under his feet? Can he erect a power superior to that which erected himself? . . . We know, and will therefore say, that kings are the servants, not the proprietors of the people. . . . The God who gave us life gave us liberty."[5]

In 1775 Jefferson was elected as a Virginia delegate to the Continental Congress, and made two trips to Philadelphia to attend meetings of that body. The following year he was again in Philadelphia and won lasting renown as author of the Declaration

---

[3] William E. Curtis, *The True Thomas Jefferson*, 68.

[4] Jefferson's entry for May 11, 1766, in his garden book records that he "went journey to Maryland, Pennsylva, New York."—Edwin M. Betts (ed.), *Thomas Jefferson's Garden Book*.

[5] Paul Leicester Ford (ed.), *The Writings of Thomas Jefferson*, I, 445–47.

of Independence. In the fall of 1776 he left Congress and returned to Virginia, where he entered the House of Delegates and initiated his program of law reform. His service in the legislature continued until his election as governor in 1779.

Succeeding Patrick Henry, Jefferson was the second governor of Virginia as an independent commonwealth, after its liberation from English rule. While he was in office, the Old Dominion was invaded by the British Army. The task of resisting and eluding the enemy obliged him to spend many hours on horseback. That by experience and study he had acquired a comprehensive knowledge of his native state was manifested in Jefferson's *Notes on Virginia*, written shortly after he retired as governor.

This work was originally prepared for the information of Barbé-Marbois, French consul in Philadelphia; its publication in Europe several years later won for its author considerable reputation as a man of learning. In accordance with the habits of industry and precision acquired in Wythe's office, it was Jefferson's practice, in conversation with persons of any station in life, to discuss the topic most familiar to those with whom he talked and to reduce to writing any information thus obtained which he thought might later on prove useful. Not only did he prepare the *Notes on Virginia* from such memoranda, but when traveling in Europe he similarly recorded his observations.

After the death of his wife, in 1782, when for the third time Congress chose him to undertake a diplomatic mission abroad, Jefferson accepted the appointment. He spent several months in Philadelphia and Baltimore attempting to find a vessel to take him across the Atlantic. But when news came that the peace negotiations terminating the Revolutionary War were already so far advanced that his attendance would not be required, Jefferson returned home.

Little over a month later he was re-elected to Congress. At Princeton, New Jersey, on November 4, 1783, he took his seat in that body, which adjourned the same day to reconvene at Annapolis. In 1784, Jefferson was appointed as an envoy to act with John Adams and Benjamin Franklin in negotiating treaties of commerce with foreign nations. Leaving Annapolis on May 11, he made a point of informing himself about the commerce of the states through which he passed on his way to embark for France. He sailed from Boston on July 5, 1784, and reached Paris a month and a day later.

With him went his daughter Martha, not yet twelve. He left his younger children, Mary, aged six, and Lucy, two, in the care of their maternal aunt, Mrs. Eppes. The youngest died shortly thereafter, and in the summer of 1787 Mary joined her father and elder sister in Paris.

In 1785, Jefferson succeeded Franklin as minister plenipotentiary to the French court. While stationed in Paris, he made three noteworthy trips. In 1786 he joined Adams in England in order to participate in diplomatic negotiations. In 1787 he made a tour of southern France and northern Italy. In 1788 he hastened to The Hague to find Adams and conclude arrangements for a loan from the Dutch bankers at Amsterdam who financed the struggling American government. From Holland he returned to Paris by way of Germany.

Jefferson remained abroad until 1789. In that year he became secretary of state in the cabinet of George Washington. From March to September, 1790, he was in New York, where the seat of the new government was first located. In August he accompanied President Washington on a brief visit to Rhode Island. In November he arrived in Philadelphia, then the temporary capital of the nation. With James Madison he made a trip through New England during the summer of 1791.

On December 31, 1793, Jefferson resigned as secretary of state, but on March 4, 1797, was sworn in as vice president of the United States. In 1800 the pastoral city of Washington became the capital of the United States. The following year Jefferson was inaugurated as president. At the end of his second term, in 1809, he retired to Monticello, where he passed the remainder of his days and died on the Fourth of July, 1826.

Jefferson constantly combined business with sightseeing. On his first trip to Philadelphia to be vaccinated, he went on to New York. Traveling through New England with Madison, he found time to report to President Washington about conditions along the Canadian border. When he had settled the affairs which brought him posthaste to Holland from Paris, he returned leisurely by the round-about route through Germany. Called to London, he proceeded to make a methodical tour of the countryside, with Whately's book on gardening in his hand. When, after an injury to his wrist, he was advised by his physician to try the effect of mineral waters as a remedy, he chose those of Aix-en-Provence in preference to others, because from that place he could commence a tour of the French seaports concerned in commerce with America. From Aix he wrote to his daughter Martha: "My journey hitherto has been a very pleasing one. It was undertaken with the hope that the mineral waters of this place might restore strength to my wrist. Other considerations also concurred—instruction, amusement, and abstraction from business, of which I had too much at Paris."[6] Indeed, the characteristic many-sidedness of the man, by his enemies called duplicity, revealed itself in the adroit management of Jefferson the tourist no less than in the skillful maneuvers of Jefferson the political leader.

Doubtless the dangers and discomforts which beset the wayfarer in those days were sufficient to discourage Jefferson from undertaking any unnecessary travel. To be sure, highway robbery was all but unknown in America, if Jefferson's reply to a Frenchman submitting a scheme for suppressing that evil is to be believed.[7] In France travelers went armed; Jefferson's passport authorized him to carry the usual weapons. Even in the United States a gun might be helpful in protecting a stranger from indignities.

But the roads, though not infested by brigands, were ill de-

[6] To Martha Jefferson, Aix-en-Provence, March 28, 1787 (Sarah N. Randolph, *The Domestic Life of Thomas Jefferson*, 115).
[7] To M. Claviere, Paris, July 6, 1787 (Ford, *Writings*, IV, 402).

fined and often impassable. On the main thoroughfare between Philadelphia and Baltimore the ruts and gullies were so deep that, in order to keep the stage coach from upsetting, the passengers were obliged to lean to the right or left in unison at the driver's direction. Often they had to descend and walk in the mud, occasionally helping to push the coach when the horses' efforts were not sufficient. When progress became impossible, a new roadway was opened by felling trees. In some places there were a dozen such routes to the same spot, all full of stumps, rocks, and trees.

Near the close of the Revolution, the French traveler de Chastellux got lost in the woods while on the road to Monticello to visit Jefferson. In 1800, Mrs. John Adams met with the same predicament on her way from Baltimore to the new capital at Washington, wandering aimlessly through forest land for two hours until set aright by directions from a straggling black. Jefferson himself seems to have encountered similar difficulty while traveling to Philadelphia in 1775 to attend the Continental Congress. His account book shows that more than once he was obliged to employ guides.

In Europe the condition of the highways was hardly superior, though their location was not so uncertain. Indeed, entries in Jefferson's account book of sums paid for repairs to carriage or harness appear oftener during his journeys abroad than at home. In 1796 he informed Madison: "The roads of America are the best in the world except those of France and England."[8]

About to return from Amsterdam to the French capital, Jefferson wrote to William Short,[9] his *élève* and secretary at Paris:

---

[8] To Madison, Monticello, March 6, 1796 (Lipscomb and Bergh, *Writings*, IX, 325).

[9] The little-known but romantic career of William Short is sketched in an article by Marie Kimball, "William Short, Jefferson's Only 'Son,' " in *North American Review*, Vol. CCXXIII, No. 3 (September–October–November, 1926), 471–86, and in a note in *William and Mary College Quarterly* (2d series), Vol. XI, No. 3 (July, 1931), 249–50. See also Beatrix Cary Davenport (ed.), *A Diary of the French Revolution by Gouverneur Morris*, I, 512, 564, 566; II, 255, 344, 435, 512, *et passim*. Short was a member of the original chapter of Phi Beta Kappa and was the

"What route I shall take will depend on information not yet received relative to the roads, and partly too on the weather's becoming milder than it now is."[10] Jefferson finally determined to follow the Rhine as far as Strasbourg if the roads would permit, but to turn toward Paris whenever they became impassable. A letter to Short from Frankfort-on-the-Main narrates the vicissitudes of the trip: "I arrived here on the 6th. inst., having been overtaken at Cleves by the commencement of a storm of rain, hail & snow which lasted to this place, with intermissions now and then. The roads however continued good to Bonne, there beginning to be clayey & to be penetrated with the wet. They became worse than imagination can paint for about 100 miles which brought me to the neighborhood of this place where the chaussee began."[11] The heavy road tax Jefferson "paid cheerfully, however, through the territory of Frankfort and thence up the Rhine, because fine gravelled roads are kept up; but through the Prussian, and other parts of the road below Frankfort, the roads are only as made by carriages, there not appearing to have been ever a day's work employed on them."[12]

In his tour of France Jefferson had also been troubled by bad weather. A letter from Lyons informed Short: "So far all is well. No complaints; except against the weather-maker who has pelted me with rain, hail & snow, almost from the moment of my departure to my arrival here."[13] Two weeks later, at Aix-en-Prov-

---

first officer to be appointed under the federal constitution and commissioned by George Washington. "He put himself under my guidance at nineteen or twenty years of age; he is to me therefore as an adopted son," declared Jefferson in a letter to Trumbull on June 1, 1789 (*Autobiography, Reminiscences, and Letters of John Trumbull*, 156). Enamored of a French noblewoman whose husband was slain by revolutionists, Short spent the latter part of his life in retirement in Philadelphia, after serving in a number of diplomatic posts.

[10] To Short, Amsterdam, March 13, 1788 (Library of Congress, Jefferson Papers).

[11] To Short, Frankfort-on-the-Main, April 9, 1788 (*ibid.*). Cf. to Martha Jefferson Randolph, Washington, January 7, 1805, and January 21, 1805, in the Pierpont Morgan Library, MS Collections.

[12] Lipscomb and Bergh, *Writings*, XVII, 277.

[13] To Short, Lyons, March 15, 1787 (Library of Congress, Jefferson Papers).

ence, Jefferson again complained of the constant storm of wind, hail, snow, and rain that pursued him.[14] To cross the Alps it was necessary to travel ninety-three miles on mules, "as the snows are not yet enough melted to admit carriages to pass. I leave mine here, therefore, preparing to return by water from Genoa."[15] Writing to his daughter Martha, he described the hardships of mountain and sea travel: "From Genoa to Aix was very fatiguing—the first two days having been at sea, and mortally sick—two more clambering the cliffs of the Appenines, sometimes on foot, sometimes on a mule, according as the path was more or less difficult—and two others travelling through the night as well as day without sleep. I am not yet rested, and shall therefore shortly give you rest by closing my letter."[16]

Jefferson was extremely susceptible to cold. "I have often wondered," he declared, "that any human being should live in a cold country who can find room in a warm one. I have no doubt but that cold is the source of more sufferance to all animal nature than hunger, thirst, sickness, and all the other pains of life and of death itself put together. I live in a temperate climate, and under circumstances which do not expose me often to cold. Yet when I recollect on one hand all the sufferings I have had from cold, and on the other all other pains, the former preponderate greatly. What then must be the sum of that evil if we take in the vast proportion of men who are obliged to be out in all weather, by land and sea."[17] Sojourning in southern France he exclaimed: "I am now in the land of corn, vines, oil, & sunshine. What more can man ask of heaven? If I should happen to die in Paris I will beg of you to send me here, and have me exposed to the sun. I am sure it will bring me to life again." He wondered why anyone possessing sufficient means to live in that pleasant region

[14] To Short, Aix-en-Provence, March 29, 1787 (*ibid.*).

[15] To Short, Nice, April 12, 1787 (Lipscomb and Bergh, *Writings*, VI, 110).

[16] To Martha Jefferson, Marseilles, May 5, 1787 (Randolph, *Domestic Life*, 120–21).

[17] To Wm. Dunbar, Washington, January 12, 1801 (Lipscomb and Bergh, *Writings*, X, 191–92).

should remain in Paris, for though "money will carry to Paris most of the good things" of that section, "it can not carry thither its sunshine, nor procure any equivalent for it."[18]

In October, 1791, Jefferson and Washington had to push on "through five days of North East storm" in order to reach Philadelphia before the opening of Congress, which took place a week earlier than anticipated. Fortunately, Mrs. Washington had taken possession of Jefferson's young daughter, Mary, at Mount Vernon and restored her to her father only after their arrival. Another peril enlivened the earlier portion of the trip. "The first part of our journey was pleasant, except some hair-breadth escapes by our new horse occasioned in going down hill the first day or so, after which he behaved better, and came through the journey preserving the fierceness of his spirit to the last."[19]

On his trip to New York in 1766 Jefferson's horse ran away with him twice, and he was nearly drowned in fording one of the twelve rivers between Monticello and his destination. Between Monticello and Washington, Jefferson wrote to his attorney general in 1801, "of eight rivers . . . five have neither bridges nor boats. When the one on which I live is fordable it will be a signal that the others are. This may be to-day, and in that case if it has ceased to rain, I shall set out and be with you on the fourth day."[20] Five days later, Jefferson had arrived at Washington and was sending word to Madison about the condition of the roads. There

---

[18] To Short, Aix-en-Provence, March 27, 1787 (*William and Mary College Quarterly* [2d series], Vol. XI, No. 3 [July, 1931], 246). The artificial sun lamp had not yet been invented. That contrivance would have appealed to Jefferson enormously, for he took delight in every sort of peculiar gadget.

[19] To T. M. Randolph, Jr., Philadelphia, October 25, 1791 (Library of Congress, Jefferson Papers).

[20] To Levi Lincoln, Monticello, April 25, 1801 (*ibid.*). Cf. with letter to H. Tazewell, Monticello, November 28, 1797, in *ibid.* Rain delayed Jefferson's departure from Monticello for Philadelphia in 1797. "I have for some time had my trunk packed & issued my last orders, & been only waiting for it to cease raining. But it still rains. I have a bad prospect of rains & roads before me. Your sister removed to Belmont about three days ago. The weather ever since has kept us entirely asunder. If tomorrow permits my departure I shall be in Philadelphia on the 9th a week from this time."—To Mary Jefferson, Monticello, August 2, 1797 (Hunt-

was a stretch of two miles, he thought, which a carriage could not safely traverse. He had passed a wagon stuck in the mud and was of the opinion that no four-wheeled vehicle could have gotten through that spot without suffering the same fate.[21] While in Philadelphia as head of the Department of State, he wrote on one occasion to a friend living at Stenton, on the outskirts of the city: "Th: Jefferson presents his compliments to Dr Logan, and is sorry that a great mass of business just come on him will prevent him the pleasure of waiting on him tomorrow. The hope of dryer roads is some consolation for postponing the visit awhile."[22]

In Virginia the highways were execrable. The best extended from Williamsburg to Richmond, a distance of sixty-three miles, which could be covered in two days. The last seventeen miles on the way from Philadelphia to Monticello were so hilly that when coming home in 1792, Jefferson feared that this bad stretch of road would injure his horses more than all the rest of the trip. Accordingly, he directed that plow or wagon horses should meet him to undertake the final stage of his journey.[23] Coaches were rarely seen in Virginia; traveling was almost exclusively by horseback. At the time the Constitution was ratified, there were thousands of respectable men in the state who had never seen any other four-wheeled vehicle than a wagon, and there were thousands who had never even seen a wagon. When going to Philadelphia in 1766, Jefferson rode in a one-horse chair. In 1775 he traveled in a phaeton, with two spare horses. Later on, when he had to make regular and frequent trips from his country estate

---

ington Library, MS Collections). Jefferson was apprehensive when his daughters were on the road in rainy weather, as is indicated in his letters to Mary Jefferson Eppes, Monticello, July 4, 1800; to Mary Jefferson Eppes, Washington, January 18, 1803; and to Martha Jefferson Randolph, Washington, January 27, 1803; all in the Huntington Library.

[21] To James Madison, Washington, April 30, 1801 (Library of Congress, Jefferson Papers).

[22] To Dr. Logan, Philadelphia, May 4, 1793 (Historical Society of Pennsylvania, MS Collections, Maria Dickinson Logan Papers). Cf. *Garden Book*, 187–88.

[23] To Martha Jefferson Randolph, Philadelphia, July 3, 1792 (Morgan Library, MS Collections).

to the seat of government, it was his practice to travel by the public stage in bad weather and in his own carriage when practicable.[24]

Some of Jefferson's stopping places on his way between Monticello and the seat of government are identified by markers erected by the Roads Commission of Maryland. These include Spurrier's Tavern (spelled "Spuryear's" by Jefferson, who visited it frequently, as did George Washington), Van Horn's Tavern, Rhodes's Tavern, and the Red Lion Tavern. Rodgers's Tavern, east of the Susquehanna River, is still standing.

In March, 1790, when he had come to New York to take up his duties as secretary of state, Jefferson wrote to his son-in-law: "I arrived here on the 21st. instant, after as laborious a journey, of a fortnight from Richmond, as I ever went through; resting only one day at Alexandria and another at Baltimore. I found my carriage and horses at Alexandria; but a snow of eighteen inches deep falling the same night, I saw the impossibility of getting on in my own carriage; so left it there, to be sent to me by water, and had my horses led on to this place, taking my passage in the stage, though relieving myself a little sometimes by mounting my horse. The roads, through the whole way, were so bad that we could never go more than three miles an hour, sometimes not more than two, and in the night but one."[25]

Jefferson could have gone faster on foot. In a curious memorandum made while in France, he records his rate of walking. "I walk a French mile in 17½ minutes. A French mile is 1.21 or 1¼ English miles. I walk then at the rate of 4 3/20 miles or 4 miles 264 yards an hour." Noting further that he paces off a French mile in 1254 steps, "walking moderately in the summer,"

---

[24] To Madison, August 25, 1793 (Ford, *Writings*, VI, 398); to J. W. Eppes, Monticello, April 25, 1801 (Alderman Library, University of Virginia, Jefferson Collection); to T. M. Randolph, Jr., Philadelphia, December 8, 1793, and June 14, 1798 (Huntington Library, MS Collections).

[25] To T. M. Randolph, Jr., New York, March 28, 1790 (Lipscomb and Bergh, *Writings*, VIII, 7–8). See also the letter to George Mason, New York, June 13, 1790, in Kate Mason Rowland, *The Life of George Mason*, II, 328.

he reckons that an English mile would require 2066½ steps, which "the brisk walk of winter" would reduce to 1735, a difference of 331 steps.[26]

A week to ten days usually sufficed Jefferson for the trip from Monticello to Philadelphia. From the Quaker City to New York was a two days' journey. Annapolis was four days distant from Philadelphia. The same interval separated Monticello from Washington. Traveling in leisurely fashion, Jefferson spent almost a fortnight on the road between New York and Boston; although the highway between those cities was considered the best in the country and was usually covered in a week.

Travel was not only laborious but expensive as well. In the winter of 1793 Congress met in Germantown. The city of Philadelphia was then suffering the ravages of yellow fever. Leaving Monticello on October 25, Jefferson rode on horseback to Fredericksburg. From that place his servants, James and Bob, returned with the horses, while their master went on to Baltimore by public stage. There Jefferson joined President Washington, and the two were obliged to hire a private conveyance to bring them to their destination. On November 2, Jefferson wrote to his son-in-law: "After having experienced on my journey the extremes of heat, cold, dust & rain, I arrived here yesterday. I found at Baltimore that the stages run no further North, and being from that circumstance thrown into the hands of the harpies who prey upon travellers, was pretty well fleeced to get here. I think from Fredericksburg here with a single servant cost me upwards of seventy dollars."[27] From his meticulously kept account book it appears that the precise sum was $77.65. The same day Jefferson wrote warning Madison and Monroe to be on their guard against a similar fate. The usual charge for passengers on

[26] Library of Congress, Jefferson Papers, 41941.

[27] To T. M. Randolph, Jr., Germantown, November 2, 1793 (Library of Congress, Jefferson Papers); Charles Francis Jenkins, *Jefferson's Germantown Letters*, 30–32. See also *ibid.*, xii–xiii, 160–64, and the letter to James Madison, November 2, 1793, in *ibid.*, 27.

the stage was six cents a mile, and the distance from Monticello to Philadelphia was two hundred and sixty miles.[28]

Experiences of the same sort had befallen Jefferson in Europe. He affirmed that Rousseau had wronged the inhabitants of a certain French city in singling them out as a people accustomed to victimize strangers, for the practice was common everywhere among the menial class of "hackneyed rascals" with whom a traveler is most frequently in contact. "I have not yet been to Montpelier, but I can pronounce that Rousseau has done it injury in ascribing to it the character of pillaging strangers, as if it was peculiar to that place. It is the character of every place on the great roads along which many travellers pass. He should also have confined the character to postillions, voituriers, tavern keepers, waiters, & workmen. The other descriptions of people are as good to strangers as any people I have ever met with."[29]

This evil was not a purely French trait. When the advisability of locating the temporary seat of government at Princeton, New Jersey, was being considered, Jefferson commented on the deficiency of accommodations there, "exposing ye attending members to the danger of indignities & extortions discouraging perhaps the fitest men from undertaking the service & amounting to a prohibition of such as had families from which they would not part."[30] While attending the Continental Congress at Princeton, Madison complained to Jefferson: "I am obliged to write in a position that scarcely admits the use of any of my limbs, Mr.

---

[28] Henry Adams, *A History of the United States during the Administration of Thomas Jefferson*, I, 14; Paul Wilstach, *Jefferson and Monticello*, 79. Money-changers also profited at the expense of travelers. Each state had its own currency until Jefferson, as secretary of state, brought about the introduction of the decimal system with the dollar as the unit. (Ford, *Writings*, I, 73–75; III, 446–57.) When supplying his daughters with funds for "expenses of the road," Jefferson advised them to change the bills and gold for silver, which would be more readily received. —To Mary Jefferson Eppes and Martha Jefferson Randolph, Washington, October 18, 1802 (Huntington Library, MS Collections).

[29] To Short, Marseilles, May 5, 1787 (Library of Congress, Jefferson Papers). The quotation from Rousseau is given in a letter from Short to Jefferson, Paris, April 4, 1787 in *ibid*.

[30] Ford, *Writings*, III, 458.

THOMAS JEFFERSON

From the portrait by Mather Brown (London, 1786)

Grille to the stone N.º 3   1172. steps.
Grille to Neuilly - - - - - - - - -   2430
Grille round the ☐ of the Rond & gr.chem. 2394
Grille to Statue Louis XV   820
~~Statue~~ Statue Lou. XV. to Chat. Thuilleries 475
Grille to Château des Tuilleries   1295

I step a French mile of 1000 toises = 6408 in 1053. steps.
      this yields 3f. 4.½ I. English to the step & 1735 steps 6 mile
I walk a French mile in 17½ minutes. a
      a French mile is = 1. 21. or 1¼ Eng. miles
      I walk then at the rate of 4 ³⁄₂₀ miles or 4 - 266 an hour

walking moderately in the summer I walked
a Fr. mile of 1000 = 6400 f. in 1256. steps. & in 26
that gives 2.557 to the step
and 2066¾ steps to the Eng. mile
1735. the brisk walk of winter
───────
331. difference

Jefferson's memorandum on rate of walking

Jones & myself being lodged in a room not 10 feet square and without a single accommodation for writing."[31]

Jefferson's experience with the Princeton townsmen may have colored his impressions of the college there. Although the degree of LL.D. had been conferred on him by that institution in 1791, Jefferson did not refrain from declaring to an inquiring parent that: "As far as I am acquainted with the colleges and academies of the U. S., and I will say more especially of Princeton, which you name, I have found their method of instruction very superficial & imperfect, carrying their pupils over the ground like race horses to please their parents and draw custom to their school."[32]

An English traveler, who likewise considered "Princetown, a place more famous for its college than its learning," resolved to make the best of the notoriously deficient accommodations which American hostelries provided and not to grumble. But in Philadelphia he could not resist the superior attractions offered by the establishment of a French innkeeper. In a southern state, the same traveler consumed without complaint a dinner of cornmeal mush, without milk, or sugar, or even molasses. "Beshrew the Traveller," he exclaims, "who would let fall a reflection over the dinner I here made. Though plain, it was wholesome; and, instead of wishing it was better, I thanked God it was not worse."[33]

Another Englishman was compelled to dance by a group of

[31] Madison to Jefferson, Princeton, September 20, 1783 (Gaillard Hunt [ed.], *The Writings of James Madison*, II, 22). According to Princeton tradition, Jefferson (as well as Washington and other distinguished guests) often visited the Stocktons at Morven. Mr. Stockton was a signer of the Declaration of Independence; Mrs. Stockton, like Jefferson, was an Ossian enthusiast. Her brother, Elias Boudinot, was president of the Congress and made Morven his official residence for a time. (V. Lansing Collins, *Princeton Past and Present*, 28; Jacob N. Beam to the author, December 26, 1939.)

[32] To Elizabeth Trist, November 23, 1816 (Roy J. Honeywell, *The Educational Work of Thomas Jefferson*, 112).

[33] John Davis, *Travels of Four Years and a Half in the United States of America*, 35, 39, 119. From Davis came the story that Jefferson at his inauguration "rode on horseback to the Capital without a single guard or even servant in his train, dismounted without assistance, and hitched the bridle of his horse to the palisades."—*Ibid.*, 177.

17

wagoners at a tavern, who wielded their whips when he hesitated to comply with their commands. Upon the arrival of his groom, the irate Briton, taking his guns from the saddlehorse, turned the tables on his tormentors. He was greatly complimented by the landlord in consequence of this feat.[34] The Indian Queen, where Jefferson sometimes stopped in Philadelphia, was on one occasion the scene of a robbery in which several Congressmen lost their linen and thirty thousand dollars' worth of securities.[35]

One journeying by water was not immune from molestation by "the harpies who prey upon travellers." Just before sailing from Cowes for America, Jefferson advised his bankers that his final draft on them would be for a larger sum than had been anticipated, since he must go by a particular ship or lose passage that season.[36] The terms which the shipowner exacted provided that the cost of passage for ship and ship's provisions should be 100 guineas; that the passenger should at his own expense furnish any fresh provisions, wines, and delicacies desired; and that he should forfeit 50 guineas for detention of the ship in case of his failure to reach Cowes during the three days the ship was to wait there for him.[37]

Navigation, moreover, had its own drawbacks and perils. Favorable winds were necessary. Jefferson's departure from Europe was delayed three weeks on this account. Certain times of the year were most propitious for passage. "By advice of those skilled in sea voiages" Jefferson chose the period between the autumnal equinox and winter for his departure. March and September,

[34] Sir Augustus Foster, *Quarterly Review*, Vol. LXVIII, No. 135 (June, 1841), 49.

[35] Claude G. Bowers, *Jefferson and Hamilton*, 120; Seth Ames, *Works of Fisher Ames*, I, 88–89.

[36] To Willinks, van Staphorsts & Hubard, Cowes, October 14, 1789 (Library of Congress, Jefferson Papers).

[37] Jonathan Trumbull to Jefferson, London, October 10, 1789 (*ibid.*).

"the boisterous equinoctial months," he regarded as the most disagreeable seasons to be passed at sea.[38]

Even coastwise sailing was apt to prove difficult. While on his way to the seat of government to assume his duties as vice president, Jefferson wrote from Chestertown, Maryland, to his daughter: "I have got so far, my dear Martha, on my way to Philadelphia which place I shall not reach till the day after to-morrow. I have lost one day at Georgetown by the failure of the stages, and three days by having suffered myself to be persuaded at Baltimore to cross the bay & come by this route as quicker & pleasanter. After being forced back on the bay by bad weather in a first attempt to cross it, the second brought me over after a very rough passage, too late for the stage.—So far I am well, tho' much fatigued."[39] Likewise, adverse winds on Lake Champlain compelled Jefferson and Madison to turn back during the course of their tour through New England in 1791.

Hostile sea power constituted another hazard to ocean travel. Jefferson's inability to get to Europe as envoy in the winter of 1782–83 was due chiefly to the British blockade. Passage on a French ship, the *Guadeloupe*, was offered Jefferson; but after observing that "she sweats almost continually on the inside, in consequence of which her commander and several of the crew are now laid up with rheumatism," he concluded that it would not be right to jeopardize a ship belonging to a friendly nation by exposing it to the danger of falling into enemy hands.[40]

A danger not dissimilar existed in time of peace. The Barbary pirates were a menace to the ships of nations which had not purchased immunity by paying tribute. Those on board the captured vessels were made prisoners and held for ransom. The principal maritime powers of Europe—England, France, Spain, and the

[38]To Mrs. Church, Paris, February 15, 1789 (Missouri Historical Society, Bixby Collection).

[39] To Martha Jefferson Randolph, Chestertown, February 28, 1797 (Morgan Library, MS Collections).

[40] To James Madison, Baltimore, February 7, 1783 (Lipscomb and Bergh, *Writings*, IV, 431–32).

States-General of Holland—submitted to these degrading conditions and bought off the pirates. Jefferson, while at the French court, sought to form a combination of the lesser maritime powers to protect their commerce by patrolling the Barbary coast with a fleet of a half-dozen frigates. Congress failed to furnish its quota of one frigate, however, and the plan fell through.[41] It was not until Jefferson's administration as president that the pirates were subdued by the American Navy.

When making arrangements for his younger daughter, Mary, to be brought to France, Jefferson believed it would be prudent to "confide my daughter only to a French or English vessel having a Mediterranean *pass*. This attention, though of little consequence in matters of merchandise, is of weight in the mind of a parent which sees even possibilities of capture beyond the reach of any estimate. If a peace be concluded with the Algerines in the mean time, you shall be among the first to hear it from myself. I pray you to believe it from nobody else, as far as respects the conveyance of my daughter to me."[42]

The anxious father likewise prescribed strict standards of seaworthiness for the ship which was to carry his child: "I must now repeat my wish to have Polly sent to me next summer. This, however, must depend on the circumstance of a good vessel sailing from Virginia in the months of April, May, June, or July. I would not have her set out sooner or later on account of the equinoxes. The vessel should have performed one voyage at least, but not be more than four or five years old. We do not attend to this circumstance till we have been to sea, but there the consequence of it is felt. I think it would be found that all the vessels which are lost are either on their first voyage or after they are five years old; at least there are few exceptions to this. . . . I

---

[41] Lafayette is said to have been told by Vergennes that both France and England profited by the piratical system and would not allow it to be suppressed (Edward E. Hale, *Franklin in France*, II, 339).

[42] To Mr. Eppes, Paris, January 7, 1786 (Randolph, *Domestic Life*, 106–107).

would rather live a year longer without her than have her trusted to any but a good ship and a summer passage."[43]

And then there was seasickness. Jefferson was nearly always a sufferer from this malady when traveling by water. At the time of his return to the United States from France, he was willing to pay twenty to thirty guineas more if the ship would carry him directly from a French port and spare him the ordeal of crossing the English Channel.[44]

If the dangers and discomforts confronting the traveler by land or water were not sufficient to discourage Jefferson from voyages undertaken exclusively for pleasure or gratification of his curiosity, the tranquil felicities of domestic life at Monticello would have dissuaded him. He never tired of contrasting the burdens of public office with the charms which he found in his family, his friends, his farms, and his books.[45]

The attractiveness of his own fireside increased with the passing years. As a young man he felt the wish to travel. In 1764, when he was a student at Williamsburg, he was unwilling to make a categorical proposal of marriage to his youthful flame, Rebecca Burwell, because he desired first to go abroad. "I shall visit particularly England, Holland, France, Spain, Italy (where I would buy me a good fiddle) and Egypt," returning home by way of Canada, he wrote to his confidant, John Page. The young lady was not inclined to postpone matrimony for two or three years until Jefferson's return from Europe (although in fact two decades were to elapse before he set foot on foreign soil), and she promptly married Jacquelin Ambler. The bridegroom, it is said, unwittingly or unfeelingly asked Jefferson to be best

<hr/>

[43] To Mr. Eppes, Paris, August 30, 1785 (*ibid.*, 105–106).

[44] To Mr. Cutting, Paris, September 24, 1789 (Library of Congress, Jefferson Papers).

[45] To Mr. Warden, Washington, February 25, 1809 (*ibid.*); to Mme de Corny, Washington, March 2, 1809 (Gilbert Chinard, *Trois Amitiés françaises de Jefferson*, 228–29); to Mr. Donald, February 7, 1788 (Randolph, *Domestic Life*, 133); to Madison, June 9, 1793 (*ibid.*, 218); to Mrs. Church, November 27, 1793 (*ibid.*, 224); to M. Odit, October 14, 1795 (Lipscomb and Bergh, *Writings*, IX, 312).

man at the wedding.[46] A daughter of the couple later became the wife of Jefferson's lifelong enemy, Chief Justice John Marshall.

But although the thought of separation from Miss Burwell did not deter Jefferson from planning an extensive voyage, absence from home was far less endurable after the wedding ceremony of New Year's Day, 1772, when the comely widow, Martha Wayles Skelton, became mistress of Monticello. Twice Jefferson refused appointment as a diplomatic envoy on account of the precarious condition of his wife's health. To Lafayette, who communicated the news of his appointment the second time and offered to be useful to him in France, Jefferson avowed: "I lose an opportunity, the only one I ever had, and perhaps ever shall have, of combining public service with private gratification, of seeing countries whose improvements in science, in arts, and in civilization, it has been my fortune to admire at a distance, but never to see."[47]

The attractions of Paris, when Jefferson at length was able to gratify his wish to go there, did not diminish his eagerness to hear the news of everything that happened "in the neighborhood of Monticello" or his affection for "my lazy & hospitable countrymen." He wistfully affirmed: "I often wish myself among them, as I am here burning the candle of life without present pleasure, or future object. A dozen or twenty years ago this scene would have amused me, but I am past the age for changing habits." To a European friend he declared: "I am now of an age which does not easily accomodate itself to new manners and new modes of living; and I am savage enough to prefer the woods, the

[46] To John Page, Shadwell, January 20, 1763; to Page, Shadwell, July 15, 1763; to Page, Devilsburg, January 19, 1764; to Wm. Fleming, Williamsburg, March 20, 1764 (Ford, *Writings*, I, 347, 348, 354, 357). Chinard says that Jefferson was best man at his rival's wedding (*Thomas Jefferson: the Apostle of Americanism*, 17); but see letters to Wm. Fleming, Williamsburg, March 20, 1764, and to John Page, Devilsburg, April 9, 1764 in Ford, *Writings*, I, 357, 359.

[47] To Lafayette, August 4, 1781 (Lipscomb and Bergh, *Writings*, IV, 184–85).

wilds, and the independence of Monticello, to all the brilliant pleasures of this gay capital."[48]

Even to sojourn in Philadelphia was painful. While attending the Continental Congress Jefferson exclaimed: "I have never received the script of a pen from any mortal in Virginia since I left it, nor been able by any inquiries I could make to hear of my family. . . . The suspense under which I am is too terrible to be endured. If anything has happened, for God's sake let me know it."[49] In the midst of political quarrels which embittered personal relations and social intercourse in the Pennsylvania metropolis during the period preceding Jefferson's election to the presidency, he averred: "I envy those who stay at home enjoying the society of their friendly neighbors." Philadelphia he found "a dreary scene; where envy, hatred, malice, revenge, and all the worst passions of men, are marshalled to make one another as miserable as possible." He fumed with "impatience to leave this place, and every thing which can be disgusting, for Monticello and my dear family, comprising every thing which is pleasurable to me in this world."[50]

Toward the close of his administration as president, Jefferson awaited with eagerness "the day of retirement" to the pleasures of private life, although he was grateful to his constituents for their support and good will.[51] "But I am tired of a life of contention, and of being the personal object for the hatred of every man, who hates the present state of things," he declared to his daughter Martha. "I long to be among you where I know nothing but love & delight, and where instead of being chained to a

[48] To Archibald Stuart, Paris, January 25, 1786 (Ford, *Writings*, IV, 187); to Mrs. Elizabeth Trist, Paris, December 15, 1786 (*ibid.*, 330); and to Baron Geismer, Paris, September 6, 1785 (Lipscomb and Bergh, *Writings*, V, 128–29).

[49] To Francis Eppes, Philadelphia, November 7, 1775 (Ford, *Writings*, I, 490).

[50] To Martha Jefferson Randolph, Philadelphia, December 27, 1797 (Henry S. Randall, *The Life of Thomas Jefferson*, II, 379); February 8, 1798, and May 31, 1798 (Randolph, *Domestic Life*, 248, 250).

[51] To Martha Jefferson Randolph, Washington, July 6, 1806 (Morgan Library, MS Collections). See also letter of October 20, 1806.

writing table I could be indulged as others are with the blessings of domestic society & pursuits of my own choice."[52]

"Nature intended me for the tranquil pursuits of science by rendering them my supreme delight," the statesman confessed at the end of his political career.[53] "The whole of my life has been a war with my natural taste, feelings & wishes. Domestic life & literary pursuits were my first & my latest inclination, circumstances and not my desires led me to the path I have trod. And like a bow tho long bent, which when unstrung flies back to its natural state, I resume with delight the character and pursuits for which nature designed me."[54] To a friend abroad he declared: "I at length detach myself from public life which I never loved to retire to the bosom of my family, my friends, my farms and books, which I have always loved."[55]

An occasional letter from an old acquaintance, however, revived fond memories of other scenes and other days, particularly "recollections of our charming coterie in Paris,"[56] and of the

[52] To Martha Jefferson Randolph, Washington, November 23, 1807 (*ibid.*).

[53] To Du Pont de Nemours, Washington, March 2, 1809 (Lipscomb and Bergh, *Writings*, XII, 260).

[54] Margaret Bayard Smith, "Washington in Jefferson's Time," *Scribner's Magazine*, Vol. XL, No. 3 (September, 1906), 309.

[55] To Mme de Corny, Washington, March 2, 1809 (Chinard, *Trois Amitiés*, 228). Less than a week earlier Jefferson had written: "I shall within a few days divest myself of the anxieties & the labors with which I have been oppressed, & retire with inexpressible delight to my family, my friends, my farms and books. There I may indulge at length in that tranquillity and those pursuits from which I have been divorced by the character of the times in which I have lived, & which have forced me into the line of political life under a sense of duty, and against a great and constant aversion to it. In retirement I shall be happy to hear from you."—To David B. Warden, Washington, February 25, 1809 (*Mississippi Valley Historical Review*, Vol. XXVIII, No. 2 [September, 1941], 227). Nine years later he said: "My life has been one of unremitting labor, and that in a line entirely foreign to the sciences. It was my lot to be cast into being at the period of the commencement of a political convulsion, which has continued since to agitate the whole civilized globe. That commencement was in my own country, and under circumstances which placed in a state of requisition all the energies of the body and mind of every citizen. It's [*sic*] necessities dragged me from a life of retirement and contemplation, to which my natural propensities strongly inclined, to one of action and contention, and in the field of politics from which I was most averse."—To Francis A. van der Kemp, Monticello, February 9, 1818 (Frank H. Severance [ed.], "A Bundle of Thomas Jefferson's Letters," *Publications of the Buffalo Historical Society*, VII [1904], 23).

[56] To Trumbull, Monticello, January 10, 1817 (Chinard, *Trois Amitiés*, 170).

dauntless band of patriots at Philadelphia in that stirring era when American independence was declared. But in the midst of these delightful reveries was heard the mournful voice of Lafayette: "You remember our happy hours, and animated conversations at Chaville—how far from us those times, and those of the venerable Hotel de la Rochefoucauld! And we who still number among the living, do we not chiefly belong to what is no more?"[57]

[57] Lafayette to Jefferson, La Grange, August 14, 1814 (*ibid.*, 74–75).

CHAPTER II

The Neighborhood of Monticello

APOSTLE of Americanism and citizen of the world though he was, Jefferson remained nonetheless a "Virginian of the Virginians." The welfare of his native commonwealth was always a matter of deep concern to him; and services to it, as author of the Statute of Virginia for religious freedom and as founder of the University of Virginia, constituted two of the three outstanding achievements which he wished to be recorded on his tombstone. Since most of his life was spent in Virginia, there are in that state many localities having associations with Jefferson.

On an imposing hilltop in Albemarle County stands Monticello, the beloved home which Jefferson spent a lifetime building and remodeling. Of that pleasant abode, overlooking the neighboring city of Charlottesville, little need be said here. Many writers have described its ingenious architecture, its attractive surroundings, its tasteful furnishings, and its agreeable society, for which Jefferson sighed when absent from his family circle. It should be remarked, however, that many architectural innovations were embodied in the structure of the dwelling as the result of Jefferson's observations abroad. Perhaps the most notable of these is the striking dome, which was suggested by Rousseau's Hôtel de Salm at Paris, now the Palace of the Legion of Honor. Moreover, on all his journeys Jefferson was constantly in search of information which could be utilized at Monticello.

During his years abroad he was always accumulating articles for Monticello. These he sent home whenever he could find a means of conveyance. He brought more than fifty cases of luggage himself when he returned to America, and eighty-six packing cases of furniture and books followed him from Paris. Jefferson's belongings were scattered when after his death his property passed into other hands. In 1923 Monticello was purchased by the Thomas Jefferson Memorial Foundation, and has since then been maintained as a historical shrine, open to the public. In refurnishing the house, only articles of undisputed authenticity, known to have been possessions of the Virginia statesman, have been placed there. But of course not all of these were bought by Jefferson himself while traveling abroad.

Of the articles purchased in Europe which are now at Monticello, perhaps the most striking is the pair of mirrors placed on either side of the entrance door to the octagonal salon. In the same room hangs Simon Vouet's "Herodiade Bearing the Head of St. John on a Platter," one of the paintings acquired by Jefferson in Paris. The lamp suspended by brass chains in the entrance hall, as well as a sturdy pair of cylinder lamps, likewise came from France. Some of Jefferson's personal belongings may also be seen at Monticello. These include the silver, the brass, and the conch-shell buttons which he wore in France, as well as his stock buckles, one of which is set with brilliants and was part of his costume when he appeared at court. Fragments of a fancy waistcoat have been preserved and also a red quilt which Jefferson obtained in Europe. On display, too, are visiting cards used by him while abroad, and the ivory memorandum tablets which he bought in London. The library at Monticello contains Jefferson's guidebook to Paris, together with several music books belonging to his daughter Martha, which date from her school days in the French capital.

From Monticello, through his telescope, Jefferson could view the handsome grounds of the University of Virginia and supervise construction of the impressive buildings he had designed. Also within sight of Monticello is Ashlawn, where James Monroe found refuge from the demands of public life. A little to the south lies Morven, which belonged to William Short.[1] A few miles further is Colonel Edward Carter's Blenheim, where Jefferson and his bride stopped on their way to their future home. Not far away, in the direction of Orange County Court House, is Montpelier, the abode of James Madison and his charming wife.

Near Monticello is Shadwell, Jefferson's birthplace.[2] In the same vicinity is Edgehill, the residence of his daughter Martha after her marriage. Eppington, the ancestral estate of his daughter Mary's husband, is located in Chesterfield County, up the Appomattox River from its junction with the James. In Goochland County, close to the confluence of the Rivanna River with the James, is situated Elk Hill, a plantation belonging to Jefferson, where he occasionally resided.

Other Virginia estates often visited by Jefferson are many.[3] Perhaps the best known of these, now a national shrine, is George Washington's Mount Vernon, overlooking the Potomac. At Gunston Hall, the residence of George Mason, author of the Virginia bill of rights, a guest room is pointed out as Jefferson's. According to one tradition, it was in the library there that the first draft of the Declaration of Independence was prepared by these two statesmen. A similar tradition says that it was in the cupola on

[1] Jefferson probably named the estate for the Stocktons' Morven at Princeton. Morven was deeded to Short by William C. and Maria Carter. The deed, written and signed by Jefferson, dated December 8, 1796, is said to be in the Albemarle County records at Charlottesville Court House, according to Josephine P. Marshall in "Morven" (in Edith Tunis Sale [ed.], *Historic Gardens of Virginia*, 271). I have been unable to locate that deed, but have found a deed of bargain and sale dated December 18, 1782, from Jefferson to Short containing a proviso that if Short did not become a resident and within seven years build a house on the land granted it should revert to the grantor (Albemarle County Deeds, VIII, 61). The signature in the deed book may have been written by Jefferson.

[2] Regarding Shadwell, see Fiske Kimball, "In Search of Jefferson's Birthplace," *Virginia Magazine of History and Biography*, Vol. LI, No. 4 (October, 1943), 313–25; and Marie Kimball, *Jefferson: The Road to Glory*, 21–23.

[3] Robert A. Lancaster, Jr., *Historic Virginia Homes and Churches*; Edith Tunis Sale, *Interiors of Virginia Houses of Colonial Times*; Sale (ed.), *Historic Gardens of Virginia*; Susanne W. Massie and Frances A. Christian (eds.), *Homes and Gardens in Old Virginia*; and *Virginia, A Guide to the Old Dominion*.

the top of Rosewell, John Page's stately dwelling in Gloucester County, that Jefferson drafted the Declaration, reading and discussing it with his host, before going to Philadelphia. Page's house on York River (near its junction with Carter's Creek), was not far from Fairfield (on Carter's Creek), where Rebecca Burwell lived. This proximity was doubtless a circumstance influencing Jefferson during his college days to confide in Page as his intermediary in making love to her. When Jefferson himself was in that neighborhood, he found much to enjoy, for he wrote to Page: "I reflect often with pleasure on the philosophical evenings I passed at Rosewell in my last visits there."[4]

In Bedford County, near Lynchburg, is located Poplar Forest, the plantation Jefferson was in the habit of visiting in order to escape the swarm of uninvited guests at Monticello. At some distance from Lynchburg may be seen the famous Natural Bridge, situated on property owned by Jefferson, and vividly described by him in his *Notes on Virginia.*

"The most sublime of nature's works," as Jefferson characterized the Natural Bridge, was often visited by him. "Though the sides of this bridge are provided in some parts with a parapet of fixed rocks," he writes, "yet few men have resolution to walk to them, and look over into the abyss. You involuntarily fall on your hands and feet, creep to the parapet, and peep over it. Looking down from this height about a minute, gave me a violent headache. If the view from the top is intolerable, that from below is delightful in an equal extreme. It is impossible for the emotions arising from the sublime to be felt beyond what they are here; so beautiful an arch, so elevated, so light, and springing as it were up to heaven! The rapture of the spectator is really indescribable!"[5]

---

[4] To John Page, Charlottesville, February 21, 1770 (Lipscomb and Bergh, *Writings*, IV, 20). Regarding Jefferson's visits to Gunston Hall, see Rowland, *The Life of George Mason*, II, 324, 328, 329, 363.

[5] Lipscomb and Bergh, *Writings*, II, 30–32. See also Randolph, *Domestic Life*, 61; and Edmund P. Tompkins and J. Lee Davis, *The Natural Bridge and Its Historical Surroundings*, 3–4, 5, 7–8. At the back of Jefferson's account book for 1767,

But, as is usually the case, such transports of delight were experienced only by tourists, and not by those who had the opportunity to enjoy the spectacle daily. Of the spot where, at its junction with the Shenandoah, the Potomac passes through the Blue Ridge, Jefferson declares: "This scene is worth a voyage across the Atlantic. Yet here, as in the neighborhood of the Natural Bridge, are people who have passed their lives within half a dozen miles, and have never been to survey these monuments of a war between rivers and mountains, which must have shaken the earth itself to its centre."[6]

Speaking of his *Notes on Virginia* in a letter from Paris, Jefferson said: "You will find in them that the Natural Bridge has found an admirer in me also. I should be happy to make with you the tour of the curiosities you will find therein mentioned. That kind of pleasure surpasses much, in my estimation, whatever I find on this side the Atlantic. I sometimes think of building a little hermitage at the Natural Bridge (for it is my property) and of passing there a part of the year at least."[7] The state of his finances, however, compelled him to consider selling the site, and at length it was leased to Dr. William Thornton, a signer of the Declaration of Independence and architect of the Capitol at Washington, for the purpose of establishing a shot factory.[8]

Nature's handiwork in Virginia impressed Jefferson more than the structures erected by his countrymen. "The only public buildings worthy of mention are the capitol, the palace, the col-

---

now in the Library of Congress, belonging to General Jefferson Randolph Kean, there is a more prosaic description of the bridge with a diagram. Besides remarking the possible danger from large cracks and loose pieces of rock, Jefferson noted that "just where the bridge joins the precipice . . . there grows a cluster of cedars" and that "at the bottom by the waterside is a tree growing which when you are under it appears to be a large tree, but when on the bridge you find that it scarcely reaches more than half way."

[6] Lipscomb and Bergh, *Writings*, II, 25.

[7] To Mr. Carmichael, Paris, December 26, 1786 (*ibid.*, VI, 29–30).

[8] To Archibald Stuart, Washington, October 22, 1808 (*ibid.*, XIX, 171); to William Caruthers, Monticello, December 3, 1814 (*ibid.*, XIX, 221). Regarding Thornton, see Ihna T. Frary, *They Built the Capitol*, 71.

lege, and the hospital for lunatics, all of them in Williamsburg, heretofore the seat of our government. The capitol is a light and airy structure, with a portico in front. . . . Yet, on the whole, it is the most pleasing piece of architecture we have. The palace is not handsome without, but it is spacious and commodious within, is prettily situated, and with the grounds annexed to it, is capable of being made an elegant seat. The college and hospital are rude, misshapen piles, which, but that they have roofs, would be taken for brick-kilns. There are no other public buildings but churches and court-houses, in which no attempts are made at elegance. . . . The genius of architecture seems to have shed its maledictions over this land. Buildings are often erected, by individuals, of considerable expense. To give these symmetry and taste, would not increase their cost. . . . But the first principles of the art are unknown."[9]

Jefferson himself did his best to remedy the architectural shortcomings of his native state. Besides his home and the public buildings which were products of his skill, there are many other structures which were undoubtedly built, in whole or in part, from designs by him. These, it is said, range from mansions for his friends to jails, and even chicken coops.[10]

Williamsburg was the capital of Virginia when Jefferson was a student at William and Mary. In 1780, largely through his efforts, the seat of government was moved to Richmond; but in 1934 the legislature again met in Williamsburg, which had been restored, at great expense and after painstaking research, to its appearance in colonial times.[11] In correspondence with his college chum, John Page, Jefferson playfully designates the town as "Devilsburg." From March 25, 1760, to April 25, 1762, he was

[9] Lipscomb and Bergh, *Writings*, II, 212–13.

[10] Harold J. Coolidge, *Thoughts on Thomas Jefferson*, 20.

[11] The Act of February 24, 1934, provided: "The General Assembly may, by joint resolution, direct the holding of such session or sessions in the Restored Capitol at Williamsburg, Virginia, as to it may seem proper."—*Acts of the General Assembly of the Commonwealth of Virginia*, 1934, 99.

enrolled in the college; but thereafter he continued to study law, and to hold public office, so that "for practically the next nineteen years Jefferson's home was in Williamsburg."[12]

Very little is known, however, regarding the location of the places where he lived. It is presumed that while he was in college he stayed in what is now called the Wren Building.[13] During his governorship he resided in the Palace.[14] His expense book shows that on October 6, 1770, he "entd into R. Adams's rooms @ £ 12–10 pr. ann." Another entry, on June 11, 1772, reads: "pd Singleton for altern. of door in the house I formerly lived in 11/6 as per rect. Still due to him 1/6." A granddaughter of Governor Tyler is reported as saying that from the front door of her parents' dwelling in Williamsburg she "could point out . . . the very spot where the house stood" in which Jefferson, Tyler, and Frank Willis of Gloucester County used to study together in the same room.[15] In 1776, after his return from Philadelphia, the author of the Declaration of Independence and his wife occupied the home of George Wythe, who urged Jefferson to make use of the house, servants, and furniture. "I shall be happy if any thing

[12] Julian A. C. Chandler, "Jefferson and William and Mary," *William and Mary College Quarterly* (2d series), Vol. XIV, No. 4 (October, 1934), 304.

[13] Letters to the author from J. S. Bryan, president of William and Mary College, September 28, 1937; H. D. Farish, director of research, Colonial Williamsburg, Inc., May 20, 1940. The accounts of John Blair, Jr., the bursar of the college, show that from March 25, 1760, to April 25, 1762, Jefferson incurred a board bill of £ 27-1-8 which was paid June 10, 1762. A note is appended that: "Mr. Jefferson tells me he left the college abt. 25th April."—Lyon G. Tyler, *Williamsburg, The Old Colonial Capital*, 157.

[14] The day after Jefferson was chosen as governor, his friend Page, who had been his rival for the office, writing to congratulate him, said: "I attended at your Lodgings, today as soon as our Board adjourned, but you were not at home."—John Page to Jefferson, June 2, 1779 (Library of Congress, Jefferson Papers). Jefferson's papers in the Library of Congress contain an inventory of the household furniture in the Palace, dated June 16, 1779. A legislator wrote to Jefferson denying a report that he intended "to impeach your Excellency before the general assembly, of illegal conduct relative to the palace furniture."—James Jones to Jefferson, Richmond, June 20, 1780 (*ibid.*). A report to Governor Jefferson in January, 1781, regarding "damage done by the enemy at the Palace" is mentioned in *Calendar of Virginia State Papers*, I, 477.

[15] Lyon G. Tyler, *The Letters and Times of the Tylers*, I, 55.

MONTICELLO

Octagonal salon of Monticello, showing Paris purchases

Photograph by Charles Gaush

of mine can contribute to make your and Mrs Jefferson's residence in Williamsburg comfortable."[16]

It was during his law-student days that Jefferson stood at the door of the House of Burgesses and heard Patrick Henry debate the famous Resolutions of 1765 against the Stamp Act. In Jefferson's estimation Henry seemed to speak as Homer wrote.

Other diversions enjoyed by Jefferson as a young man, in Williamsburg or in the towns where he attended county court as an itinerant attorney, included visits to the "play house" and the "coffee house" at the capital, games of "cross & pile" or "backgammon," and consumption of "punch" or "arrack." When he came to Staunton, the county seat of Augusta County, he usually revisited the same taverns or places of entertainment: "T. Bowyer's," "Mrs. Wallace's," "McLanahan's," and "S. Matthews's." When court was held in Albemarle County, at Charlottesville, Jefferson was often to be found imbibing "toddy at Jouett's" or dining at that tavern. In Williamsburg, where the general court and the court of oyer and terminer met, he frequented the establishments kept by "Robert Anderson," "Richd. Charlton," "Christopher Ayscough," "Mrs. Vobe," and "Mrs. Campbell."

"About one hundred paces distant from the Capitol" stood the Raleigh Tavern. In the Apollo Room there young Jefferson danced merrily with Rebecca Burwell in agreeable company; but, when he sought to win her heart by means of carefully premeditated speeches in moving language, he succeeded only in uttering a few broken sentences interrupted with pauses of uncommon length. Years later, when in 1769, 1773, and 1774 the royal governor dissolved the House of Burgesses because of their bold sentiments, Jefferson and other members of the Assembly repaired to the same Apollo Room to unite in political conclave.[17]

[16] George Wythe to Jefferson, Philadelphia, October 28, 1776, and November 18, 1776 (Library of Congress, Jefferson Papers).
[17] Lipscomb and Bergh, *Writings*, I, 182; to John Page, Williamsburg, October 7, 1763 (Ford, *Writings*, I, 353); Lipscomb and Bergh, *Writings*, I, 6, 8, 10, 182.

Williamsburg was likewise the meeting place of Jefferson, Wythe, and Pendleton in February, 1779, when they came together to prepare their notable revision of the laws of Virginia. They had first met at Fredericksburg, on January 13, 1777, to settle the plan of operation and distribute the work.[18]

The educational advantages of Williamsburg were pointed out to an inquiring parent by Jefferson in 1788: "Williamsburg is a remarkably healthy situation, reasonably cheap, and affords very genteel society. I know no place *in the world,* while the *present professors remain,* where I would so soon place a son." Most illustrious of the teachers thus eulogized was Chancellor Wythe. "He is one of the greatest men of the age. . . . He gives lectures regularly, and holds moot courts and parliaments wherein he presides, and the young men debate regularly in law and legislation, learn the rules of parliamentary proceeding, and acquire the habit of public speaking."[19] Furthermore, Jefferson pointed out, "there are many individuals in Williamsburg, and its vicinity, who have already attained a high degree of science, and many zealously pursuing it."[20]

In 1779 Jefferson had been visitor of William and Mary while governor of Virginia, and effected some reforms in the curriculum of the institution. Late in his life, when there was talk of removing William and Mary to Richmond as a substitute for the plan Jefferson had at heart of establishing a seat of higher learning at Charlottesville, near his home, he eloquently exclaimed: "When the professors, their charter and funds shall be translated to Richmond, will they become more enlightened there than at the old place? Will they possess more science? be more capable of communicating it? . . . Or has Richmond any

[18] *Ibid.,* I, 62, 66. Jefferson's account book shows on January 16, 1777: "pd Smith, tavern keeper Fredsbgh. entt. £ 4-4." On the seventeenth: "pd Smith's tavern (on the road) entertt. 5/9" and "pd Bell, Orange C. H. dinner 5/."

[19] To Mr. Izard, Paris, July 17, 1788 (Lipscomb and Bergh, *Writings,* VII, 71). Among Wythe's pupils in law, besides Jefferson, were numbered Henry Clay and Chief Justice John Marshall.

[20] To G. C. de la Coste, Washington, May 24, 1807 (*ibid.,* XI, 207).

peculiarities more favorable for the communication of sciences generally than the place which the legislature has preferred and fixed on for that purpose? This will not be pretended. . . . But Richmond thinks it can have a hospital which will furnish subjects for the clinical branch of medicine. The classes of people which furnish subjects for the hospitals of Baltimore, Philadelphia, New York and Boston, do not exist at Richmond. . . . I will ask how many families in Richmond would send their husbands, wives, or children to a hospital, in sickness, to be attended by nurses hardened by habit against the feelings of pity, to lie in public rooms harassed by the cries and sufferings of disease under every form, alarmed by the groans of the dying, exposed as a corpse to be lectured over by a clinical professor, to be crowded and handled by his students to hear their case learnedly explained to them, its threatening symptoms developed, and its probable termination foreboded? In vindication of Richmond, I may surely answer that there is not in the place a family so heartless, as, relinquishing their own tender cares of a child or parent, to abandon them in sickness to this last resource of poverty; for it is poverty alone which peoples hospitals, and those alone who are on the charities of their parish would go to their hospital. Have they paupers enough to fill a hospital? and sickness enough among these?"[21]

It is interesting to note that a similar proposal made in recent years to transfer to Richmond the medical school of the University of Virginia caused another illustrious Virginia statesman, Woodrow Wilson, to protest against the proposed removal, in a letter which has been placed on exhibition in the dormitory room occupied by President Wilson when he was a student at the University of Virginia in Charlottesville.

From his earliest days Jefferson was doubtless familiar with Richmond. As a child he lived for seven years at Tuckahoe, a few miles up the James River from there. Likewise, on his way

[21] To J. C. Cabell, Monticello, May 16, 1824 (*ibid.*, XVI, 36–38).

from Albemarle County to Williamsburg in order to attend college or sessions of the legislature, he undoubtedly passed through Richmond. It was not always his lot to find congenial society at that place. He wrote in 1763: "From a crowd of disagreeable companions among whom I have spent three or four of the most tedious hours of my life, I retire into Gunn's bed-chamber to converse in black and white with an absent friend."[22] This letter was doubtless penned from James Gunn's yellow house on the high ground later selected as the site of the capitol building.[23]

In the vicinity of Richmond are clustered many historic mansions where Jefferson was once a familiar figure. His boyhood home at Tuckahoe, a splendid specimen of colonial craftsmanship and design, still stands on the spot where it was originally erected. Two other noteworthy houses have been recently transplanted. Ampthill, in Chesterfield County, the abode of patriotic Archibald Cary,[24] and Wilton, on the opposite side of the river,

[22] To William Fleming, Ri[chmond, late in September, 1763] (Ford, *Writings*, I, 351).

[23] James Buchanan and William Hay, on behalf of the Directors of Public Buildings, wrote to Jefferson, who was in France, on March 20, 1785: "We have laid down the ground, it being fully in your power to describe it, when we inform you that the Hill on which Gunns yellow house stands, and which you favoured as the best situation, continues to be preferred by us: and that we have located 29 half acre lots including Marsdens tenement, and Minzies' lots in front of Gunns."—Fiske Kimball, *Thomas Jefferson and the First Monument of the Classical Revival in America*, 11. The capitol was built on lot 392, belonging to John Gunn, whose residence was on the diagonally adjacent lot 404. Lots 405 and 391 also belonged to Gunn, a house occupied by a tenant standing on lot 391. The suggestion has been made that Jefferson while governor lived in the Gunn dwelling, that being one of the few houses then standing on Shockoe Hill. (R. W. Gunn to Edward V. Valentine, February 15, 1926 [information supplied by Miss Helen G. McCormack of the Valentine Museum, Richmond, to the author, October 6, 1940].) John Gunn inherited the property from his father, James Gunn, who died in 1775 (R. W. Gunn to the author, November 2, 1940). Jefferson's index to his account book for 1774 lists under "Gunn's ordinary" payments made January 3 and April 25, the first being for "entertt. at Gunn's 1/" and the second to "James Gunn in part £ 2." Entries under date of May 17 and December 12, 1773, and March 22, 27, and 28, 1775, also show that Jefferson stopped at Gunn's tavern. He likewise patronized (as shown by entries under date of May 22, 1777, and December 18, 1781) Gabriel Galt's City Tavern, on the northwest corner of Main and Nineteenth streets (Alexander W. Weddell, *Richmond, Virginia, in Old Prints*, 34, 225). Payments for "punch" at "Mrs. Younghusband's" and "Cooley's" are likewise recorded (March 20 and 23, 1775).

[24] Jefferson often visited Ampthill. After Mrs. Jefferson's death he took his

where doubtless Jefferson called on Anne Randolph (a belle mentioned as "Nancy Wilton" in his letters, to distinguish her from a cousin of the same name),[25] have now been rebuilt on new sites. The Forest, in Charles City County, was the scene of Jefferson's wedding. However, the hospitable merriment and fiddle playing which accompanied that occasion can be recaptured only in imagination, for a visitor who makes his way to that place at the present time finds nothing but a tangle of weeds and bushes overrunning the ruined substructure of an edifice destroyed years ago by fire.[26] Further down the James River in the direction of Williamsburg are situated Shirley, Westover, and Brandon. These beautiful estates, when Jefferson beheld them, were occupied by the Carters, the Byrds, and the Harrisons. Shirley, indeed, the home of Robert E. Lee's mother, never passed into the hands of strangers, but has remained continuously in the possession of members of the family ever since it was built, early in the eighteenth century. To visit Shirley was a lifelong source of de-

children there to be inoculated. His acquaintance with Cary began at William and Mary. Cary won perennial renown by his threat to slay Patrick Henry if the eloquent orator were made dictator. (Robert K. Brock, *Archibald Cary of Ampthill*, 65–66, 103–104.) The Du Pont rayon plant now embraces the site of Ampthill. Some of the trees which surrounded the mansion still stand, and plans preserved by the Du Pont Company show the exact site where the house stood. (George R. Beach, Jr., of the Du Pont Company to the author, June 28, 1940). The house was taken down in 1929 and rebuilt on a site west of Richmond by Mr. Hunsdon Cary, its present owner.

[25] To John Page, Shadwell, January 20, 1763 (Lipscomb and Bergh, *Writings*, IV, 7): "I hear that Ben Harrison has been to Wilton: let me know his success"; to John Page, Ri[chmond, late September 1763] (*ibid.*, IV, 223): "[Jenny Taliaferro] is in my opinion a great resemblance of Nancy Wilton, but prettier." Cf. Mary Newton Stanard, *Richmond Its People and Its Story*, 38–39. Wilton is now maintained by the Society of Colonial Dames.

[26] The site of The Forest is now part of a tract of timber land belonging to the present owner of Shirley. On trips to The Forest, Jefferson's account book shows he often patronized "Lorton's ferry" and James Vaughan's tavern. On January 1, 1772, the bridegroom "gave revd. W. Coutts £ 5" and "borrowed of Mr. Coutts 20/." The next day he "gave revd mr. Davies marriage fee £5." On the third he "gave a fidler 10/." On December 30, 1771, he "inclosed to M. Debman for marriage license 40/," and on January 18, 1772 he "inclosed to James New for marriage license 40/." Jefferson was married on New Year's Day.

light to the revered Confederate commander, who had spent many happy days there as a young man.[27]

Jefferson was in Richmond, attending the second Virginia convention, when that body met on March 20, 1775, in St. John's church. It was there that Patrick Henry uttered his memorable cry: "Give me liberty or give me death!"

Of the much-vaunted seven hills of Richmond, perhaps the most renowned for its memorable events and personages is the one on which stands the historic place of worship where Henry spoke. Now called Church Hill, it was then known as Richmond Hill, probably because in those days the town hardly extended beyond the vicinity of that hill. A great deal of land in the neighborhood was owned by Colonel Richard Adams. He lived on Richmond Hill at the southwest corner of Twenty-second and Grace Streets. Here, it is said, Jefferson was a frequent guest. However, according to tradition, the Colonel's warm friendship for Jefferson was turned into lifelong enmity as a result of disappointment over the location of the Capitol Square when the seat of government was moved from Williamsburg. Adams was anxious for the public buildings to be erected on Richmond Hill so that his property would increase in value. Jefferson, according to the story, promised to use his influence in favor of Richmond Hill. Apparently, however, Jefferson preferred the site on Shockoe Hill which was ultimately selected, after considerable controversy regarding the rival locations.[28]

As early as 1776 Jefferson had proposed removal of the capital from Williamsburg to Richmond; but the measure did not prevail in the legislature until the summer of 1779, and the actual transfer of the executive offices was effected in the spring of

[27] Douglas S. Freeman, *R. E. Lee, A Biography*, IV, 365.

[28] The story was related by Mrs. Eliza Griffin Carrington, a granddaughter of Colonel Adams, in her eighty-third year as "an authentic tradition of her childhood."—Robert A. Brock, *The Vestry Book of Henrico Parish*, 184–85; Robert A. Brock, "The Adams Family," in the *Richmond Standard*, December 11, 1880. Regarding the location of the capitol on Shockoe Hill, see William W. Hening, *The Statutes at Large*, X, 317; Journal of the House of Delegates for 1783, 91–92; and n. 23 *supra*.

1780 while he was governor.[29] Besides the fact that Williams-burg was no longer the center of population, "its situation was so exposed that it might be taken at any time in war."[30] However, despite its supposed advantages, Richmond was seized on January 5, 1781, by British troops under the command of Benedict Arnold, and held for twenty-four hours, during Jefferson's governorship. Not many months later, fearing another attack, the legislature abandoned Richmond. On May 10, 1781, they adjourned to Charlottesville. But from there, too, they were obliged to flee. The invading forces took possession of that town and almost captured Jefferson, when on June 4, 1781, the "British horse came to Monticello." It was doubtless painful to the pride of Virginians to see their capital profaned by the traitor Arnold as well as their legislature repeatedly dispersed; and Jefferson did not escape criticism.[31] But he believed that, in view of the circumstances of the crisis with which he had been confronted, there was nothing blameworthy or extraordinary in his having failed to prevent "the surprise of an open and unarmed place, although called a city, and even a capital."[32]

But although adequate fortifications were lacking, Richmond was not altogether bereft of public works and architectural attractions. In 1789, after his return from abroad, Jefferson wrote to William Short: "There is one street in Richmond (from the bridge on towards Currie's) which would be considered as handsomely built in any city of Europe."[33] To this result Jefferson

[29] *Official Letters of the Governors of the State of Virginia*, II, 115. A notice in the *Virginia Gazette* of March 25, 1780, stated that business in the executive department would cease to be transacted in Williamsburg on April 7 and would commence in Richmond on April 24. Jefferson's official correspondence in Williamsburg stops on the seventh and resumes in Richmond on the tenth. The act for the removal of the seat of government was passed on June 5, 1779, by the House of Delegates, which on June 12, 1779, concurred in the Senate's amendments. (Journal of the House of Delegates for 1779, 36, 44.)

[30] Lipscomb and Bergh, *Writings*, I, 60.

[31] John P. Little, *History of Richmond*, 66–67.

[32] To Henry Lee, Monticello, May 15, 1826 (Ford, *Writings*, X, 388).

[33] To William Short, Eppington, December 14, 1789 (*ibid.*, V, 137). Dr. Currie's house was on Broad Street opposite the old City Hall (Weddell, *Richmond in Old Prints*, 39).

himself had largely contributed. In the "Act for locating the publick squares, to enlarge the town of Richmond, and for other purposes," he was named first of the nine Directors of the Public Buildings.[34] He took an active part in planning the new capital of Virginia, just as later he did in laying out the new capital of the nation at Washington. While abroad, he made arrangements for statues of Washington and Lafayette by the eminent French sculptor Houdon.[35] These were to adorn the capitol at Richmond, of which Jefferson himself was the architect.

Construction had already begun before Jefferson's plans were received. However, he persuaded the Virginia authorities to make a fresh start, adopting his "simple & sublime" designs, "copied from the most precious, the most perfect model of antient architecture remaining on earth." This model was the Maison Carrée at Nîmes, an edifice "which has been the admiration of sixteen centuries; which has been the object of as many pilgrimages as the tomb of Mahomet"; and which is unsurpassed by "the beautiful monuments of Greece, Rome, Palmyra, and Balbec." The event was of great architectural significance. The Virginia capitol was "the first building destined specifically for a modern republican government, and the first to give such a government a monumental setting."[36]

In his later life Jefferson seems to have had little contact with Richmond. Referring to that place, he wrote in 1815: "But altho I once lived there and knew nearly every body in it, yet I have been there but twice or thrice within the last 30. years, and think there is not a single person living there now who was an inhabi-

[34] Hening, *Statutes*, X, 318.

[35] Charles Henry Hart and Edward Biddle, *Memoirs of the Life and Works of Jean Antoine Houdon*, 193.

[36] To Dr. James Currie, Paris, January 18, 1786 (Ford, *Writings*, IV, 133); to Madison, Paris, February 8, 1786 (Lipscomb and Bergh, *Writings*, V, 282); to Madison, Paris, September 20, 1785 (*ibid.*, V, 135); Kimball, *Jefferson and the Classical Revival*, 44–45. (For Jefferson's praise of the Maison Carrée, see letters to Buchanan and Hay, Paris, January 26, 1786, in *ibid.*, 13.) See also Fiske Kimball, *Thomas Jefferson, Architect*, 40–42.

tant when I was."[37] He may have avoided visiting Richmond because he found it uncongenial. Perhaps he disliked the city because it was a Federalist stronghold, where his antagonists John Marshall and Aaron Burr were honored, or because it had been the scene of British military exploits, even the recollection of which was distasteful to him. He may have remembered also with displeasure that on December 7, 1789, the Richmond city fathers voted upon a motion "that an Address be prepared to be presented to His Excellency Thomas Jefferson Late Ambassador to the Court of France upon his return to his native country; and the question being put thereon, the same was negatived" by eight to three.[38]

When he had completely retired from public life, however, the inhabitants of Richmond found it possible to abandon partisan restraint, and to welcome him with cordiality upon his return to their midst. In 1809, on the occasion of one of his infrequent visits to the city on private business[39] during the later years of his life, he was honored by repeated tributes of respect.[40] Ar-

[37] To Samuel Thurber, Monticello, January 2, 1815.—Mo. Hist. Soc., Bixby Collection.

[38] Richmond City Hall, Records No. 1, July 3, 1782–December 22, 1792, 200.

[39] Besides his dealings with Richmond merchants, Jefferson owned property in the city. The tax books for 1782 and 1784 show him as owner of lot 335. That location is on Cary Street, on the south side of the block, between Fourteenth and Fifteenth Streets. Coffee warehouses are now situated there. In the Huntington Library is an extract from a deed of Charles Carter to Jefferson, to which the date of December 27, 1773, is attributed, conveying part of a lot "adjacent to the river," to the road laid off from Shockoe Warehouse to the wharf, to the portion of the lot belonging to Robert Cary Nicholas, and to lot No. 334 owned by Patrick Coutts. According to information in folder 547 of the Lawyers Title Insurance Company (courteously made available by Mr. Laurie Smith), on August 6, 1897, P. R. Carrington had possession of the unrecorded original deed to Jefferson from Charles Carter of Shirley, surviving trustee of William Byrd III, dated in 1782. Jefferson's account book under date of November 9, 1777 states: "Chas. Carter (surviving trustee for Colo. Byrd) executed deed to me for part of a lot in Richmond, for which I am to pay Mr. Wayles's Estate £25, as of this day & endorse it on the protested bill due from Byrd to the estate." Entries for October 9, 1774, and January 24, 1775, show that Colonel T. M. Randolph "is also to build me a ware house at Shockoes" and that "John Mayo is to saw me stuff for a warehouse at Richmond." Again, in 1810–12 the tax books show Jefferson as owning lot 25, on Broad Street, on the north side, between Twenty-ninth and Thirtieth Streets.

[40] Information regarding Jefferson's visit to Richmond in 1809 is found in W.

riving on Thursday, October 19, he stopped at the Swan Tavern, situated on the northwest corner of Broad and Ninth Streets. The next day, he was invited to dine at the armory by the officers of the Nineteenth Regiment of Virginia Militia, who, at their drill muster on the Capitol Square that morning, had learned of his presence in the city. Together with the Governor and other dignitaries, he was escorted from the Swan at the hour for dinner, and conducted through the files of the officers. Among the volunteer toasts drunk during and following the repast was one by Jefferson to: "The militia of the United States—the bulwark of our Independence."

The Eagle Tavern, at the southeast corner of Main and Twelfth Streets, was the scene of a subscription dinner given in Jefferson's honor on Saturday the twenty-first. Governor Tyler tendered the invitation on behalf of "the Council of State, and many gentlemen." Arrangements were in the hands of a committee chosen at a meeting of the citizens at the capitol on Friday. An address to be presented to the illustrious guest was prepared by the same committee. In reply to the address Jefferson said: "I claim no other merit than that of having, with my best endeavors contributed, together with my fellow citizens at large, to the establishment of those rights, without which, man is a degraded being."

The Governor presided at the banquet, assisted by Dr. William Foushee, who had served in the Revolutionary War and had been first mayor of the city of Richmond. Other guests included former Governor Cabell, members of the Executive Council, and the three judges of the Court of Appeals. According to the account published in an unfriendly newspaper, there were about seventy-five persons present, of whom less than a dozen were Federalists.

Asbury Christian, *Richmond, Her Past and Present,* 73; Tyler, *The Tylers,* I, 228–30; extracts from *Richmond Enquirer,* and from *Virginia Gazette and General Advertiser* for Tuesday, October 24, 1809 (furnished the author by courtesy of Professor Maude H. Woodfin of the University of Richmond).

After dinner a number of toasts were drunk, "accompanied with music from the Band of the Rifle Company, and discharges from the Artillery Company." The toast proposed by Jefferson was: "The Freedom of the Seas." It was planned to fire a six-pounder after each toast; but after the third discharge of the cannon so many windows were shattered that "a stop was put to the firing by some of the citizens." It was estimated that between eighty and ninety panes of glass had been broken.

On the day following the affair at the Eagle Tavern, Jefferson was entertained at the "Palace," as the ramshackle frame house where the Governor lived was then called. Governor Tyler had instructed his son (who later became president of the United States) to be sure that there was a good dinner for the distinguished guest, but all details had been left to the young man's supervision. However, when two smoking plum puddings were set on the table, the astonished Governor expressed his amazement at this extraordinary circumstance. The youthful superintendent of household arrangements admitted that it was extraordinary for two plum puddings to be served, but he explained, rising and bowing deferentially to Jefferson, that the occasion was also extraordinary.

Probably at the time of this visit Jefferson could notice the dilapidated condition of the Governor's dwelling. Not long afterwards Governor Tyler complained to the legislature that the house was rapidly deteriorating, "having been originally badly built," and was "intolerable for a private family." Besides being too small, it was exposed on three sides to public thoroughfares. A cluster of dirty tenements immediately in front of it added to its unsightliness.[41] It was a plain wooden building of two stories, with two rooms of moderate size on each floor. On three sides there were porticoes. For many years it was unpainted. A cheap

[41] Message of Governor Tyler, December 3, 1810, Journal of the House of Delegates for 1810, 9.

wooden fence partly enclosed the yard, but the palings were usually in bad repair, and goats grazed on the grounds.[42]

This unpretentious residence fell far short of the magnificence of which the legislature had dreamed while writing on Virginia's statute books that two squares with the intervening street were to be reserved for the use of the governor, and that the houses were to be "built in a handsome manner with walls of brick or stone, and porticoes where the same may be convenient or ornamental, and with pillars and pavements of stone."[43]

The furniture was of the plainest kind, in keeping with the democratic simplicity of the house and its occupants. In an inventory of articles left in the "Palace" by Governor Harrison, he recorded:

"8 table cloths there were 14 but six stolen 3 Days before I left Government
1 old bed of little value being worn out by militia & recovered from some low creature in the town."[44]

Governor Tyler's complaints bore fruit. After satisfying themselves of the "ruinous decay"[45] of the structure, the law-

---

[42] Christian, *Richmond*, 35, 75; S. Mordecai, *Richmond in By-Gone Days*, 59.

[43] In May, 1779, the Act for the Removal of the Seat of Government provided: "Two others [squares] with the intervening street, shall be reserved for the use of the governour of this Commonwealth for the time being, and the remaining square shall be appropriated to the use of the publick market. The said houses shall be built in a handsome manner with walls of brick or stone, and porticoes where the same may be convenient or ornamental, and with pillars and pavements of stone."— Hening, *Statutes*, X, 86. Provision for temporary buildings (not mentioning a house for the governor) was made in the same act: "But whereas from the great expence attending the just and necessary war this commonwealth is at present engaged in, the difficulties of procuring the materials for building, and the high price for labour it will be burthensome to the inhabitants if the said publick buildings be immediately erected: *Be it therefore enacted*, That the directors aforesaid shall, with all convenient speed, cause to be erected or otherwise provide some proper and temporary buildings for the sitting of the general assembly, the courts of justice, and the several boards before described."—*Ibid.*, 88. In the *Williamsburg Gazette* for July 5, 1779, the directors gave notice of a meeting at Hogg's tavern in Richmond for the purpose of providing temporary buildings (Christian, *Richmond*, 17). The temporary capitol was located at the northwest corner of Cary and Fourteenth Streets (*ibid.*, 19). The Assembly met in the new capitol on October 28, 1788 (*ibid.*, 35).

[44] Inventory in Virginia State Archives.

[45] Journal of the House of Delegates for 1810–11, 91.

makers made provision for its replacement by a new edifice. Pursuant to this legislation, the materials of the "house in which the former Governors resided" were sold for $530.[46] The present Governor's Mansion was completed in 1813. Governor James Barbour was its first occupant.[47]

It seems unlikely that Jefferson had ever lived in the old "Palace" himself.[48] When he came to Richmond as governor, he "got possession of Colo Turpin's house" on April 17, 1780, according to his account book. That "house on the hill" belonged to Colonel Thomas Turpin of Powhatan County, who was a kinsman of Jefferson's and a direct ancestor of the novelist James Branch Cabell.[49] Jefferson rented it for one year. Under his arrangement with Turpin, he was personally liable for the rent, but he believed that the state ought to bear that expense as a public charge. Hence he referred the matter to Governor Benjamin Harrison when Turpin demanded the amount due. The Executive Council authorized payment "according to Mr. Jefferson's contract, out of the first public tobacco" available for that purpose,[50] and Governor Harrison notified Jefferson accordingly.[51] Apparently it is impossible to determine the site of Turpin's

[46] The sale was made to Charles Copland on April 20, 1811, under the Act of February 13, 1811.

[47] Earle Lutz, *A Richmond Album*, 20. Governor Barbour served from January 3, 1812, to December 1, 1814 (information supplied by Miss Helen G. McCormack of the Valentine Museum, Richmond, to the author, October 24, 1940).

[48] See Appendix II regarding Jefferson's residence in Richmond.

[49] Robert Armistead Stewart, "Jefferson and His Landlord," *The Researcher*, Vol. I, No. 1 (October, 1926), 5; William Clayton Torrence, "Thomas and William Branch of Henrico and Some of Their Descendants," *William and Mary College Quarterly* (1st series), Vol. XXV, No. 2 (October, 1916), 110–11; James B. Cabell to the author, May 31, 1940.

[50] On September 24, 1782 it was resolved: "A demand being made by Colo. Turpin of eight thousand weight of Tobacco for the rent of his house for the use of the Governor: The Commercial Agent is desired to discharge the same according to Mr. Jefferson's contract, out of the first public tobacco he may receive."—Council Journal 1781–82 (No. 13), 249.

[51] "Payment has been some time order'd for the rent of the House you lived in whilst Governor of the State and Colo Turpen may receive the Money whenever he pleases to apply to the Agent."—Harrison to Jefferson, October 3, 1782 (*Official Letters of the Governors of Virginia*, III, 336–37).

house which Jefferson occupied. It may have been located on the southeast corner of Broad and Governor Streets, where the Memorial Hospital now stands.

In addition to the places already mentioned, Jefferson's account book shows that in Richmond he patronized Hogg's tavern[52] and Formicola's.[53] Both of those establishments were on Main Street. Likewise Ege's old stone house, now maintained as the Edgar Allan Poe shrine, stands on the north side of Main Street, between Nineteenth and Twentieth Streets. That landmark, thought to be the oldest building in Richmond, is said to have been at one time in use as a tavern, and Jefferson is reported as having stopped there.[54]

[52] According to information at the Valentine Museum, that tavern was located (in 1783) on lot 327 at the southwest corner of Main and Fifteenth Streets. It was kept by Richard Hogg, who, according to the tax book of September 1782, was thirty-seven years of age and had been a tavern keeper for eleven years. In the *Williamsburg Gazette* of July 5, 1779, the Directors of Public Buildings gave notice that they would meet in Richmond at Hogg's tavern to make arrangements for temporary buildings (Christian, *Richmond*, 17). Jefferson's account book shows payments to Hogg on March 11, 1780, May 14, 1781, and December 22, 1781.

[53] The tax book of September, 1782, shows that Serafino Formicola had been a resident for only nineteen months. He was thirty-nine years of age, his wife Matilda was twenty-eight, and their daughter Eve was two. According to information at the Valentine Museum, in 1783 he kept tavern in a house belonging to the estate of Joshua Storrs, on the south side of Main Street between Fifteenth Street and Shockoe Creek (Seventeenth Street); but by May 7, 1789, he had removed to the Eagle Tavern at the southeast corner of Main and Twelfth Streets. On January 7, 1784, the Richmond city fathers named a committee "to view and report upon that part of the main street passing Mr. Formicola's Tavern" and on March 16, 1784 directed the "Committee for Streets to view the situation of the street opposite Formicola's Tavern & to give such directions as to them shall seem proper, to the Surveyor of Streets for diverting the course of the Water near the said Formicola's House & securing it from farther danger, and that the said Committee do report to the Hall any Damages he may have sustained thereby."—Richmond City Hall, Records, No. 1, July 3, 1782 to December 22, 1792, 51, 55–56. Formicola was said to be a descendant of the doges of Venice, in which city he had married. The Marquis de Chastellux, who enjoyed his visit at Formicola's tavern, said that "Formicalo" was a Neapolitan who had come to Virginia as maître d'hôtel for Lord Dunmore (*Voyages de M. le Marquis de Chastellux dans l'Amérique septentrionale*, II, 119–21). Jefferson's account book shows payments to Formicola on May 14 and 15, 1781, and on December 22, 1781; likewise on December 8, 1789, when Jefferson was returning from France.

[54] Benson J. Lossing, *The Pictorial Field-Book of the Revolution*, II, 233: "Washington, Jefferson, Madison, and Monroe (four of the presidents of the United States) have all been beneath its roof." Cf. Weddell, *Richmond in Old Prints*, 12; Little, *History of Richmond*, 172; and Lutz, *Richmond Album*, 6.

CHAPTER III

Law under His Feet

AT the age of twenty-three Jefferson first traveled beyond the frontiers of the Old Dominion. Philadelphia was his destination. He went there in the spring of 1766 to be inoculated for smallpox. This trip was an eventful one. The first day his horse ran away twice. The next day he rode in a drenching rain from morning until night without coming to a habitation in which he could take shelter. On the following day he came near being drowned while fording the swollen Pamunkey River. However, the journey brought pleasure as well as hardships. He called at the country seats of several acquaintances and enjoyed a reunion with some of his old college associates. He also stopped at Annapolis, where the General Assembly of Maryland was then in session. Writing to his friend Page, he contrasted the behavior of that body with the dignified proceedings of the Virginia legislature. Comparing Annapolis with the capital of his own state, he observed: "The houses are in general better than those in Williamsburg; but the gardens more indifferent. The two towns seem much of a size. They have no public buildings worth mentioning, except a Governor's House, the hall of which, after being nearly finished, they have suffered to go to ruin. I would give you an account of the rejoicings here on the repeal of the stamp act, but this you will probably see in print before my letter can reach you. I shall proceed to-morrow to Philadelphia, where I shall make the stay necessary for inoculation; thence going on to New York, I shall return by water to Williamsburg, about the middle of July."[1]

In Philadelphia, Jefferson "was placed in a cottage house, back from the city, near to the Schuylkill. It was then that Charles Thomson first became acquainted with him."[2] In New York Jefferson made the acquaintance of Elbridge Gerry, a young man from Massachusetts who was staying at the same boardinghouse. In later years, both Thomson and Gerry were his intimate friends and associates in political life.

In 1775 Jefferson was elected deputy delegate to the Continental Congress. On June 11 he left Williamsburg for Philadelphia, where he arrived on the twentieth. His lodging places en route were King William Court House, Fredericksburg, Port Tobacco, Upper Marlborough, Annapolis, Rockhall, and Wilmington. It is to be hoped that at Port Tobacco Jefferson escaped the unpleasant experiences which there befell a traveler from New England on a trip to visit Jefferson at Monticello. "We asked the landlady," writes the young man from Massachusetts, "what we could have for supper; the answer was, 'anything we pleased,' and after many useless selections, we were compelled to be contented with some miserable corn bread, a glass of milk and a piece of cheese, which we obtained in about two hours." The guests slept on a bag of feathers, and used a coverlid from the landlord's bed, after professing that they did not wish the sheets which were said to be drying. "I suspect there were no sheets, but our host wished the refusal to come from us."[3]

In Philadelphia Jefferson stayed with Benjamin Randolph,

[1] George Tucker, *The Life of Thomas Jefferson*, I, 44. To John Page, Annapolis, May 25, 1766, in the New York Public Library. This visit to Philadelphia is not mentioned in Joseph Jackson, "Thomas Jefferson in Philadelphia," *Encyclopedia of Philadelphia*, III, 788–90.

[2] John F. Watson, *Annals of Philadelphia and Pennsylvania in the Olden Time*, II, 373. Thomson was a cousin of Deborah Logan (*ibid.*, I, 573). Jefferson had a letter of introduction to Dr. John Morgan from George Gilmer, dated May 11, 1766. This letter is preserved in the Historical Society of Pennsylvania, Gratz Collection, case 7, box 29.

[3] Francis Calley Gray, *Thomas Jefferson in 1814*, 40–41.

The Forest, Charles City County, Virginia,
where Jefferson was married

From a photograph taken in 1890 by Cook, Richmond

The Fountain Inn, Baltimore

a cabinetmaker, who may have been a relative, and whose place of business was on Chestnut Street between Third and Fourth. The young statesman took most of his meals at the City Tavern, in Second Street north of Walnut.[4]

On August 1 he left Philadelphia for Virginia. At Richmond he attended the Virginia Convention, and was re-elected a member of the Continental Congress. On September 25 he "set out from Monticello for Philadelphia," arriving there October 1. While in the city on this visit, he lodged at Randolph's with a group of colleagues, and his account book frequently refers to sums "put into Common stock for housekeeping" or "for house rent" or "provisions." On December 28 he departed for Virginia, and arrived at Monticello on January 9, 1776. His route was through Bushtown, Baltimore, Upper Marlboro, Piscataway, Port Tobacco, and Fredericksburg. Returning to Philadelphia in 1776, Jefferson took a more westerly route, through York and Lancaster, in Pennsylvania. Leaving Monticello on May 7, he reached Philadelphia a week later.

The Declaration of Independence was written by Jefferson during this sojourn in Philadelphia. The monarch who had put "all law under his feet" was duly brought to book in an arraignment that became immortal; the nation he had wronged assumed its rightful station among the powers of the earth. With good cause, Jefferson regarded his authorship of the Declaration as the foremost achievement of his career.

Although upon his arrival in Philadelphia, Jefferson stopped

[4] Joseph F. A. Jackson, *Market Street Philadelphia*, 119. Jefferson's account books indicate other places where he was entertained. These include: "Center house," "Province isld.," "on Jersey shore," "at falls of Schuylkill," "Byrne's," and "Biddle's." Additional places visited in the fall of 1775 include: "Mullins's," "Blue bell," "Indian Queen," "Bird in hand," "Sadler's arms in Germantown," and "Duff's." Additional places visited in 1776 include: "Greentree's," "at Frankfurt," "Marks's," "Rising sun," and "Indian King." Some of those establishments can be readily identified. See Joseph Jackson, "Washington in Philadelphia," *Pennsylvania Magazine of History and Biography*, Vol. LVI, No. 222 (April, 1932), 121–25; James G. Barnwell, "Some of the Alleys, Courts and Inns of Philadelphia, 1767–1790," *ibid.*, Vol. XXXVII, No. 145 (January, 1913), 115; Jackson, *Encyclopedia of Philadelphia*, I, 304, II, 407, IV, 1046; Jackson, *Market Street*, 31, 59, 69.

again at Benjamin Randolph's for over a week, he soon began to look for more comfortable quarters. Writing to a friend in Virginia, he reported: "I am at present in our old lodgings, though I think, as the excessive heats of the city are coming on fast, to endeavor to get lodgings in the skirts of the town where I may have the benefit of a freely circulating air."[5] Though continuing to dine at Smith's City Tavern, the youthful patriot on May 23 "took lodgings at Graaf's," on the southwest corner of Seventh and Market Streets. Here, for thirty-five shillings a week, he obtained the whole second floor of a new brick house, three and one-half stories high. The owner was a newly married bricklayer of German extraction. The entrance was on Seventh Street, and the house was numbered 2. It was also known then as 230 High Street, later as 700 Market Street. It had five windows on the east side of the second story and two windows on the north. The back room served as a bedroom, and the apartment that opened upon Market Street was the study or sitting room where conferences with the other members of the committee took place and the Declaration was written.[6]

The folding desk which Jefferson used for that purpose was designed by him and made by Benjamin Randolph, the cabinetmaker with whom he had at first lodged. It is now to be seen in the National Museum at Washington, in the same room as "The Spirit of St. Louis," the plane in which another American pioneer, Colonel Charles A. Lindbergh, traversed the Atlantic Ocean.

The building in which Jefferson penned the immortal proclamation of American liberties was demolished in 1883. It had been for many years used for commercial purposes. Among its owners had been two brothers of Rebecca Gratz, who was the original of the character Rebecca in Scott's *Ivanhoe*.

[5] To Thomas Nelson, Philadelphia, May 16, 1776 (Lipscomb and Bergh, *Writings*, IV, 254).
[6] Jackson, *Market Street*, 120–21; Thomas Donaldson, *The House in Which Thomas Jefferson Wrote the Declaration of Independence*, 56, 69, 72, 82; John H. Hazelton, *The Declaration of Independence: Its History*, 151.

At the conclusion of his service in Congress, Jefferson left Philadelphia on September 2, 1776, arriving at Monticello a week later. He did not thereafter, until after the death of his wife on September 6, 1782, hold any public office requiring him to leave Virginia. He then accepted a diplomatic appointment but could not obtain passage to Europe when he went to Philadelphia and Baltimore for that purpose. Departing from Monticello on December 19, 1782, he reached Philadelphia two days after Christmas.

Jefferson's landlady in Philadelphia during this visit was a Mrs. House. She was the mother of Samuel House, whose residence is given as 368 Chestnut Street in Macpherson's directory for the city and suburbs of Philadelphia published in 1785.[7]

Setting out for Baltimore on January 26, 1783, Jefferson was absent a month from the Pennsylvania metropolis. He lodged in Baltimore with a Mrs. Langston and a Mrs. Ball. He also patronized "Grant's" in that city. The latter hostelry was the famous Fountain Inn, on the northeast corner of Light Street and Lovely Lane (now Redwood Street). For many years that tavern was one of the historic landmarks of Baltimore. It was probably erected during the Revolution, and stood until 1872 when the Carrollton Hotel was built. The site is now occupied by the Southern Hotel, opened in 1918. In December, 1782, Daniel Grant removed from the Indian Queen Tavern on the corner of Hanover and Baltimore Streets to "his large, new, and elegant house, in Light lane, between Market street and Ellicott's wharf, where the Fountain Inn is opened for the reception and entertainment of such gentlemen and ladies, travellers or others, as shall be pleased to honor his house with their company."[8] Besides Jef-

---

[7] Samuel House to Jefferson, Philadelphia, May 28, 1785 (Massachusetts Historical Society, Jefferson Papers). When Washington came to Philadelphia in 1787, he planned to lodge with a Mrs. Mary House at Fifth and Market Streets, according to Joseph Jackson in "Washington in Philadelphia," *Pennsylvania Magazine of History and Biography*, Vol. LVI, No. 222 (April, 1932), 139.

[8] John T. Scharf, *The Chronicles of Baltimore*, 206; John T. Scharf, *History of Baltimore City and County*, 514.

ferson, many other illustrious guests, including Lafayette and Washington, were welcomed there.

The Fountain Inn was at first the gathering place of Jefferson's followers, but later catered to the Federalists. The explanation for this may be found in a story told in Baltimore to the effect that on one occasion a horseman, much bespattered with mud, arrived at the Inn and was told that there was no lodging available without sharing accommodations with another guest. The lone rider was Jefferson. Without a word he turned away and patronized the Fountain's nearest rival. That night a fire broke out in the rival's stable, in which a number of horses were lost, including that of Jefferson. The incident thus became a matter of public discussion.[9]

Whatever the reason may have been, it is certain that in later years Jefferson did patronize the Indian Queen. It was situated at the southeast corner of Hanover and Baltimore Streets. The premises extended from Baltimore Street to Redwood Street. Men's clothing and tailoring establishments, as well as other shops, are now located there. In addition to Jefferson, many other presidents and statesmen were entertained at that historic tavern. When Andrew Jackson was there with the celebrated Indian warrior, Black Hawk, the crowd of curious spectators was so large that the defeated chieftain had to be taken to Fort McHenry. It was at the Indian Queen, in a spacious chamber with two fireplaces, that the Continental Congress met in 1776 when it abandoned Philadelphia because of British military successes. Rejoicing in 1814 over the repulse of the same foe when Baltimore was attacked, Francis Scott Key completed writing "The Star-Spangled Banner" in a room at the Indian Queen.[10]

[9] Matthew Page Andrews, "At the Sign of the Fountain 1773–1930," page 15 (typewritten memorandum consulted by courtesy of Mr. A. J. Fink, managing director of the Southern Hotel).

[10] Jefferson's account book shows that he was at "Grant's" on July 16, 1792, and at "Brydon's" on February 26, 1797. Daniel Grant and James Bryden were proprietors of the Fountain Inn. He was at "Starck's" on January 8, 1794; and at "Evans's" on May 9, 1797, December 10, 1797, and December 23, 1798. Jacob Starck and William Evans were proprietors of the Indian Queen. After Evans re-

Leaving Philadelphia on April 12, 1783, Jefferson traveled by way of Baltimore, Upper Marlboro, Portroyal, Hanover, Richmond (where he stayed a fortnight), and Tuckahoe, to Monticello. He arrived there on May 15.

Jefferson's willingness to return to public life having been thus manifested, it was not long until he was again attending the Continental Congress as a representative of the Old Dominion. On his way to Philadelphia in the fall of 1783, he took the most westerly route which he ever traversed, passing through Woodstock, Winchester, Harper's Ferry, Frederick, Tawneytown, McAlistertown, Susquehanna, and Lancaster.[11] He left Monticello on October 16, and reached Philadelphia on October 29.

It was on this trip that Jefferson ascended the height back of the tavern at Harper's Ferry and viewed the impressive spectacle presented by the passage of the Potomac through the Blue Ridge, which he described in his *Notes on Virginia*.[12]

According to local tradition, "Jefferson's rock," as it is called, is the spot from which he surveyed the landscape. Since only the Shenandoah River can be seen from there, and the junction of the Potomac and the Shenandoah is not visible, it seems more likely that he stood at a higher point, probably near where the McMahon house now stands. In that dwelling another famous president, Grover Cleveland, is said to have stayed overnight at Harper's Ferry.

---

tired, he leased the hotel to various tavern keepers until it was closed in 1832. The property is still owned by descendants of Evans's son-in-law, Colonel James Piper of the Maryland Guard, who took part in the battle of North Point. (Scharf, *History of Baltimore*, 514; Henry M. Hyde, in the *Baltimore Evening Sun* of January 24, 1927; Charles F. Adams [ed.], *The Works of John Adams*, II, 433; *Journals of the Continental Congress*, VI, 1027; letters to the author from William B. Marye, of the Maryland Historical Society, July 26, 1940, and September 18, 1940; from Louis Gordon, September 20, 1940; and from James Piper, October 7, 1940, and October 24, 1940.)

[11] Jefferson later advised a friend in Philadelphia that "the road by Baltimore & Havre de grace is the best, and 80 miles shorter than by Lancaster."—To John Barnes, Monticello, September 12, 1801 (Huntington Library, MS Collections).

[12] To Horatio G. Spafford, Monticello, May 14, 1809 (Lipscomb and Bergh, *Writings*, XII, 280).

The rock, a huge inverted pyramid, was once so balanced that it would move at the pressure of a child's hand. For many years it has been supported by pillars placed under it by order of one of the superintendents of the armory which formerly embraced an extensive site at Harper's Ferry. One ledge of the rock appears to have been detached from it, and leans against it.

The story is told that in 1799, during a bitter feud between Federalists and Republicans, a certain Captain Henry, of General Pinckney's army which was quartered on Camp Hill, one day took his company to Jefferson's rock and ordered them to overthrow the favorite seat of Jefferson, his political enemy. The men succeeded in separating from the top of the rock a large boulder, which rolled down the steep hillside to Shenandoah Street, where it lay for many years, a monument of stupid bigotry. Captain Henry was challenged to mortal combat by an equally zealous Republican; but the duel was prevented by General Pinckney, much to the regret of the sensible people of the town who believed that if it had been permitted to proceed there would have been at least "one fool the less at Harper's Ferry."

Jefferson's interest is also said to have been attracted by a nest of eagles in an oak tree across the Shenandoah River from the rock. At his request, after his election as president, the son of Mr. Perkins, the superintendent of the armory, with two other young men, climbed the tree and captured three eaglets. The birds were shipped to Jefferson, who sent one of them as a gift to the King of Spain. That monarch thereupon presented Jefferson with an Andalusian ram, which was kept in the White House grounds as a curiosity.[13]

Jefferson arrived at Princeton, where he took his seat in Congress, on November 4, 1783. The following day he turned back toward Philadelphia, arriving on the seventh. Two weeks later

[13] Joseph Barry, *The Strange Story of Harper's Ferry*, 6, 20; Josephus Junior [Barry], *Annals of Harper's Ferry*, 5–6, 11.

he departed thence for Annapolis, to which place Congress had adjourned. He arrived on November 26.

While Jefferson was attending Congress in Annapolis, his daughter Martha was enjoying the educational advantages of Philadelphia. Regarding her studies while she stayed with Mrs. Hopkinson in that city, Jefferson said: "Her time in Philadelphia will be chiefly occupied in acquiring a little taste and execution in such of the fine arts as she could not prosecute to equal advantage in a more retired station." However, the prudent parent desired his daughter also to be familiar with "the graver sciences" and with such accomplishments as music, dancing, drawing, and belles lettres, inasmuch as "the chance that in marriage she will draw a blockhead I calculate at about fourteen to one" and accordingly "the education of her family will probably rest on her."[14]

Less than a decade later Jefferson's younger daughter, Mary, likewise obtained her schooling in Philadelphia, while her father was secretary of state and the Pennsylvania metropolis was the seat of the national government. He took her there with him in the fall of 1791. Writing to the family at Monticello, he said: "Maria is immersed in new acquaintances; but particularly happy with Nelly Custis, and particularly attended to by Mrs. Washington. She will be with Mrs. Pine a few days hence."[15] Several weeks later he wrote: "Maria is fixed at Mrs. Pine's, and perfectly at home. She has made young friends enough to keep herself in a bustle with them, and she has been honored with the visits of Mrs. Adams, Mrs. Randolph, Mrs. Rittenhouse, Sarjeant, Waters, Davies, &c so that she is quite familiar with Philadel-

[14] Edward Dumbauld, "Thomas Jefferson and Pennsylvania," *Pennsylvania History*, Vol. V, No. 3 (July, 1938), 158. See also Randolph, *Domestic Life*, 68; and Randall, *Jefferson*, I, 390. Both of Jefferson's children went to school in Philadelphia. Likewise, he sent his grandson there because "There are particular branches of science, which are not so advantageously taught anywhere else in the United States as in Philadelphia."—To Casper Wistar, Washington, June 21, 1807 (Lipscomb and Bergh, *Writings*, XI, 243).

[15] Randolph, *Domestic Life*, 207. See also *ibid.*, 222; and Randall, *Jefferson*, II, 223.

phia."[16] Six months later he lamented that: "Mrs. Pine has determined to go to England, so that I shall be obliged to send Maria to Mrs. Brodeau's, a better school, but much more distant from me. It will in fact cut off the daily visits which she is able to make me from Mrs. Pine's."[17] However, Mary frequently enjoyed pleasant holidays with her father.

At Annapolis Jefferson lodged with a "Mrs. Gheeseland," where he paid 15 shillings a day, itemized as follows: lodging and breakfast, 5/; dinner, 2/6; wood, 5/; servant, 2/6. He also paid her a shilling apiece for making six cravats. On February 25, 1784, he "moved to Mr. Dulany's house." Monroe shared his quarters, and continued there when Jefferson left Annapolis on May 11, 1784, after being appointed to go on a diplomatic mission to Europe.[18] In his account book that day Jefferson noted: "sold Colo Monroe my books & household things at Annap. He is to pay Mr Dulany my house rent £ 5-6-9 and Frazer stable rent £ 6." A French servant named Partout was in charge of the household arrangements, and Monroe felt the need of an interpreter after Jefferson's departure.[19]

The dwelling occupied by Jefferson may have been the Lloyd Dulany house on the east side of Conduit Street, between Southeast Street (now Duke of Gloucester Street) and Church Street (now Main Street). That house, used at present by the Masonic

[16] To Martha Jefferson Randolph, Philadelphia, November 13, 1791 (Morgan Library, MS Collections).

[17] To Martha Jefferson Randolph, Philadelphia, May 11, 1792 (*ibid.*).

[18] "On motion of Mr. Hardy, seconded by Mr. Gerry,

"*Resolved*, That a minister plenipotentiary be appointed, in addition to Mr. John Adams and Mr. Benjamin Franklin, for the purpose of negotiating treaties of commerce.

"Congress proceeded to the election, and, the ballots being taken,

"Mr. Thomas Jefferson was elected, having been previously nominated by Mr. Hardy."—*Journals of Congress*, Philadelphia, 1800, IX, 146 (Friday, May 7, 1784).

"On motion of Mr. Stone, seconded by Mr. Read,

"*Resolved*, That the agent of marine provide suitable accommodations for Mr. Jefferson's passage to Europe."—*Ibid.*, 147 (Tuesday May 11, 1784).

[19] Monroe to Jefferson, Annapolis, May 14, 1784 (Library of Congress, Jefferson Papers).

Lodge, is said to have been built in 1730. The premises were sold in 1783 to George Mann as confiscated British property, and became a hotel. On December 31, 1783, Jefferson "pd George Mann in full to this day exclusive £ 18-13," and again on May 10, 1784, he "pd Mann in full 31⅓ Dol." The "Gheeseland" house where Jefferson lived was perhaps the brick residence of Mary Ghiselin, widow of Reverdy Ghiselin, situated on the north side of West Street, not far from St. Anne's Church, where the Telephone Building now stands.[20]

Outstanding among the official activities in which Jefferson participated at Annapolis was the occasion when General Washington resigned his command on December 23, 1783, and received the plaudits of a grateful people. Washington also called on Jefferson at Annapolis to discuss the Cincinnati. "It was a little after candlelight, and he sat with me till after midnight, conversing almost exclusively on that subject."[21] Popular sentiment regarded the formation of that society, composed of army officers who had served in the Revolutionary War, as a menace to democratic institutions and a steppingstone to the creation of an order of hereditary nobility. Hence both statesmen felt that the organization ought to disband.

Before going abroad, Jefferson made a tour of the New England states, familiarizing himself at first hand with their economic conditions, in order to prepare himself for his task of negotiating

---

[20] Information from the Hall of Records at Annapolis, supplied by Miss Louise E. Magruder of that city, shows the sale on September 2, 1783, of the Lloyd Dulany house to George Mann (Confiscated British Property 1781–85, folio 59), as well as a conveyance of the property in West Street on November 26, 1770, from Anthony Stewart to Reverdy Ghiselin, whose will was probated on April 24, 1775 (Anne Arundel County, Deeds, IB#3, folio 20; Wills, 40, folio 194). When passing through Annapolis in 1775, according to entries under date of June 18, 1775 and August 4, 1775 in Jefferson's account book for that year, he stopped at "Middleton's."

[21] Randall, *Jefferson*, I, 409. In advance of this interview, Washington had asked Jefferson his opinion and that of Congress regarding the Cincinnati (Washington to Jefferson, Mount Vernon, April 8, 1784, John C. Fitzpatrick [ed.], *The Writings of George Washington*, XXVII, 388–89). He had previously written requesting that some valuable packages expected from Lafayette be kept for him at Jefferson's lodgings (*ibid.*, 368).

treaties of commerce with foreign countries. He announced to a Virginia correspondent: "I mean to go thro' the Eastern States in hopes of deriving some knoledge of them from actual inspection and inquiry which may enable me to discharge my duty to them somewhat the better."[22]

Upon leaving Annapolis, he reached Philadelphia on May 14, 1784. Two weeks later he departed from Philadelphia, arriving at New York on the thirtieth. He left New York on June 5, and visited Fort Washington, Stamford, Fairfield, Stratford, New Haven, Middletown, Hartford, Bolton, Lebanon, Norwich, New London, South Kingston, Newport, and Providence. Upon setting out from that place for Boston, according to newspaper accounts, Jefferson "was attended a few miles from town by a number of the principal inhabitants."[23] After passing through Dedham, he arrived at Boston on June 18. On the twenty-first he left the Massachusetts capital on a jaunt to Charlestown, Winnisimet, Salem, Ipswich, Hampton, Portsmouth, Exeter, Newberry, Salem, and Marblehead, returning to Boston on the twenty-sixth. In that city he lodged with a "Colonel Ingersol." This was probably Joseph Ingersoll, a tavern keeper. The house where Jefferson stopped may have been located at the south corner of Tremont and Court Streets, on the site now occupied by the Hemenway Building.[24]

From Boston he wrote to Madison: "After visiting the principal towns through Connecticut, Rhode Island, this state and

[22] To Edmund Pendleton, Philadelphia, May 25, 1784 (New York Public Library, MSS Division). Jefferson had informed the same correspondent that "it is very essential for us to obtain information of facts, of opinions, & of wishes from our own country." To Edmund Pendleton, Annapolis, December 16, 1783 (*ibid.*).

[23] *Maryland Journal and Baltimore Advertiser*, Friday, July 9, 1784. Jefferson was at Lebanon, Connecticut, on June 11, 1784. According to Florence S. Crofut, *Guide to the History and the Historic Sites of Connecticut*, II, 698, Jefferson was among the visitors to the War Office of Governor John Trumbull at Lebanon. Perhaps a visit took place on that date.

[24] In 1789 George Washington lodged with the widow of Joseph Ingersoll. Her house was on the south corner of Tremont and Court Streets. It is likely that Jefferson's "Colonel Ingersol" was this lady's husband and lived at the same place. Stephen T. Riley, of the Massachusetts Historical Society, to the author, September 13, 1940, and September 21, 1940.

New Hampshire, in order to acquire what knowledge I could of their commerce and other circumstances, I am returned to this place, and shall sail the day after tomorrow on the Ceres bound for London; but my purpose is to get on shore in some boat on the coast of France and proceed directly to Paris. My servant being sent off today, and much on hand to prepare for my voyage, I have no time for any particular communications. Indeed, there are few I should have to make, unless I were to enter into a detail which would be lengthy, as to the country and people I have visited."[25]

On July 5, 1784, Jefferson sailed for Europe, on board the *Ceres*. "The voyage was as pleasant as fine weather, a fine ship, good company, and an excellent table could make it." While the vessel was becalmed three days on the Banks of Newfoundland, fresh codfish were caught and a tasty feast enjoyed by the passengers.[26] Half a decade, filled with stirring events, both in the Old World and the New, was to pass before Jefferson's return to his native land.

[25] To Madison, Boston, July 1, 1784 (Lipscomb and Bergh, *Writings*, IV, 458). In Boston, Jefferson informed Gerry, "no small part of my time has been occupied by the hospitalities and civilities of this place, which I have experienced in the highest degree."—To Elbridge Gerry, Boston, July 2, 1784 (James T. Austin, *The Life of Elbridge Gerry*, I, 453–54). In later years the wife of Samuel Adams remembered "the pleasure and entertainment you offered us when you were about to embark for France."—Samuel Adams to Jefferson, Boston, April 24, 1801 (William V. Wells, *The Life and Public Services of Samuel Adams*, III, 372). At Philadelphia Jefferson had conferred with David Humphreys, who was to accompany him to Europe as secretary of mission; and in New Haven he had paid a visit to Ezra Stiles, the president of Yale College (Frank L. Humphreys, *Life and Times of David Humphreys*, I, 300, 306; Franklin B. Dexter, *Literary Diary of Ezra Stiles*, III, 124–25).

[26] Randolph, *Domestic Life*, 73.

CHAPTER IV

Blue Lamp Chimneys and
Invincible Silence

❁

O N July 25, 1784, Jefferson first set foot on foreign soil. The *Ceres*, owned by Nathaniel Tracey, a fellow-passenger with Jefferson, and commanded by Captain St. Barbe, arrived at Cowes after a voyage of nineteen days from land to land. Not being able, as he had hoped, "to get on shore in some boat on the coast of France and proceed directly to Paris," Jefferson was obliged to disembark in England.

He was detained at Portsmouth several days by the illness of his daughter Martha, who was visited by a physician, Dr. Meek, on the twenty-seventh and twenty-eighth. Meanwhile, Jefferson on the twenty-ninth made an excursion to Farnham, Titchfield, and Gosport. In the course of this jaunt he paid a visit to the home of a lady from Virginia who had married a British naval officer, Captain Thompson. She was the daughter of John Blair of Williamsburg.

Through the fault of a stupid servant, as Jefferson later learned, Mrs. Thompson experienced the "mortification . . . of not seeing my old friend, and acquaintance Mr Jefferson, when he did me the favor of calling." Instead of being told that she was confined upstairs, Jefferson was informed that she was not at home. "But had I known *you* was in the *house* I should not have denied my self the pleasure of seeing you, and should certainly have introduced you into my Bed Chamber," she wrote to Jefferson. "Captn. T. set out the next day in hopes of meeting you, but had the mortification of hearing you was gone: I dont know that I was ever more vexed, for believe me I should have rejoyced much to see you."[1] Upon receiving this explanation of the circumstances, Jefferson replied: "Certainly if I had suspected your being in the house I should have pressed for a permission to see you. The accident of my daughter's being taken ill a little before we made land, occasioned my going ashore on your side of the channel to procure medical aid, and the gentleman who attended her, gave me the first information of your living in the neighborhood. . . . My history, since I had the pleasure of seeing you last, would have been as happy a one as I could have asked, could the objects of my affection have been immortal. But all the favors of fortune have been embittered by domestic losses. Of six children I have lost four, and finally their mother."[2]

On July 30 Jefferson settled his hotel bill of £ 5-16 at Bradley's Crown Inn at Portsmouth. The next day, having crossed the Channel, he arrived at Havre de Grace. Proceeding by way of Bolbec, Aliquerville, Yvetot, Barentin, Rouen, Point Saint-Ouen, Vaudreuil, Gaillon, Vernon, Bonnieres, Mantes, Meulan, Triel, St. Germain, Marly, and Nanterre, he reached Paris on August 6. He took lodgings at the Hôtel d'Orléans in the Rue de Richelieu, but moved on the tenth to another hotel of the same name situated in the Rue des Petits Augustins.[3] Soon he rented from Gueraud a handsome house in the Cul-de-sac "Têtebout," which he held from October 16, 1784, to March 10, 1786. The Hôtel Landron, as this dwelling was called, was near the Italian Comedy. During his occupancy of this house, Jefferson found it advisable to remodel two rooms, and a plan drawn by him for this work has been preserved.

The Cul-de-sac Taitbout, as shown by a plan of Paris in 1786,

[1] Elizabeth Thompson to Jefferson, Titchfield, January 10, 1787 (Worthington C. Ford [ed.], *Thomas Jefferson Correspondence Printed from the Originals in the Collections of William K. Bixby*, 19).

[2] To Elizabeth Thompson, Paris, January 19, 1787 (*ibid.*, 20-22). A similar experience is mentioned in a letter to Mrs. Kinloch, Paris, July 1, 1787, in the Mass. Hist. Soc., Jefferson Papers.

[3] A guide book published in 1777 lists the Hôtel d'Orléans in the Rue des Petits Augustins among the hotels of first rank, where "seigneurs étrangers" lodge (*Almanach Parisien en faveur des étrangers et des personnes curieuses*, 141, 143).

branched off from the Rue Taitbout toward the Rue de la Chaussée d'Antin, but came to a dead end. The Rue de la Chaussée d'Antin was at that time a newly developing fashionable quarter, and Jefferson's friends Louis-Dominique Ethis de Corny and Mme de Corny lived there, not far away from Jefferson's house. In 1799 the Cul-de-sac Taitbout was prolonged southward to the Boulevard des Italiens, and the street renamed Rue du Helder in honor of a victory over the English. The site of Jefferson's dwelling is therefore at present located on the northern segment of the Rue du Helder (IX*ème arrondissement*), in the vicinity of the Opéra.[4]

On October 17, 1785 Jefferson moved to a house near the Grille de Chaillot, at the corner of the Grande Route des Champs Élysées and Rue Neuve de Berry, where he remained during his residence in France. The site has been marked. A plaque, designed by Maurice Colomb, was placed there by alumni of the University of Virginia serving overseas in the United States Army during World War I. At the unveiling ceremonies on April 12, 1919, the presentation was made by Brigadier General Jefferson Randolph Kean, a direct descendant of Jefferson. Secretary of the Navy Josephus Daniels, representatives of the City and the University of Paris, and other dignitaries also participated in the proceedings. The modern structure thus adorned stands at the northeast corner of the Rue de Berri and the Champs Élysées on the right-hand side halfway up the rise between the Rond Point and the Arc de Triomphe de l'Étoile.[5]

To Abigail Adams, wife of the New England statesman whose diplomatic activities had shortly before been transferred to London from the French capital, Jefferson announced, among

[4] Edward Dumbauld, "Where Did Jefferson Live in Paris?" *William and Mary College Quarterly* (2d series), Vol. XXIII, No. 1 (January, 1943), 64–68.

[5] *Alumni Bulletin of the University of Virginia* (3rd series), Vol. XII, No. 3 (July, 1919), 217–53. See also lease and other papers dated September 5, 1785, October 10, 1788, June 19, 1790, and letters of Short to Jefferson, Paris, July 7, 1790, August 15, 1790, and September 9, 1790 (Library of Congress, Wm. Short Papers).

other items of Paris news in the autumn of 1785, that: "I have at length procured a house in a situation much more pleasing to me than my present, it is at the grille des Champs Elysees, but within the city. It suits me in every circumstance but the price,—being dearer than the one I am now in,—it has a clever garden to it."[6]

The rent was 7,500 livres a year. The house belonged to M. le Comte de Langeac. Garnishment proceedings instituted from time to time by that nobleman's creditors annoyed Jefferson, who preferred to have dealings with only a single party and to make payments of rent as usual directly to the Count. The American diplomat soon found that he was being overcharged and gave notice to terminate the lease. He entertained the "thought of taking a little country house opposite the plaine des sablons for the moment" if he could not come to terms with his landlord or find a suitable house elsewhere.

The Hôtel de Langeac had been built for the mistress of one of the ministers of Louis XV by the famous architect Chalgrin, designer of the Arc de Triomphe. Nevertheless alterations had to be made in order to suit Jefferson's requirements. Architect's drawings by Jefferson show that two small rooms were combined to make a large room along the Champs Élysées at the east corner of the house. Work began in December, 1785, and continued until February, 1786.

Jefferson also kept rooms at the Carthusian Monastery on Mount Calvary, where silence was enjoined, and he could work without interruption. In 1789 he requested and received protection for his house, which had been robbed three times. His daughters were placed in a convent school at the Abbaye Royale de Panthemont, on the Rue de Grenelle.

At the time of Jefferson's arrival in France, Lafayette, who was himself revisiting "the blessed shores of liberty," wrote from America extending a fraternal welcome.[7] Franklin and his friends

---

[6] To Mrs. Adams, Paris, September 4, 1785 (Hale, *Franklin in France*, II, 379).
[7] Lafayette to Jefferson, Hartford, October 11, 1784 (*ibid.*, II, 329, 330).

also received warmly the illustrious Philadelphian's future successor at the French court. Jefferson, Franklin, and Adams were in almost daily contact. Dazzled by an unbounded admiration for America, the French public had the opportunity to behold, within less than a decade after the Declaration of Independence, three of its renowned draftsmen and signers reunited in a foreign capital.

Jefferson's mode of life at the Hôtel de Langeac has been described by fellow countrymen who visited him there. One of these was a Virginia neighbor, Philip Mazzei, who came to Paris in the summer of 1785. He relates in his memoirs: "I went at once to see Jefferson, who lived in a beautiful *villetta* with a charming garden, at the end of the Champs Elysees, within gunshot distance of the city wall passed on going to Versailles. I took an enjoyable and interesting walk, arriving about an hour before dinner. I had informed him of my arrival at Lorient, as soon as I landed; and I wrote to him from Nantes also. So he expected me daily. Nevertheless, our meeting was moving to both. We had many things to say, and we had a great deal of time at our disposal, for on that day no one came to dine with him, and his secretary, Mr. Short, was at dinner with the Countess de Tessé, cousin of the Marquis de la Fayette. After discoursing on public matters, we spoke about our own affairs." The following day they called on Marmontel, and the Abbé Morellet came in before they left; then they paid their respects to Lavoisier, Condorcet, and the Duc de Rochefoucault, and returned home to dine with Short.[8]

A wealthy Pennsylvanian with a wooden leg, who arrived in Paris four years later, was perhaps the most prominent of the Americans welcomed by Jefferson at the Grille de Chaillot. This

[8] "Memoirs of the Life and Voyages of Doctor Philip Mazzei," translated by Dr. E. C. Branchi, *William and Mary College Quarterly* (2d series), Vol. X, No. 1 (January, 1930), 14, 15. See also *Memoirs of the Life and Peregrinations of the Florentine Philip Mazzei, 1730–1816*, translated by Howard R. Marraro, 291–93; and Richard C. Garlick, Jr., *Philip Mazzei, Friend of Jefferson: His Life and Letters*, 98.

Ceremonies at the site of the Hôtel de Langeac,
Jefferson's house in Paris, on April 12, 1919

Left to right (on the balcony): M. Raux, Préfet de Police; M. Chas-
saigne-Goyon, President du Conseil Municipal; Ambassador William G.
Sharp; Secretary of the Navy Josephus Daniels; M. Autrand, Préfet de
la Seine; M. Lucien Poincaré, Vice-Recteur de l'Université de Paris;
Lt. Commander Charles O. Maas; Major Armistead H. Dobie

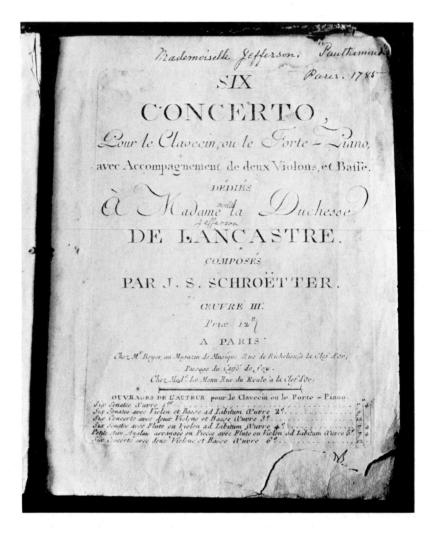

Mademoiselle Jefferson's music book

was the witty and amorous Gouverneur Morris. He bore a letter of introduction from George Washington,[9] who later appointed him as minister to France after Jefferson's return to America. Though the aristocratic Philadelphian's political sentiments (which offended French public opinion and ultimately led to his recall from that post) were decidedly unlike the democratic doctrines to which Jefferson adhered, Morris respected the Virginian's ability.[10] Both statesmen had a reputation for literary talent. Jefferson had won fame in Philadelphia as author of the Declaration of Independence; Morris had earned distinction by perfecting the style and language of the Constitution. In Paris they were congenial companions.

At Jefferson's house on the Champs Élysées, where Morris was a frequent caller, or at the latter's lodgings in the Rue de Richelieu, they often discussed business, politics, and news from America. Morris thought that Jefferson's estimates of character were defective in that he assigned too many persons to the humble rank of fools, whereas in actual life every individual is endowed with a combination of strength and weakness peculiar to himself, and the gradations of ability are infinite. These conversations were sometimes lengthy. On one occasion, Morris felt that his visit, which lasted an hour, had been at least fifty minutes too long; for he noticed that Jefferson's daughters, who had left the room upon his coming, seemed only to be awaiting his departure to return. Perhaps he found it hard to leave because the house was warm and comfortable. On cold and rainy days he was glad to find a good fire at Jefferson's.[11]

Morris's diary records that he often took "a Family Dinner" or "a Dish of Tea" at Jefferson's home. Sometimes he dined there with Lafayette and other Frenchmen of high rank. At other

[9] Beatrix Cary Davenport (ed.), *A Diary of the French Revolution by Gouverneur Morris*, I, xxxii, xxxiv.

[10] *Ibid.*, 159. Morris was surprised to hear Frenchmen in England speak slightingly of Jefferson (*ibid.*, 476, 525).

[11] *Ibid.*, 29, 100, 106, 108. Morris records that late in July Jefferson had a fire (*ibid.*, 160).

times the guests were mostly Americans. On the day of the procession to Longchamps, Morris and Jefferson dined early in order to witness the spectacle. After breakfast at Jefferson's one morning they went to Versailles, where the American diplomat presented Morris to the French Minister of Foreign Affairs and other notables. They returned to Paris in time for dinner at Madame de Tessé's. Another friend of Jefferson's, Madame de Corny, was regarded by Morris as "a lively, sensible woman." It was at her house that a supper party gave him an opportunity to further his acquaintance with the captivating Madame de Flahaut.[12]

Morris's witty sallies often amused the company at Jefferson's hospitable table. On one occasion, he displayed his gallantry and gaiety at the expense of the poet Joel Barlow. The man of letters was enamored of an American colonel's lady, whose beauty was somewhat on the wane. After Morris, by his attentions to her, had succeeded in arousing Barlow's jealousy, he promptly set another officer to laughing at the discomfited poet's ill humor. On another occasion, having just received letters from America as he stepped into the carriage to go to Jefferson's, Morris was in such good spirits that he found he was better company for girls of sixteen than he had thought possible. Entertainment was furnished that evening by one of the guests, a young lady who played and sang (at her mother's request), although she seemed aware that music was not her forte.

Jefferson and Morris enjoyed walks and drives together, on errands and for pleasure. They went twice to the Palais Royal to have their profiles taken. The first time they arrived too late, and the next day they could get only one ticket. With this they went to the Rue Croix des Petits Champs, where Jefferson sat for the artist. From there they proceeded to the Place des Victoires to

---

[12] *Ibid.*, 28. It was there, too, that he first heard the news that Jefferson had left Paris for America; though the departing Virginian had not trusted himself to take leave of Madame de Corny in person, preferring to convey his adieux less painfully by letter (*ibid.*, 234).

purchase a watch for General Washington. Morris posed as a model for the bust of Washington in the statue by Houdon now in the Virginia capitol at Richmond. The same sculptor also executed a mold of Morris's face, and a bust of Jefferson.[13]

In the course of their excursions together Jefferson would point out beauties which the less discriminating eye of Morris had failed to discern. On one of their walks Jefferson took his companion to see a very beautiful view of a house and garden opening on the Champs Élysées which had escaped the latter's notice entirely. Returning from a ride in the Bois de Boulogne, at Jefferson's suggestion they went to look at the Pont de Neuilly. Jefferson declared that this bridge was the handsomest in the world. But although Morris had crossed it four times, he had never observed, until the structure was called to his attention, how strikingly it displayed solidity and lightness as perfectly combined as possible.

The details of Jefferson's activities in Paris need not be recounted here. Historians and biographers have not neglected that topic. In his unending negotiations in behalf of American commerce, whale-oil and tobacco occupied a prominent place. To conciliate European creditors when America owed war debts was not an easy task and caused him considerable concern. In addition to public business, a wide range of fascinating pursuits claimed Jefferson's attention. He could ramble daily in the solitude of the Bois de Boulogne, or join the crowds frequenting fashionable shops and places of amusement. He was able to gratify his taste for architecture, art, and music. To universities, learned societies,

[13] *Ibid.*, 107, 109. Signed original busts of Jefferson by Houdon in plaster are preserved in the collections of the New York Historical Society and the American Philosophical Society (Hart and Biddle, *Memoirs of Houdon*, 248-49). The Boston Museum of Fine Arts has a marble bust of Jefferson (Edwin J. Hipkiss, "Portrait Sculpture by Houdon," *Bulletin of the Museum of Fine Arts*, Vol. XXXII, No. 193 [October, 1934], 70–74). See also Georges Giacometti, *Le Statuaire Jean-Antoine Houdon et son Époque*, II, 236–40; and Fiske Kimball, "The Life Portraits of Jefferson and Their Replicas," *Proceedings* of the American Philosophical Society, Vol. LXXXVIII, No. 6 (December, 1944), 505–507.

and acquaintances in America, he communicated matters of interest in mechanical, botanical, literary, and intellectual realms. He enjoyed thoroughly the *esprit* and elegance of French life.

Jefferson was intimate with characters conspicuous in the momentous events which marked the outbreak of the French Revolution. His house served as a meeting place for Lafayette and other prominent French statesmen. He counseled them regarding the reforms in their government which he believed it would be possible to achieve. He attended daily at Versailles the sessions of the States-General. On July 14, 1789, at the house of Madame de Corny he heard from her husband, who had just returned from the Bastille, a first-hand account of that day's happenings. Jefferson had witnessed, two days earlier, an ominous occurrence in one of the public squares of Paris. The people assembled in the Place Louis XV, confronting a body of troops which had been posted there, allowed the American plenipotentiary in his carriage to proceed without interruption through the lane they had formed. But the moment after Jefferson had passed, they attacked the troops with stones; and the soldiers, though mounted, were obliged to retreat. This incident was perhaps symbolic of Jefferson's connection with the French Revolution. The savage fury of the populace did not burst forth until after he had left the scene. When he returned to America in 1789, he thought that the strife in France would end happily and within a year. He regarded it as a sequel to the American Revolution, a continuation of the struggle for the rights of man which had begun in the United States; and he believed that the outcome of that contest would vitally affect the success of the American experiment in free government. For such a cause, he felt, stupendous sacrifice was justified. Though Jefferson deplored the sanguinary violence of the conflict in France, he viewed its victims as soldiers who perished on the field of battle for their country's welfare. Never was so great a prize won, he declared, with so little loss of innocent lives; the tree of liberty must inevitably be watered from time to time with the blood of patriots and tyrants.

A better opportunity to know England than that obtained while in transit came to Jefferson in the spring of 1786. John Adams, then United States minister at London, invited Jefferson to participate in diplomatic negotiations at the English capital. Colonel William Stephens Smith, secretary of legation at London and soon to be Adams's son-in-law,[14] was the bearer of an urgent entreaty from Jefferson's colleague across the channel. "Mr. Jefferson has long projected a visit to England, and this will be a good opportunity," Adams informed John Jay, the American secretary for foreign affairs. "No notice will be taken of it, publicly, in America, and his real errand will be concealed from the public here."[15]

Jefferson and Colonel Smith set out from Paris on the morning of March 6. On the eighth they reached Calais, traveling by way of Chantilly, Breteuil, Abbeville, and Montreuil. On his return journey Jefferson took a different route from Calais to Paris, passing through St. Omer, Royes, and Bourget. He counseled Colonel Smith: "Whenever you come again to Paris come by way of St. Omer and Arras. By this means you do not travel one foot of the road you have always passed, and you see the whole way one of the most lovely countries imaginable, except on the D'Oise where there are a few miles of barrens, being in the skirts of the forest of Chantilly."[16]

On March 11, the travelers arrived in London. Their expenses for the journey from Paris totalled £ 49-14-3. Jefferson took lodgings at No. 14 Golden Square, then a fashionable quar-

[14] On July 12, 1786, Colonel Smith and Abigail Amelia Adams were married by the Bishop of Asaph (Lipscomb and Bergh, *Writings*, XVIII, 180). For portraits of Colonel Smith and his wife by Mather Brown, and of the former by Trumbull, see Clarence W. Bowen, *The History of the Centennial Celebration of the Inauguration of George Washington as First President of the United States*, 528, and opposite pages 18, 260, and 41.

[15] John Adams to Jay, Grosvenor Square, London, February 20, 1786 (Adams, *The Works of John Adams*, VIII, 376). A letter of February 22, 1786, states that Colonel Smith departed the day before (*ibid.*, 379).

[16] To Col. W. S. Smith, Paris, May 4, 1786 (Library of Congress, Jefferson Papers).

ter.[17] A letter to William Short describes the trip: "We had a cold journey to Calais, but made it in less time than we expected, having lodged at Breteuil & Montreuil. We were detained at Calais a day and a half, & then had a passage of nine hours & a half; so that on the whole we were six days getting here. I have lost a great deal of time in ceremony, returning visits, &c; so that I have done & seen less than I ought, & probably this will be the fate of the few remaining days."[18]

As usual, a multiplicity of motives lay behind Jefferson's visit. Writing to Jay, he gives the following account of his purposes in going to England: "The date of a letter from London will doubtless be as unexpected to you as it was unforeseen by myself a few days ago. On the 27th of the last month, Colo. Smith arrived in Paris with a letter from Mr. Adams informing me that there was at this place a minister from Tripoli having general powers to enter into treaties on behalf of his state, and with whom it was possible we might do something in our Commission to that power and that he gave reason to believe he could also take arrangements with us for Tunis: he further added that the minister of Portugal here had received ultimate instructions from his court, and that probably that treaty might be concluded in the space of three weeks were we all on the spot together. He therefore pressed me to come over immediately. The first of these objects had some weight in my mind, because as we had sent no person to Tripoli or Tunis I thought if we could meet a minister from them on this ground our arrangements would be settled much sooner & at less expence. But what principally decided with me was the desire of bringing matters to a conclusion with Portugal before the term of our commission should expire or any new turn in the negotiations of France & England should abate their willingness to fix a connection with us. A third motive

---

[17] Ford, *Jefferson Correspondence in Collections of Bixby*, 17. Regarding the neighborhood, see Edwin Beresford Chancellor, *The History of the Squares of London*, 129, 136.

[18] To William Short, London, March 28, 1786 (*William and Mary College Quarterly* [2d series], Vol. XI, No. 4 [October, 1931], 336).

had also it's [*sic*] weight. I hoped that my attendance here, and the necessity of shortening it, might be made use of to force a decisive answer from this court. I therefore concluded to comply with Mr. Adams's request. I went immediately to Versailles and apprised the Count de Vergennes that circumstances of public duty called me hither for three or four weeks, arranged with him some matters and set out with Colo. Smith for this place, where we arrived last night, which was as early as the excessive rigour of the weather admitted. I saw Mr. Adams immediately, & again to-day. He informs me that the minister of Portugal was taken ill five or six days ago, has been very much so, but is now somewhat better. It would be very mortifying indeed should this accident, with the shortness of the term to which I limit my stay here, defeat what was the principal object of my journey, and that without which I should hardly have undertaken it. With respect to this country, I had no doubt but that every consideration had been urged by Mr. Adams which was proper to be urged. Nothing remains undone in this way. But we shall avail ourselves of our journey hither as if made on purpose, just before the expiration of our commission, to form our report to Congress on the execution, of that Commission, which report they may be given to know cannot be formed without decisive information of the ultimate determination of their court. There is no doubt what that determination will be; but it will be useful to have it; as it may put an end to all further expectations on our side of the water, and shew that the time is come for doing whatever is to be done by us for counteracting the unjust & greedy designs of this country. We shall have the honour, before I leave this place, to inform you of the results of the several matters which have brought me to it."[19]

Before leaving Paris, as stated in his letter to Jay, Jefferson had asked for an audience with Vergennes, adding the intercession: "I cannot omit to mention how pleasing it would be to me

[19] To Jay, London, March 12, 1786 (Lipscomb and Bergh, *Writings*, V, 288–90).

to be enabled (before my departure) to convey to the American prisoners at St. Pol de Leon such mitigation of their fate as may be thought admissible." These luckless sailors had been driven by storm into a French port with a cargo of tobacco, importation of which was prohibited. Jefferson instructed his banker, Grand, to supply the prisoners with funds during his absence.[20]

Jefferson likewise sent word to his daughter Martha at her convent school: "I shall be absent so short a time that any letter you would write to me would hardly get to London before I should be coming away; and it is the more discouraging to write as they open all letters in the post office. Should however sickness or any other circumstance render a letter necessary, send it here to Mr. Short & he will direct & forward it."[21]

Before his departure Jefferson was also careful to make arrangements for the admission of articles he expected to bring with him from England. To M. de Reyneval, a subordinate in the foreign office, he addressed the following letter:

His Excellency Count de Vergennes having been pleased to say he would give orders at Calais for the admission of certain articles which I wish to bring with me from England, I have thought it best to give a description of them before my departure. They will be as follows:

1. A set of table furniture consisting in China, silver & plated ware, distributed into three or four boxes or canteens for the convenience of removing them.
2. A box containing small tools for wooden & iron work, for my own amusement.
3. A box of books.
4. I expect to bring with me a riding horse, saddle etc.

The mathematical instruments will probably be so light that I may bring them in my carriage, in which case I presume they will pass with my bag-

---

[20] To Vergennes, Paris, February 28, 1786 (*ibid.*, V, 287); to Grand, Paris, March 4, 1786 (Library of Congress, Jefferson Papers).

[21] To Martha Jefferson, Paris, March 6, 1786 (Morgan Library, MS Collections).

gage under the authority of the passport for my person. If these orders can be made out in time I would willingly be the bearer of them myself.[22]

That he did not at the time succeed in obtaining in England all the items he desired appears from a communication on the same subject written three years later: "Being about to take a journey to London a little before the death of the Count de Vergennes, I asked from him a passport for several objects which I had a thought of bringing from thence. He first satisfied himself from the Marquis de la Luzerne, upon the point of reciprocity, that the Minister of France in America is allowed to import every thing, for his own use, duty-free, without any restriction of time, place, or quantity, and then gave me the passport. I brought however but one or two small objects. A carriage was one of those named in the passport, and not brought. I ordered it to be made; but partly from the tardiness of the workman, partly from the difficulty of finding a person coming to Paris and who would undertake to bring it, I never received it till the beginning of the present year. In the meantime the former passport had been given in to the Douane when I returned from England. I now ask a renewal of it as to the carriage which has come to hand."[23]

On being reproached by his friend Lafayette for using goods of English manufacture, Jefferson replied that what he required was not obtainable in France. "The reason for my importing harness from England is a very obvious one. They are plated, and plated harness is not made at all in France, as far as I have learnt. It is not from a love of the English but a love of myself that I sometimes find myself obliged to buy their manufactures."[24]

Two days after Jefferson's arrival in London, Adams sent a note to the minister of foreign affairs informing him of the fact: "Mr. Adams presents his Compliments to the Right Honourable

[22] To M. de Reyneval, Paris, March 3, 1786 (Library of Congress, Jefferson Papers).

[23] To M. du Rival, Paris, April 13, 1789 (*ibid.*).

[24] Gilbert Chinard, *The Letters of Lafayette and Jefferson*, 108.

The Marquis of Carmarthen & acquaints His Lordship that Mr. Jefferson, minister Plenipotentiary of the United States at the Court of Versailles, is now here, and as they have something to communicate to His Lordship, relative to the affairs of the United States, they request a Time when they may have the honor to pay their respects to his Lordship, before the levee on Wednesday."[25]

It was Jefferson's opinion of the British that "of all nations on earth, they require to be treated with the most hauteur. They require to be kicked into common good manners."[26] This belief may have taken root during his reception at the court. "The King turned his back upon the American Commissioners, a hint which, of course, was not lost upon the circle of his subjects in attendance."[27] In his autobiography Jefferson wrote of this incident: "On my presentation as usual to the King and Queen at their levees, it was impossible for anything to be more ungracious than their notice of Mr. Adams & myself. I saw at once that the ulcerations in the narrow mind of that mulish being left nothing to be expected on the subject of my attendance; and on the first conference with the Marquis of Caermarthen, his Minister of foreign affairs, the distance and disinclination which he betrayed in his conversation, the vagueness & evasions of his answers to us, confirmed me in the belief of their aversion to have anything to do with us. We delivered him however our Projét, Mr. Adams not despairing as much as I did of it's [sic] effect. We afterwards, by one or more notes, requested his appointment of an interview and conference, which without directly declining, he evaded by pretences of other occupations for the moment. After staying there seven weeks, till within a few days of the expiration of our commission, I informed the minister by note that my duties in Paris required my return to that place, and that I should with

[25] Library of Congress, Jefferson Papers, 3321.

[26] To W. S. Smith, Paris, September 28, 1787 (Lipscomb and Bergh, *Writings*, VI, 324).

[27] Adams, *The Works of John Adams*, I, 420. Jefferson's account book states, under date of March 17, 1786: "pd porters at St. James on my being presented 42/."

pleasure be the bearer of any commands to his Ambassador there.[28] He answered that he had none, and wishing me a pleasant journey, I left London the 26th. arrived at Paris on the 30th. of April."[29]

During Jefferson's stay in England, a treaty with Portugal was duly concluded. In order not to delay Jefferson's return to France, the American plenipotentiaries affixed their signatures before the Portuguese envoy, Pinto, had received his powers to sign. Negotiations for a treaty of peace with the Tripolitan pirates led to nothing, as the amount of tribute demanded was so great that what the Americans were authorized to offer was but a drop in the bucket. And with England nothing could be done.

The course of negotiations with the British is described by the American diplomats in a report to Jay. At their first meeting with Carmarthen to submit their credentials, they handed him their proposed draft of a treaty with England. This he undertook to lay before the ministry and the King. In a few days, chancing to encounter one of the envoys, Carmarthen suggested that another project, containing nothing but regulations relating to commerce, should be proposed. He professed to find in the American draft provisions of a political character, instead of purely commercial stipulations. The Americans followed up this suggestion, and proposed as a treaty of commerce four or five articles extracted from their former project.[30] But nothing came of it. In a letter to Jay, Jefferson declares: "Six weeks have elapsed without

[28] Jefferson's farewell note reads:
"Mr. Jefferson has the honor of presenting his respects to the right honourable, the Marquis of Carmarthen; he had that of calling at his house to take leave on his departure for Paris; from which place the arrangements he had taken do not permit his longer absence. He shall be happy if he can be useful to his Lordship in being the bearer of his commands for that Capital.
the right honourable
     the M. of Carmarthen
          &c &c &c."—Library of Congress, Jefferson Papers, 8875.

[29] Paul Leicester Ford (ed.), *Autobiography of Thomas Jefferson*, 97–98.

[30] John Adams and Thomas Jefferson to Jay, London, April 2[25], 1786 (Library of Congress, Jefferson Papers). The draft was accompanied by a note dated April 4, 1786 (*ibid.*).

one scrip of a pen, or one word from a minister, except a vague proposition at an accidental meeting. We availed ourselves even of that, to make another essay to extort some sort of declaration from the court. But their silence is invincible."[31]

Jefferson's visit to England convinced him that, except for a few enlightened individuals without influence on government policy, the entire English people were still enemies of America. "Even the opposition dare not open their lips in favor of a connection with us, so unpopular would be the topic."[32] The situation was certainly one to inspire misgivings. "The animosities of sovereigns are temporary, and may be allayed; but those which seize the whole body of a people, and of a people too who dictate their own measures, produce calamities of long duration. I shall not wonder to see the scenes of ancient Rome and Carthage renewed in our day; and if not pursued to the same issue, it may be because the republic of modern powers will not permit the extinction of any one of its members. Peace and friendship with all mankind is our wisest policy; and I wish we may be permitted to pursue them. But the temper and folly of our enemies may not leave this in our choice."[33]

Jefferson repeatedly declared that the English were unalterably determined not to conclude a commercial treaty with the United States. This was not because the British merchants were unmindful of the importance of trade with America, but because they felt confident that they could monopolize it without making any concessions to the infant republic. "I found the king, ministers and nation of England hostile, and averse to all arrangement with us. Not that they undervalue our commerce, but that they are secure of keeping it on their own terms. They think their commerce indispensable to us. . . . They think we cannot unite to retaliate upon them. I hope we can."[34]

[31] To Jay, London, April 23, 1786 (Lipscomb and Bergh, *Writings*, V, 297).
[32] To Jay, London, April 23, 1786 (*ibid.*, V, 296).
[33] To Dumas, Paris, May 6, 1786 (*ibid.*, V, 310).
[34] To W. T. Franklin, Paris, May 7, 1786 (Library of Congress, Jefferson

Accordingly, Jefferson was indefatigable in his efforts to promote American commerce with France. He continually sought to encourage direct exchange of American commodities for French products. He wished to supplant British middlemen and carriers. As a Virginian, he was well acquainted with the exactions of British merchants, and knew that an American planter, once indebted to an English trader, could never free himself from debt; for no matter what economies he might practice, he could never receive for his crops a price exceeding that which he was required to pay for the articles he imported. Moreover, Jefferson believed that France's friendship during the Revolutionary War and afterwards deserved a different recompense than did the continued enmity of England. In this respect Jefferson epitomized the foreign policy for which he strove during his public life when he said: "We owe gratitude to France, justice to England, goodwill to all, and subservience to none."[35]

In accordance with his usual practice when traveling, Jefferson did not fail to inform himself about the condition of the working people. He found French laborers worse off than those in England. "They pay about one half their produce in rent; the English, in general, about a third."[36] The toilers' status was one of "abject oppression," Jefferson believed. "The population of England is composed of three descriptions of persons. . . . These are, 1. The aristocracy, comprehending the nobility, the wealthy commoners, the high grades of priesthood, and the officers of government. 2. The laboring class. 3. The eleemosynary class,

Papers). Cf. to Nicholas Lewis, London, April 22, 1786 (*ibid.*): "All attempts to induce this nation to enter into such arrangements as may place our commerce on equal terms, are absolutely fruitless. This is now decided. They think they can have our trade on their own terms. They rely that the Southern states will never interest themselves in a case where the Northern are principal sufferers, that all our states cannot be induced to place the regulation of their commerce in a single body, and that while it is in the hands of thirteen legislatures they need not fear an union in their proceedings. It remains for us to shew whether they are true prophets."

[35] To Col. Arthur Campbell, Monticello, September 1, 1797 (Lipscomb and Bergh, *Writings*, IX, 421).

[36] To John Page, Paris, May 4, 1786 (*ibid.*, V, 304).

or paupers, who are about one-fifth of the whole. The aristocracy, which have the laws and government in their hands, have so managed them as to reduce the third description below the means of supporting life, even by labor; and to force the second, whether employed in agriculture or the arts, to the maximum of labor which the construction of the human body can endure, and to the minimum of food, and of the meanest kind, which will preserve it in life, and in strength sufficient to perform its functions. To obtain food enough, not only their whole strength must be unremittingly exerted, but the utmost dexterity also which they can acquire; and those of great dexterity only can keep their ground, while those of less must sink into the class of paupers. . . . The less dexterous individuals, falling into the eleemosynary ranks, furnish materials for armies and navies to defend . . . the domination and vicious happiness of the aristocracy. In their hands the paupers are used as tools to maintain their own wretchedness, and to keep down the laboring portion whenever the desperation produced by the cravings of their stomachs drives them into riots. Such is the happiness of scientific England."[37]

Meanwhile Jefferson had not permitted statecraft to engross all his attention. He was a frequent visitor to the theater, at Drury Lane and Covent Garden. He attended dinner parties.[38] He also found time to patronize a London tailor,[39] and to sit for a portrait. This was the first portrait ever painted of Jefferson. The artist, Mather Brown, "a Bostonian who went early to London and remained there," received £ 10 for it.[40] Copley, West,

---

[37] To Thos. Cooper, Monticello, September 10, 1814 (*ibid.*, XIV, 180–82).

[38] Adams, *The Works of John Adams*, III, 393, 396; Charles Francis Adams (ed.), *Letters of Mrs. Adams, Wife of John Adams*, 280. Cf. to R. H. Lee, London, April 22, 1786 (Lipscomb and Bergh, *Writings*, V, 293). See also Archibald B. Shepperson, *John Paradise and Lucy Ludwell of London and Williamsburg*, 196–212.

[39] To Colonel Wm. S. Smith, Paris, September 13, 1786 (*More Books, The Bulletin of the Boston Public Library*, Vol. XVIII, No. 4 [April, 1943], 156).

[40] Ford, *Writings*, V, 2; Samuel Isham, *The History of American Painting*, 124. John Adams on May 12, 1786, paid the artist for a duplicate of this portrait, according to Bowen in *Centennial Celebration*, 486. For a reproduction of the painting belonging to Adams, and now owned by former Secretary of the Navy

and Trumbull were consulted by Jefferson regarding the statue of George Washington which was being designed for the state of Virginia, and they all concurred in the conclusion that it should depict him in modern dress rather than classical garb.

Jefferson was delighted by the ingenuity of English artisans. "The mechanical arts in London are carried to a wonderful perfection," he declared. Particularly deserving of notice, because "likely to have extensive consequences," was the use of steam as a motive power.[41] Jefferson supplied his friends with cleverly constructed lamps and other inventions. He sent a bundle of feminine finery to his sister Nancy and another lady.[42] Among his purchases were "blue lamp chimneys and printed muslin." And of course he did not overlook the booksellers. To Madame de Corny he remarked that "the splendor of their shops . . . is all that is worth looking at in London."[43]

English architecture, Jefferson believed, exhibited the most wretched style he had ever seen, "not meaning to except America, where it is bad, nor even Virginia, where it is worse than any other part of America." The city of London, though handsomer than Paris, was not so handsome as Philadelphia. But English gardens delighted him. "The gardening in that country is the article in which it excels all the earth. I mean their pleasure-gardening. This, indeed, went far beyond my ideas."[44]

Jefferson recorded his impressions in his "Memorandums made on a tour to some of the gardens in England, described by Whateley in his book on gardening." Whately's work contains descriptions of a lawn at Moor Park; of a grove at Esher Place;

Charles Francis Adams, see *ibid.*, opposite page 21. On July 2, 1788, Jefferson paid the same artist for a portrait of Adams now in the Boston Athenaeum (United States Constitution Sesquicentennial Commission, *Loan Exhibition of Portraits*, 11).

[41] To Charles Thomson, London, April 22, 1786 (Lipscomb and Bergh, *Writings*, V, 294).

[42] To Anne Scott Randolph Jefferson, London, April 22, 1786 (Ford, *Writings*, IV, 208).

[43] To Mme de Corny, Paris, June 30, 1787 (Lipscomb and Bergh, *Writings*, VI, 145).

[44] To John Page, Paris, May 4, 1786 (*ibid.*, V, 304–305).

of the water at Blenheim; of the water at Wotton; of the approach at Caversham; of the Leasowes; of Woburn Farm; of Painshill; of Hagley; of Stowe; of Persfield; of the temple of concord and victory at Stowe, at sunset.[45] As to the author's accuracy Jefferson thus testifies: "While his descriptions, in point of style, are models of elegance and classical correctness, they are as remarkable for their exactness. I always walked over the gardens with his book in my hand, examined with attention the particular spots he described, found them so justly characterized by him as to be easily recognized, and saw with wonder, that his fine imagination had never been able to seduce him from the truth." At Wotton, Jefferson noted, "there is a Palladian bridge, of which, I think, Whately does not speak."[46]

An interesting account of this tour is given by John Adams in his diary: "Mr. Jefferson and myself went in a postchaise to Woburn Farm, Caversham, Wotton, Stowe, Edgehill, Stratford upon Avon, Birmingham, the Leasowes, Hagley, Stourbridge, Worcester, Woodstock, Blenheim, Oxford, High Wycombe, and back to Grosvenor Square.

"Edgehill and Worcester were curious and interesting to us, as scenes where freemen had fought for their rights. The people in the neighborhood appeared so ignorant and careless at Worcester, that I was provoked, and asked, 'And do Englishmen so soon forget the ground where liberty was fought for? Tell your neighbors and your children that this is holy ground; much holier than that on which your churches stand. All England should come in pilgrimage to this hill once a year.'

"This animated them, and they seemed much pleased with it. Perhaps their awkwardness before might arise from their uncertainty of our sentiments concerning the civil wars."

Of the house, "as small and mean as you can conceive," in which Shakespeare was born, Adams writes: "They showed us an old wooden chair in the chimney corner where he sat. We cut off

[45] Thomas Whately, *Observations on Modern Gardening*.
[46] Lipscomb and Bergh, *Writings*, XVII, 236, 239.

a chip according to custom."[47] Jefferson's account book simply records, without comment, that he spent "for seeing house where Shakespeare was born, 1s.; seeing his tomb, 1s.; entertainment, 4s. 2d.; servants, 2s."

Austerely practical, Adams remarks of the adornments in one of the gardens visited: "A national debt of 274 millions sterling, accumulated by jobs, contracts, salaries and pensions, in the course of a century might easily produce all this magnificence.

"The temples to Bacchus and Venus are quite unnecessary, as mankind have no need of artificial incitement to such amusements."

In a more romantic mood he adds: "Lord Littleton's seat interested me, from a recollection of his works, as well as the grandeur and beauty of the scene. Pope's pavilion and Thompson's seat made the excursion poetical."[48]

On April 26 Jefferson "Set out from London for Paris." He passed through Greenwich, where he visited the observatory and hospital, Dartford, Rochester, Sittingborne, Canterbury, and Dover, where he saw the castle the following day. On the twenty-eighth he sailed for Calais. Writing to a friend in England, Jefferson said: "I arrived at Dover a little before midnight of the day I parted with you at Greenwich, and was detained for a day & a half by bad weather and unfavorable winds. However I had at length an excellent passage of three hours only, and was able to get to Paris on the 5th day of my departure from London."[49] To Colonel Smith, who had written him about matters arising since Jefferson's departure from London, he explained that "on . . . Friday, the wind became so favorable as to place me at Calais in three hours. At the moment therefore of your writing your friendly letter, to wit at a quarter before four of that day, I was

[47] Adams, *The Works of John Adams*, III, 394.
[48] *Ibid.*, 395.
[49] To Mr. Paradise, Paris, May 4, 1786 (Library of Congress, Jefferson Papers).

on the road between Calais & St. Omer. I reached Paris in 48 hours from Calais."[50]

When returning to America in 1789, Jefferson again touched England. Being unable to embark for America directly from a French port, he was obliged to cross the English Channel and sail from Cowes.

On Christmas Day at Monticello, nearly a quarter of a century later, recollections of his three visits to England were revived in Jefferson's mind. In response to an odd request asking him to state, in order to decide a bet, whether he had ever been in London and had ever seen the King, the aged statesman obligingly answered in the affirmative, by giving an account of the happenings which had occasioned his being in England and his presentation to the English monarch.[51]

[50] To Col. W. S. Smith, Paris, May 4, 1786 (*ibid.*).

[51] Thomas Williamson to Jefferson, Norfolk, December 19, 1812; Jefferson to Thomas Williamson, Monticello, December 25, 1812 (Mo. Hist. Soc., Bixby Collection).

CHAPTER V

Remains of Roman Grandeur

✿

IN 1787, Jefferson was absent from Paris on the most extensive tour he ever made. He left on February 28 and returned on June 10. The preceding autumn, on the afternoon of September 4, he had suffered an injury as the result of an accident. Returning from a walk in the country, he was joined by a friend, and while engaged in conversation, he fell and broke his right wrist. It was doubtless badly swollen by the time he reached home and called a surgeon. The fracture was never properly set; his wrist was always weak and stiff thereafter. During the time he was disabled by the accident, he learned to write with his left hand. This skill enabled him to carry on his immense correspondence with less fatigue in later years.

In accordance with his physician's advice, he undertook "a journey to the south of France, one object of which is to try the mineral waters there, for the restoration of my hand; but another is, to visit all the seaports where we have trade, and to hunt up all the inconveniencies under which it labors, in order to get them rectified. I shall visit, and carefully examine, too, the canal of Languedoc."[1] He chose the waters of Aix, in Provence, from among the half dozen or more recommended as equally benefi-

[1] To Monroe, Paris, December 18, 1786 (Lipscomb and Bergh, *Writings*, VI, 16). Jefferson was planning this trip in the fall of 1786. "This court sets out for Fontainebleau about the 10th of Octob. I propose to go there at the same time, to stay there about a week, and then employ the rest of the time of their continuance there in making a tour into the South of France, as far as the canal of Languedoc which I have a great desire to examine minutely as at some future time it may enable me to give information thereon to such of our states as are engaged in works of that kind."—To Col. Wm. S. Smith, Paris, September 13, 1786 (*More Books, The Bulle-*

cial," because they would place me at the beginning of a tour to the seaports of Marseilles, Bordeaux, Nantes and L'Orient, which I had long meditated."[2] Hence, as he observed to Madison, "if they fail to be effectual, my journey will not be useless altogether. . . . I shall be absent about three months, unless anything happens to recall me sooner, which may always be effected in ten days, in whatever part of my route I may be."[3]

In Champagne Jefferson noted that the women performed heavy labor out of doors and that the people lived in villages rather than scattered farmhouses. These phenomena were both at variance with his notions of fitness. During a short stay in Dijon, "one of the gastronomical capitals of France,"[4] he hired a good servant. Proceeding through Burgundy, he "rambled thro' their most celebrated vineyards, going through the houses of the laborers, cellars of the vignerons, & mixing and conversing with them" as much as he could.[5] He recorded minutely the results of his investigation of the wine industry. "The wines which have given such celebrity to Burgundy . . . begin at Chambertin, and go through Vougeau, Romanie, Veaune, Nuys, Beaune, Pommard, Voulenay, Meursault, and end at Monrachet. Those of the two last are white, the others red. Chambertin, Vougeau and Veaune are strongest, and will bear transportation and keeping. They sell therefore on the spot for . . . forty-eight sous the bottle. Voulenay is the best of the other reds, equal in flavour to Chambertin, etc., but being lighter, will not keep, and therefore sells for not more than . . . twelve sous the bottle. It ripens sooner than

tin of the Boston Public Library, Vol. XVIII, No. 4 [April, 1943], 156). A month later he wrote: "The lateness of the season obliges me to decline my journey to the south of France."—To Maria Cosway, Paris, October 12, 1786 (Ford, Writings, IV, 323).

2 To Adams, Paris, July 1, 1787 (Lipscomb and Bergh, Writings, VI, 146).

3 To Madison, Paris, January 30, 1787 (Ford, Writings, IV, 367).

4 Douglas Goldring, The French Riviera and the Valley of the Rhone from Avignon to Marseilles, 24.

5 To Short, Lyons, March 15, 1787 (Library of Congress, Jefferson Papers, 4902, 4919).

they do, and consequently is better for those who wish to broach at a year old. In like manner of the white wines, and for the same reason, Monrachet sells for . . . forty-eight sous the bottle. It is remarkable that the best of each kind, that is, of the red and white, is made at the extremities of the line, to-wit, at Chambertin and Monrachet. It is pretended that the adjoining vineyards produce the same qualities, but that belonging to obscure individuals, they have not obtained a name, and therefore sell as other wines. . . . The best wines are carried to Paris by land. . . . The more indifferent go by water. Bottles cost four and a half sous each."[6]

Much of this information Jefferson obtained from a wine merchant at Beaune with whom he had considerable dealings and correspondence.[7] Although white wine was chiefly consumed by Jefferson's household, considerable quantities of Voulenay were required, as well as of Meursault and Monrachet.[8] To expedite entry, Jefferson advised that shipments be marked "vins ordinaires" and sent to the Grille des Champs Élysées, although that gate to the city was the most distant from the highway. For Sauterne he wrote directly to M. d'Yquem, although having no personal acquaintance with that renowned producer as he did with those he met in the course of his journey through the wine country.[9] Good Madeira Jefferson obtained by having it shipped from New York.[10] After his return to the United States he continued to receive his favorite varieties of wine, through American consular representatives abroad, with whom he had left a list of the

---

[6] Lipscomb and Bergh, *Writings*, XVII, 157–59.

[7] To Parrain, Lyon, March 18, 1787 (Mass. Hist. Soc., Jefferson Papers).

[8] To Parent, Paris, July 21, 1787; December 17, 1787; March 11, 1789 (*ibid.*). Jefferson also ordered a supply of de la Fite.—To President Richard, Paris, February 22, 1788 (Mo. Hist. Soc., Bixby Collection).

[9] To Parent, Paris, June 14, 1787; to Diquem, Paris, December 18, 1787; to Bondfield, Paris, December 18, 1787 (Mass. Hist. Soc., Jefferson Papers).

[10] To Francis Lewis, Paris, February 9, 1786 (*ibid.*). In Washington, Jefferson sent some of his Madeira to the Spanish minister, from whom he had received a supply of champagne.—D'Yrujo to Jefferson, Capitol Hill, December 30, 1802 (Mo. Hist. Soc., Bixby Collection). Jefferson also used Marsalla, a wine much like Madeira, and St. George.—To John Woodhouse, Washington, May 5, 1805; to Peter Walsh, Monticello, March 27, 1811 (*ibid.*).

choice sources of supply. Of Italian vintages he preferred Mon-
tepulciano and Nebioule.[11] Through his good offices George
Washington and other friends obtained their requirements in the
way of wine.[12]

Attentive, as always, to "the condition of the laboring poor,"
Jefferson wrote: "At Pommard and Voulenay I observed them
eating good wheat bread; at Meursault, rye. I asked the reason
of this difference. They told me that the white wines fail in quality much oftener than the red, and remain on hand. The farmer
therefore cannot afford to feed his labourers so well. At Meursault only white wines are made, because there is too much stone
for the red. On such slight circumstances depends the condition
of man."[13]

Encountering along the way a malefactor under arrest, whom
he viewed as "perhaps a dove in the talons of a hawk," Jefferson
indulged in reflections upon the French penal system, doubtless
contrasting it in his mind with the reforms introduced by him in
Virginia. Criminal prosecutions in France, he believed, were a
form of oppression. That because of their expense they were few
in number he regarded as "a good effect from a bad cause."[14]

In the Beaujolais, thanks to letters of introduction from
friends in Paris, Jefferson passed some time at the Chateau de
Laye Epinaye. There he fell in love with "a Diana and Endym-
ion, a very superior morsel of sculpture, by Michael Angelo
Slodtz, done in the year 1740" which "carries the perfection of
the chisel to a degree of which I had no conception. It is the

[11] To C. C. Pinckney, Philadelphia, December 2, 1792 (Mass. Hist. Soc., Jefferson Papers); to Peter Kuhn, Washington, March 14, 1805; Thomas H. Storm
to Jefferson, Genoa, April 24, 1806; Jefferson to Storm, Washington, April 29,
1805; to Kuhn, Washington, March 30, 1807 (Mo. Hist. Soc., Bixby Collection).

[12] Mass. Hist. Soc., Jefferson Papers, 742; to Cathalan, Washington, November
21, 1803 (*ibid.*); to Jay, Paris, September 17, 1789 (Henry P. Johnston, *Correspondence and Public Papers of John Jay*, III, 376–77); October 8, 1787 (*ibid.*,
257); Lambert to Jefferson, Frontignan, February 10, 1791 (Mo. Hist. Soc., Bixby
Collection).

[13] Lipscomb and Bergh, *Writings*, XVII, 157.

[14] *Ibid.*, XVII, 162, 160.

only thing in sculpture which I have seen on my journey worthy of notice."[15] He was "entertained by Madame de Laye with a hospitality and goodness & ease that was charming and left here with regret." Her "attention and civilities" moved him to beseech William Short to convey to the lady's husband, as well as to Jefferson's clerical friends in Paris, the Abbés Chalut and Arnond, his gratitude for their letters of introduction.

At Lyons he was the recipient of similar courtesies, though the shortness of his stay circumscribed their extent. "A constant tempest confined me to the house the first day; the second, I determined to see everything within my plan before delivering my letters, that I might do as much, in as little time, as possible. The third & fourth have been filled up with all the attentions they would admit, & I am now on the wing, as soon as this letter is closed. I enter into these details because they are necessary to justify me to the abbés for the little time I had left to profit of the good dispositions of their friends."

"I have not visited all the manufactures of this place; because all knowledge of them would be useless, and would extrude from the memory other things more worth retaining," Jefferson wrote Short from Lyons. "Architecture, painting, sculpture, antiquities, agriculture, the condition of the laboring poor fill all my moments. Hitherto I have derived as much satisfaction, & even delight from my journey as I could propose to myself. The plan of having servants who know nothing of me places me perfectly at my ease. I intended to have a new one at every principal city; to have carried him on to serve me on the road to the next & there changed him. But the one I brought forward from Dijon is so good a one that I expect to keep him through the greater part of the journey, taking additionally a valet de place wherever I stay a day or two."[16] The statesman took pains to reassure his

---

[15] *Ibid.*, XVII, 162; to Short, Aix, March 29, 1787 (Library of Congress, Jefferson Papers).

[16] To Short, Lyons, March 15, 1787 (*ibid.*, 4902, 4919). Cf. to Chalut and Arnond, Nice, April 12, 1787 (*ibid.*).

Paris servant, Espagnol, that it was not because of any dissatisfaction with the latter's services that he had been left at home.[17]

In Dauphiné, near Vienne, Jefferson noted, "the hills come in precipices to the river, resembling then very much our Susquehanna and its hills, except that the Susquehanna is ten times as wide as the Rhone."[18] He arrived on March 19 at Nîmes, where he spent four days "gazing whole hours at the Maison Quarrée, like a lover at his mistress,"[19] and viewing the temple and fountain of Diana, and other monuments of Roman times.

At Nîmes Jefferson had an interview with an unknown Brazilian who had written from Montpellier that he wished to make a communication of importance to the American envoy. Jefferson replied "that I would go off my road as far as Nismes, under the pretext of seeing the antiquities of that place, if he would meet me there."[20] The South American sought help from the United States in promoting a revolution to free Brazil from the Portuguese yoke. Jefferson returned what he considered a discreet answer. In a similar conversation with a Mexican in Paris, he had been even more noncommittal, suspecting that his interviewer was a Spanish spy.

Jefferson was merely pretending that his interest in classical antiquities was a pretext drawing him to Nîmes. His enthusiasm was genuine. Before Jefferson himself had ever set eyes on the Maison Carrée, he had praised its beauty, and persuaded the Directors of the Public Buildings in Virginia to adopt his plan for the new capitol in Richmond which took the Maison Carrée as its model.

Jefferson was favorably impressed with Nîmes.[21] He later

[17] To Short, Nantes, June 1, 1787 (*William and Mary College Quarterly* [2d series], Vol. XI, No. 4 [October, 1931], 340).

[18] Lipscomb and Bergh, *Writings*, XVII, 163.

[19] To Mme de Tessé, Nismes, March 20, 1787 (*ibid.*, VI, 102).

[20] To Jay, Marseilles, May 4, 1787 (*ibid.*, VI, 115).

[21] In addition to his enjoyment of the antiquities of Nîmes, he found that: "The vin ordinaire is excellent and costs but 2. or 3. sous a bottle. This is the cheapest place in France to buy silk stockings."—Library of Congress, Shippen Papers.

advised a friend to visit that city in order "to see the most perfect remains of antiquity which exist on earth."[22] He playfully
suggested that Mme de Tessé should transport her residence to
that place. A well-known English traveler, Arthur Young, who
visited Nîmes a few months after Jefferson, wrote: "I like Nismes much; and if the inhabitants are at all on a par with the
appearance of their city, I should prefer it for a residence to most,
if not all the towns I have seen in France."[23] More recently a fellow countryman of Young declared: "Nimes struck me as one
of the very brightest, pleasantest towns I have ever visited, and
the one in which, if forced to live out of England, I think I could
live most happily in."[24]

What is perhaps the most exuberant expression of Jefferson's
pleasure in the midst of the vestiges of antiquity which abound
in the region of Nîmes is contained in his celebrated letter to
Mme de Tessé, Lafayette's aunt. That epistle was read by her
to Jefferson's friend Mazzei, in the same manner as she imagined
those of the apostles were read by the early Christians in their
assemblies, in order to be sure of understanding the true weight
of each word.[25] Jefferson wrote with rapture:

From Lyons to Nismes I have been nourished with the remains of
Roman grandeur. They have always brought you to my mind, because I
know your affection for whatever is Roman and noble. . . . At Orange,
too, I thought of you. I was sure you had seen with pleasure the sublime
triumphal arch of Marius at the entrance of the city. I went then to the
Arenae. Would you believe, Madam, that in this eighteenth century, in
France, under the reign of Louis XVI., they are at this moment pulling
down the circular wall of this superb remain, to pave a road? And that,

[22] To Shippen, Paris, September 29, 1788 (Lipscomb and Bergh, *Writings*, VII,
153–54).

[23] Arthur Young, *Travels in France*, 52.

[24] Sabine Baring-Gould, *In Troubadour Land: A Ramble in Provence and
Languedoc*, 216.

[25] Mme de Tessé to Jefferson, Paris, March 30, 1787 (Chinard, *Trois Amitiés*,
100–101). Doubtless the political comments Jefferson advanced were divulged to a
wide circle of acquaintances in the French capital (Randall, *Life of Jefferson*, I,
468).

too, from a hill which is itself an entire mass of stone, just as fit, and more accessible? A former intendant, a M. de Basville, has rendered his memory dear to the traveller and amateur, by the pains he took to preserve and restore these monuments of antiquity. The present one (I do not know who he is) is demolishing the object, to make a good road to it. I thought of you again, and I was then in great good humor, at the Pont du Gard, a sublime antiquity, and well preserved. But most of all here, where Roman taste, genius, and magnificence, excite ideas analogous to yours at every step. I could no longer oppose the inclination to avail myself of your permission to write to you, a permission given with too much complaisance by you, and used by me with too much indiscretion. Madam de Tott did me the same honor. But she, being only the descendant of some of those puny heroes who boiled their own kettles before the walls of Troy, I shall write to her from a Grecian, rather than a Roman canton; when I shall find myself, for example, among her Phocaean relations at Marseilles.

Loving, as you do Madam, the precious remains of antiquity, loving architecture, gardening, a warm sun and a clear sky, I wonder you have never thought of moving Chaville to Nismes. . . .

From a correspondent at Nismes, you will not expect news. Were I to attempt to give you news, I should tell you stories one thousand years old. I should detail to you the intrigues of the courts of the Caesars, how they affect us here, the oppressions of their praetors, prefects, &c. I am immersed in antiquities from morning to night. For me, the city of Rome is actually existing in all the splendor of its empire. I am filled with alarms for the event of the irruptions daily making on us, by the Goths, the Visigoths, and Vandals, lest they should re-conquer us to our original barbarism. If I am sometimes induced to look forward to the eighteenth century, it is only when recalled to it by the recollections of your goodness and friendship, and by those sentiments of sincere esteem and respect with which I have the honor to be Madam, your most obedient, and most humble servant.[26]

Indeed a poetic charm seems to color the most commonplace objects of observation: "At Nismes the earth is full of limestone. . . . Wild figs, very flourishing, grow out of the joints of the Pont

---

[26] To Mme de Tessé, Nismes, March 20, 1787 (Lipscomb and Bergh, *Writings*, VI, 102–106).

du Gard. . . . The high hills of Languedoc are covered with snow."[27]

On March 25, almost a month after leaving Paris, Jefferson arrived at Aix-en-Provence, whose medicinal waters were ostensibly the object of his journey. He departed on the twenty-ninth. "Having taken 40 douches, without sensible benefit, I thought useless to continue them. My wrist strengthens slowly; it is to time that I look as the surest remedy, & that I believe will restore it at length."[28]

Doubtless Jefferson found bathing his wrist less amusing than other occupations. In a letter written from Aix he regales William Short with an account of his activities: "In painting I have seen some good things at Lyons only. In architecture nothing anywhere except the remains of antiquity. These are more in number, & less injured by time, than I expected, and have been to me a great treat. Those at Nismes, both in dignity, & preservation, stand first."

A disquisition on the Romance languages follows. Of the *langue d'Oc* Jefferson says: "Provençale stands nearer to the Tuscan that it does to the French, & it is my Italian which enables me to understand the people here, more than my French. . . . The ballads of it's [*sic*] Troubadours were the delight of the several courts of Europe & it is from thence that the novels of the English are called Romances. Every letter is pronounced, the articulation is distinct; no nasal sounds disfigure it, & on the whole it stands close to the Italian & Spanish in point of beauty. I think it a general misfortune that historical circumstances gave a final prevalence to the French instead of the Provençale language. It loses its ground slowly and will ultimately disappear because there are few books written in it, & because it is thought more polite to speak the language of the capital. Yet those who learn that language here pronounce it as the Italians do."

[27] *Ibid.*, XVII, 169, 170, 171.
[28] To Short, Toulon, April 7, 1787 (Library of Congress, Jefferson Papers).

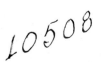

He concludes by describing a visit to the theater the night before, where the most celebrated actress of Marseilles had appeared. Approving her technique, Jefferson adds: "She is moreover young & handsome; and has an advantage over . . . some . . . of the celebrated ones of Paris, in being clear of that dreadful wheeze or rather whistle in respiration which resembles the agonizing struggles for breath of a dying person."[29]

The sunshine and the attractive appearance of Aix delighted him: "This city is one of the cleanest & neatest I have ever seen in any country. The streets are streight, from 20 to 100 feet wide, & as clean as a parlour floor. Where they are of width sufficient they have 1. 2. or 4. rows of elms from 100 to 150 years old, which make delicious walks. There are no porte-cocheres, so that the buildings shew themselves advantageously on the streets."[30]

Perhaps skeptical from the outset regarding the curative powers of the medicinal waters, Jefferson was not surprised when they did not manifest their healing properties in the four days he passed at Aix, before proceeding to Marseilles, where he spent a week. As he informed Jay: "Having staid at Aix long enough to prove the inefficacy of the waters, I came on to this place for the purpose of informing myself, as I mean to do at the other seaport towns, of whatever may be interesting to our commerce."[31]

"My journey from Paris to this place has been a continued feast of new objects and new ideas," Jefferson wrote from Marseilles to the Marquis de Chastellux. "To make the most of the little time I have for so long a circuit I have been obliged to keep myself rather out of the way of good dinners and good company. Had they been my objects I should not have quitted Paris. I have courted the society of gardeners, vignerons, coopers, farmers, & c, and have devoted every moment of every day almost to the busi-

[29] To Short, Aix, March 29, 1787 (*ibid.*, 4917, 4918, 4913).

[30] To William Short, Aix, March 27, 1787 (*William and Mary College Quarterly* [2d series], Vol. XI, No. 3 [July, 1931], 246. Moreover, in Aix Jefferson observed that "the bread at this place is equal to any in the world," and that "the oil is also considered as the best."—Library of Congress, Shippen Papers.

[31] To Jay, Marseilles, May 4, 1787 (Lipscomb and Bergh, *Writings*, VI, 111).

ness of enquiry. M. de Bergasse however united for me all objects, a good dinner, good company, and information." An additional letter of introduction was requested from the French diplomat, directed to "some one good person at Tours," where Jefferson wished to investigate certain scientific phenomena mentioned in the writings of Voltaire. "I have found the abbés in general are most useful acquaintances. They are unembarrassed with families, uninvolved in form, . . . frequently learned and always obliging. If you know any such a one at Tours you will oblige me infinitely."[32]

Besides viewing the wine cellars of M. de Bergasse at Marseilles, Jefferson found time to visit the Chateau d'If, famous in the adventures of the Count of Monte Cristo, and the Chateau Borelli, where he observed with interest "pumps worked by the wind." Diligently prosecuting his commercial inquiries, he learned that thirty-two American ships had brought cargoes to Marseilles since the peace of 1783.

But he was unable to find out why American rice, although admittedly superior to other varieties when cooked with milk and sugar, was not preferred by French consumers when prepared *au gras*. "I had expected to satisfy myself at Marseilles," he wrote, "of the causes of the difference of quality between the rice of Carolina & that of Piedmont which is brought in quantities to Marseilles."[33] Not willing to be put off with superficial answers, he was obliged to make an expedition into Italy in order to settle the matter to his satisfaction.

"I wished particularly to know whether it was the use of a different machine for cleaning which brought European rice to market less broken than ours, as had been represented to me by those who deal in that article at Paris. I found several persons who had passed thro' the rice country of Italy, but not one who could explain to me the nature of the machine. But I was given to

[32] To Chastellux, Marseilles, April 4, 1787 (Mass. Hist. Soc., Jefferson Papers). Cf. Lipscomb and Bergh, *Writings*, XVII, 178.
[33] To John Adams, Paris, July 1, 1787 (*ibid.*, VI, 147).

believe that I might see it myself immediately on entering Piedmont. As this would require but about three weeks I determined to go & ascertain this point; as the chance only of placing our rice above all rivalship in quality as it is in colour, by the introduction of a better machine, if a better existed, seemed to justify the application of that much time to it. I found the rice country to be in truth Lombardy, 100 miles further than had been represented, & that tho' called Piedmont rice, not a grain is made in the country of Piedmont. I passed thro the rice fields of the Venellese & Milanese, about 60 miles, & returned from thence last night, having found that the machine is absolutely the same as ours, and of course that we need not listen more to that suggestion. It is a difference in the species of grain, of which the government of Turin is so sensible, that, as I was informed, they prohibit the exportation of rough rice on pain of death. I have taken measures however for obtaining a quantity of it which I think will not fail & I bought on the spot a small parcel which I have with me."[34]

Jefferson's journal reveals what those measures were: "Poggio, a muleteer, who passes every week between Vercelli and Genoa, will smuggle a sack of rough rice for me to Genoa; it being death to export it in that form." Jefferson put little trust in his confederate, and carried away a supply of the rice himself, "as much as my coat & surtout pockets would hold."[35]

Other curious experiences awaited Jefferson at Marseilles. He saw "dried raisins from Smyrna without seeds," and "measured a mule, not the largest, five feet and two inches high." Mazzei's friend Soria, a Marseilles merchant to whom Jefferson had a letter of introduction, received the American visitor as civilly as the state of his mind would permit, his only son having

---

[34] To Jay, Marseilles, May 4, 1787 (*ibid.*, VI, 112–13).

[35] *Ibid.*, XVII, 192; to Edward Rutledge, Paris, July 14, 1787 (*ibid.*, VI, 170). Cf. to Wm. Drayton, Paris, July 30, 1787 (*ibid.*, VI, 193, 196). There seems to be no evidence concerning the success of the muleteer's expedition. Cf. the conflicting statements of Albert J. Nock, *Jefferson*, 171, and James Parton, *Life of Thomas Jefferson*, 308.

just eloped with jewels and money to the value of 40,000 livres.[36]

From Marseilles, carrying out the intention expressed in his letter from Nîmes to Mme de Tessé, Jefferson wrote to Mme de Tott. She was a portrait painter, of Greek extraction, with whom he had undertaken "the pleasing office of studying . . . the rythm of Homer . . . your divine countryman."[37] On the day of his departure from Paris, Jefferson had urged her "to see the superb picture now exhibiting . . . chez Mde. Drouay . . . of Marius in the moment when the souldier enters to assassinate him. It is made by her son, a student at Rome under the care of David, & is much in David's manner. All Paris is running to see it, & really it appears to me to have extraordinary merit. . . . Write me your judgment on it. It will serve to rectify my own, which, as I told you, is a bad one, & needs a guide. It will multiply too the occasions of my hearing from you."[38] Mme de Tott reported that in her opinion the appearance of the Roman hero was too delicate, and not fierce enough, although the artist had given him a very strong expression. The coloring in the picture was too uniform; the limbs and body of Marius were too pale; he leaned too nonchalantly and tranquilly on one arm.[39]

[36] Lipscomb and Bergh, *Writings*, XVII, 226, 178; to Mazzei, Marseilles, April 4, 1787 (*ibid.*, XIX, 32).
[37] Presenting to Mme de Tott a choice copy of Homer, he wrote: "To so perfect an edition then of so charming a poet, allow me to add so charming a reader." At the same time he compiled for her "the few rules of Greek prosody which must be indispensably known." These included the proposition that "The verse of Homer is called Hexameter, because it consists of six feet or measures."—To Mme de Tott, Paris, November 28, 1786 (Mo. Hist. Soc., Bixby Collection). She accepted the volume "avec reconnaissance et confusion. Qu'il me seroit doux de pouvoir vous exprimer combien je suis touchée, penetrée, de l'extreme bonté que vous avez de vous occuper de moi, combien je suis honorée de l'interêt que vous me témoignez, combien je serois fière si je pouvais croire que j'ai merité un moment cet interêt d'un homme tel que vous! Ajoutez je vous supplie a toutes les marques de bonté dont vous m'avez comblée, celle de me procurer le plutôt possible, le plaisir de vous en remercier moi même chez maman."—Mme de Tott to Jefferson, Paris, November 28, 1786 (*ibid.*). In an undated letter she thanks him for books and invites him to dine. "Les livres que vous voulez bien me donner sont d'un prix infini pour une malheureuse grecque, qui sans tous les soins que vous vous êtes donnés pour elle, se seroit reduite a l'affligeante extremité de rennoncer au bonheur de lire le divin auteur qui a immortalisé sa langue."—*Ibid.*
[38] To Mme de Tott, Paris, February 28, 1787 (*ibid.*).
[39] Mme de Tott to Jefferson, Paris, March 4, 1787 (*ibid.*).

Jefferson's sprightly letter from Marseilles to Mme de Tott, hitherto unpublished, is in the same vein as that to Mme de Tessé from Nîmes, of which it is the companion piece:

I thank you sincerely, madam, for the favor of your letter on the subject of M. Drouay's picture. It has confirmed a part of my own ideas, given me some which had escaped me, and corrected others wherein I had been wrong. The strong expression given to the countenance of Marius had absorbed all my attention, and made me overlook the slenderness of his frame, which you justly recall to my mind as faulty in this particular. Give me leave in return to rectify for you an opinion in another kind, which I suppose you to entertain, because you have not yet had time to correct all the errors of the human mind. I presume that you think, as most people think, that a person cannot be in two places at one & the same time. Yet is there no error more palpable than this. You know, for example, that you have been in Paris & it's neighborhood constantly since I had the pleasure of seeing you there. Yet I declare you have been with me above half my journey. I would repeat to you long conversations, word for word, on a variety of subjects. When I find you fatigued with conversation, sighing for your pallet and pencil, I permit you to return to Paris awhile, & in the mean time amuse myself with philosophising on the objects which occur. The plan of my journey, as well as of my life, being to take things by the smooth handle, few occur which have not something good to offer me. The Auberge for instance in which I am obliged to take refuge for the night, presents, in the first moment nothing but noise, dirt, & disorder. But the Auberge has been too much abused. True it has not the charming gardens of Chaville without, nor it's decorations, nor it's charming society within. I do not seek therefore the good things which it has not, but those which it has. A traveller, sais I, retired at night to his chamber in an inn, all his effects contained in a single portmanteau, all his cares circumscribed by the walls of his apartment, unknown to all, unheeded and undisturbed, writes, reads, thinks, sleeps just in the moments when nature & the movements of his body & mind require. Charmed with this tranquility, he finds how few are our real wants, how cheap a thing is happiness, how expensive a one pride. He views with pity the wretched rich whom the laws of the world have submitted to the cumbrous trappings of rank. He sees him labor over ingots of gold, little of which goes to feed, to clothe or cover himself; the rest gobbled up by harpies of various descriptions with which he has surrounded himself. These, & not himself, are it's real masters. He wonders that a thinking mind can be so subdued by opinion, and that he does not run away from his own crowded house and take refuge in the chamber of an inn. Indeed I wonder so too, unless he has a Chaville to retire to, and a family composed, like that of Chaville, where quiet and friendship can both be united. But between the society of real friends, & the tranquility of solitude, the mind finds no middle ground.

Thus reconciled to my auberge by night, I was still persecuted by day with the cruel whip of the postillions. How to find a smooth handle to this tremendous instrument? At length however I found it in the callous nerves of the horse, to which these terrible stripes may afford but a gentle and perhaps pleasing irritation, like a pinch of Scotch snuff to an old snuff-taker. Sometimes I amuse myself with physical researches. Those enormous boots, for instance, in which the postillion is encased, like an Egyptian mummy, have cost me more pondering than the laws of motion did Newton. I have searched their solution in his physical, & in his moral constitution. I fancied myself in conversation with one of Newton's countrymen, & asked him what he thought could be the reason of their wearing those boots? Sir, says he, it is that a Frenchman's heels are so light that without this ballast he would turn keel-up.—"If so, Sir, it proves at least that he has more gravity in his head than your nation is generally willing to allow him?"

I should go on, Madam, detailing to you my dreams & speculations, but that my present situation is most unfriendly to speculation. 4350. market women (I have counted them) brawling, squabbling, jabbering patois, 300. asses braying & bewailing to each other, & to the world, their cruel oppressions, 4. files of mule carts passing in constant succession, with as many bells to every mule as can be hung about him, all this in the street under my window, & the weather too hot to shut it. Judge whether in such a situation it is easy to hang one's ideas together. Besides, writing from a colony of your own country, you would rather I should say less of myself, and more of that. But, just dropped among them, how can I pretend to judge the legitimacy of their descent? Of beauty, you will say, one may judge on a single coup d'oeil. Of beauty, then, madam, they have a good share, as far as the public walks, the Spectacles, & the assembée of

Mademlle. Conil enable me to decide. But it is not a legitimate Grecian beauty. It is not such as yours. The reason I suppose is that yours is genuine & brought from the spot; whereas theirs has been made here, &, like all fabricated wares, is sophisticated with foreign mixtures.

Perhaps you would rather I should write you news?—Any thing to obey you.—Oil is 10. sols the cwt. almonds 2#. cacao 19″. caffe 31′. rice 21#. etc. This is not in the stile of Paris news; but I write from Marseilles, and it is the news of the place. I could continue it thro' the whole table of prices current, but that I am sure you have enough, and have already in your heart wished an end to my letter. I shall therefore annex but one preliminary condition, which is, permission to express here my respectful attachment to Made. & M. de Tessé & to assure yourself of those sentiments of friendship and affection with which I have the honor to be sincerely and constantly, madam,

your most obedt. & most humble servt
Th: Jefferson[40]

On his way toward the rice country of Italy, with Marseilles a day's journey behind him, Jefferson writes: "Hitherto my journey has been a continued feast on objects of agriculture, new to

[40] To Mme de Tott, Marseilles, April 5, 1787 (Library of Congress, Jefferson Papers). Replying, Mme de Tott wrote: "J'ai été malade assez longtems après avoir reçu la lettre que vous avez eu la bonté de m'ecrire, Monsieur, et j'ai cru depuis quelques jours que je me porte bien, que celle que je pourrois avoir l'honneur de vous ecrire ne vous parviendroit plus. J'esperois que votre retour seroit prochain, mais Mr. Short que j'ai vu aujourdhui, m'a assurée que une lettre vous parviendroit encore.—C'est avec regret et avec plaisir que je vous ecris Monsieur, devinez comment cela s'arrange, et quand vous aurez deviné permettez moi de vous remercier de la très jolie et très aimable lettre que vous m'avez ecrite de Marseille. Je n'aurois jamais imaginé que j'eusse tant de plaisir a apprendre le prix des denrées de cette ville, je n'aurois jamais imaginé que je pusse me transporter dans votre auberge et compter avec vous les quatre mille trois cent poissardes qui faisoient un vacarme si comique sous vos fenêtres, enfin je n'aurois jamais imaginé trouver un aussi grand interêt a la solution du problème concernant les postillons de poste, mais il est pourtant très vrai que j'en ai eu un très grand a lire et a relire tous les tableaux que vous avez tracés avec un crayon digne de Tenieres, et quelquefois digne de Raphael. Ne vous attendez pas Monsieur, a recevoir le pendant de tous vos jolis tableaux. Sans compter qu'un pauvre petit barbouilleur comme moi ne doit pas mesurer ses forces avec les grands hommes dont je viens de parler, il y a aussi une uniformité dans les tableaux qu'offre la vie douce et tranquille que nous menons a Chaville, qui donneroit peut-être un peu de peine au pinceau sublime du redacteur de l'acte d'independance; et pour vous en donner une idée je vous dirai seulement que Jupiter pluvieux a été suspendu sur nos têtes pendant près de six semaines, et que plusieurs fois par jour, nous allions a la suite l'un de l'autre donner un petit coup sur le baromêtre pour

me, & some of them, at least, susceptible of adoption in America. Nothing can be ruder or more savage than the country I am in, as it must have come from the hands of nature; & nothing more rich & variegated than the productions with which art has covered it. Marseilles is a charming place."[41]

Before crossing the Alps, Jefferson paused several days at Nice. While still in Paris he had planned to go there and had written to the French Minister of Foreign Affairs: "I think it possible I may go as far as Nice. As circumstances might arise under which a passport might be useful, I take the liberty of troubling your Excellency for one."[42] From Nice he penned a famous letter to Lafayette, which is of interest here:

Your head, my dear friend, is full of notable things; and being better employed, therefore, I do not expect letters from you. I am constantly roving about, to see what I have never seen before, and shall never see again. In the great cities, I go to see what travellers think alone worthy of being seen; but I make a job of it, and generally gulp it all down in a day. On the other hand, I am never satiated with rambling through the fields and farms, examining the culture and cultivators, with a degree of curiosity which makes some take me to be a fool, and others to be much wiser than I am. I have been pleased to find among the people a less degree of physical misery than I had expected. They are generally well clothed, and have plenty of food, not animal indeed, but vegetable, which is as wholesome. Perhaps they are over-worked, the excess of the rent required by the landlord obliging them to too many hours of labor in order to produce that, and wherewith to feed and clothe themselves. The soil of Champagne and Burgundy I have found more universally good than I had expected, and as I could not help making a comparison with England,

voir si la colère du Dieu s'étoit enfin apaisée, et ce prophête de malheur nous annoncait, *Grande pluie*, pour le lendemain.—Papa et maman ont été infiniment sensibles a votre souvenir ils me chargent tous les deux de vous dire milles choses tendres en vous assurant de l'impatience qu'ils ont de vous revoir. La mienne est aussi vive Monsieur, il me sera bien doux de vous assurer moi même de mon attachement et de tous les sentiments que je vous ai voués pour la vie."—Mme de Tott to Jefferson, Chaville, May 9, 1787 (Mo. Hist. Society, Bixby Collection).

[41] To Short, Toulon, April 7, 1787 (Library of Congress, Jefferson Papers).

[42] To Vergennes, Paris, February 11, 1787 (Mo. Hist. Soc., Bixby Collection).

I found that comparison more unfavorable to the latter than is generally admitted. . . . From the first olive fields of Pierrelatte, to the orangeries of Hieres, has been continued rapture to me. I have often wished for you. I think you have not made this journey. It is a pleasure you have to come, and an improvement to be added to the many you have already made. It will be a great comfort to you, to know, from your own inspection, the condition of all the provinces of your country, and it will be interesting to them at some future day, to be known to you. This is, perhaps, the only moment of your life in which you can acquire that knowledge. And to do it most effectually, you must be absolutely incognito, you must ferret the people out of their hovels as I have done, look into their kettles, eat their bread, loll on their beds under pretence of resting yourself, but in fact, to find if they are soft. You will feel a sublime pleasure in the course of this investigation, and a sublimer one hereafter, when you shall be able to apply your knowledge to the softening of their beds, or the throwing a morsel of meat into their kettle of vegetables.

You will not wonder at the subjects of my letters; they are the only ones which have been presented to my mind for some time past; and the waters must always be what are the fountains from which they flow. According to this, indeed, I should have intermixed, from beginning to end, warm expressions of friendship to you. But according to the ideas of our country, we do not permit ourselves to speak even truths, when they may have the air of flattery. I content myself, therefore, with saying once for all, that I love you, your wife and children. Tell them so, and adieu. Yours affectionately." [43]

Leaving his carriage at Nice, Jefferson proceeded on mule-back over the Alps to Turin. His route was through Scarena, Sospello, Breglio, Saorgio, Fontan, Ciandola, Tende, Limone, Cuneo, Centallo, Savigliano, Racconigi, and Poirino.

After passing Breglio he notes a striking view: "Further on, we come to the Chateau di Saorgio, where a scene is presented, the most singular and picturesque I ever saw. The castle and village seem hanging to a cloud in front. On the right, is a mountain cloven through, to let pass a gurgling stream; on the left,

[43] To Lafayette, Nice, April 11, 1787 (Lipscomb and Bergh, *Writings*, VI, 106–10).

a river, over which is thrown a magnificent bridge. The whole forms a basin, the sides of which are shagged with rocks, olive trees, vines, herds, etc."[44] This impressive spectacle affected him profoundly; for later, when counselling two young fellow countrymen about their plans for traveling in Europe, he exclaimed: "Fall down and worship the site of the Chateau di Saorgio, you never saw, nor will ever see, such another. This road is probably the greatest work of the kind which ever was executed either in ancient or modern times. It did not cost as much as one year's war."[45]

Regarding other places along the way, he observes: "Ciandola consists of only two houses, both taverns. Tende is a very inconsiderable village, in which they have not yet the luxury of glass windows; nor in any of the villages of this passage, have they yet the fashion of powdering the hair. Common stone and limestone are so abundant, that the apartments of every story are vaulted with stone, to save wood."[46]

After spending a day making excursions in the vicinity of Turin, where he arrived on April 16, Jefferson went on through Settimo, Chivasco, Ciliano, and St. Germano to Vercelli. When he had observed the methods of husking rice, he proceeded by way of Novara, Buffalora, and Sedriano to Milan, arriving on April 20. Here Jefferson was the recipient of the attentions and services of Count del Vermi. "Being restricted to pass a very short time there, he directed my attention to those objects which merited most attention."[47] At Milan Jefferson found time to visit the

[44] *Ibid.*, XVII, 185. See also Bullock, *My Head and My Heart*, 68, 102, 142.

[45] Library of Congress, Shippen Papers. With similar insight into conventional financial habits, he found "the Cathedral of Milan a worthy object of philosophical contemplation. To be placed among the rarest instances of the misuse of money. On viewing the churches of Italy it is evident without calculation that the same expense would have sufficed to throw the Appenines into the Adriatic & thereby render it terra firma from Leghorn to Constantinople."—*Ibid.*

[46] Lipscomb and Bergh, *Writings*, XVII, 186.

[47] To Gaudenzio Clerici, Paris, August 15, 1787 (Library of Congress, Jefferson Papers). Cf. to Count del Vermi, Paris, August 15, 1787 (Lipscomb and Bergh, *Writings*, VI, 283).

comedy, and inform himself regarding "a pendulum odometer for the wheel of a carriage," which he later used to measure distances in America.

Jefferson thus described his Italian journey to his old preceptor, George Wythe, a lover of the classics: "In the latter country my time allowed me to go no further than Turin, Milan, and Genoa: consequently I scarcely got into classical ground. I took with me some of the writings in which endeavors have been made to investigate the passage of Annibal over the Alps, and was just able to satisfy myself, from a view of the country, that the descriptions given of his march are not sufficiently particular to enable us at this day even to guess at his track across the Alps. In architecture, painting, sculpture, I found much amusement; but more than all in their agriculture, many objects of which might be adopted with us to great advantage. I am persuaded there are many parts of our lower country where the olive tree might be raised, which is assuredly the richest gift of heaven. I can scarcely except bread. I see this tree supporting thousands in among the Alps where there is not soil enough to make bread for a single family. The caper too might be cultivated with us. The fig we do raise. I do not speak of the vine, because it is the parent of misery. Those who cultivate it are always poor, and he who would employ himself with us in the culture of corn, cotton, & c can produce in exchange much more wine, & better than he could raise by its direct culture."[48]

Leaving Milan on April 23, Jefferson reached Pavia the same day, and Genoa on the twenty-fifth. Here he ascertained the price of marble. Two years later, wishing to know the cost for workmanship of a chimney-piece made from that material, he

[48] To George Wythe, Paris, September 16, 1787 (*ibid.*, VI, 297). While crossing the Alps, Jefferson compared the hardihood of different plants as evidenced by the altitudes where they grew.—To Wm. Drayton, Paris, July 30, 1787 (*ibid.*, VI, 203–204). One of the Italian cities not visited by Jefferson was Venice, although the statement is made in a recent biography of Dr. Samuel L. Mitchill that "His sponsoring of a particular form of covered dock, largely because Jefferson had seen such a one in Venice, smacked of subservience to the president more than of good judgment."—Courtney R. Hall, *A Scientist in the Early Republic*, 114.

wrote to William Short, who was traveling in Italy. Short was directed to make inquiries of Jefferson's informant, living "near the hotel du Cerf, where I would recommend you to lodge, for pleasantness & convenience, if you take a room looking to the sea."[49]

After visiting the suburbs of Genoa, Jefferson sailed on the twenty-eighth, and was "mortally sick" for two days on the water. At Noli, a port forty miles distant into which he was obliged to put by a change of wind, he noted: "A bishop resides here, whose revenue is two thousand livres, equal to sixty-six guineas. I heard a nightingale here."[50]

Walking along the Italian Riviera from Louana to Albenga, Jefferson was struck with the beauty of the situation: "If any person wished to retire from his acquaintances, to live absolutely unknown, and yet in the midst of physical enjoyments, it should be in some of the little villages of this coast, where air, water and earth concur to offer what each has most precious."[51] Then follows a catalogue of the fowls, sea food, and vegetables obtainable there. At Albenga the hotel accommodations were the worst he ever met with anywhere in his travels. He complained tartly of "the most detestable gite, called a tavern, that I ever saw in any part of the earth, & the dearest too."[52] At the same place there resided a bishop "whose revenue is forty thousand livres. . . . The wind continuing contrary, I took mules at Albenga for Oneglia."[53] There Jefferson paid the felucca captain and took mules to Nice, where he arrived on the first of May. Two more days brought him to Aix, and on May 4, he reached Marseilles.

---

[49] To Wm. Short, Paris, February 28, 1789 (*William and Mary College Quarterly* [2d series], Vol. XII, No. 2 [April, 1932], 151). "The back windows look to the port and sea."—Library of Congress, Shippen Papers.

[50] Lipscomb and Bergh, *Writings*, XVII, 201–202.

[51] *Ibid.*, XVII, 202.

[52] Library of Congress, Shippen Papers.

[53] Lipscomb and Bergh, *Writings*, XVII, 203. In Jefferson's opinion Oneglia and Port Maurice were towns "worth giving a day to. Your mules will be the better for this rest, & yourselves also."—Library of Congress, Shippen Papers.

Departing from that city on May 7, he passed through Aix, Avignon, Vaucluse, Nîmes, Montpellier, and Frontignan to Cette. Embarking there on the Canal of Languedoc on May 13, he proceeded to Agde. Leaving Agde on the fourteenth, he was in Carcassonne on the eighteenth. The next day from Castelnaudary he visited the "Souterrain of St. Feriol" and then continued along the canal from Castelnaudary to Toulouse. From this city, birthplace of the jurist Cujas and famous in the time of the Troubadours as the seat of the Counts of Toulouse, Jefferson followed the Garonne River to Bordeaux. He was adhering faithfully to his maxim that "Rivers are generally the best guides for travellers, because they furnish the best lands, most considerable cities, & most flourishing commerce."[54]

The Canal of Languedoc, connecting the Mediterranean and the Atlantic, was built under Louis XIV by Riquet. "To effect this noble work, of uniting the two seas, less money was expended than to besiege Turin, or to seize Strasbourg like a robber," observed the English traveler, Arthur Young, in a vein very Jeffersonian.[55] One of the main objects of Jefferson's tour was to inspect this waterway. In doing so he traveled "in the whole 200 American miles, by water; having employed in examining all its details nine days, one of which was spent in making a tour of 40 miles on horseback among the Montagnes noires, to see the manner in which water has been collected to supply the canal; the other eight on the canal itself."[56]

Jefferson proceeded along the canal in leisurely fashion. "The bark in which I go, is about thirty-five feet long, drawn by one horse, and goes from two to three geographical miles an hour."[57]

[54] To Governor Rutledge, Paris, July 12, 1788 (Library of Congress, Jefferson Papers). Cf. to Dr. Benjamin S. Barton, Monticello, March 7, 1815, in *More Books, The Bulletin of the Boston Public Library*, Vol. XVIII, No. 4 (April, 1943), 160.

[55] Young, *Travels in France*, 46. Cf. Chapter VII, n. 9, *infra*.

[56] To William Short, On the canal of Languedoc, May 21, 1787 (*William and Mary College Quarterly* [2d series] Vol. XI, No. 4 [October, 1931], 339). The distance traveled by post boats in four days "I was 9 days going, because I chose to go leisurely."—Library of Congress, Shippen Papers.

[57] Lipscomb and Bergh, *Writings*, XVII, 212.

This novel mode of travel was delightful: "I dismounted my carriage from it's wheels, placed it on the deck of a light bark, and was thus towed on the canal instead of the post road. That I might be perfectly master of all the delays necessary, I hired a bark to myself by the day, & have made from 20. to 35 miles a day, according to circumstances, always sleeping ashore. Of all the methods of traveling I have ever tried this is the pleasantest. I walk the greater part of the way along the banks of the canal, level & lined with a double row of trees which furnish shade. When fatigued I take seat in my carriage, where, as much at ease as if in my study, I read, write, or observe. My carriage being of glass all around, admits a full view of the varying scenes thro' which I am shifted, olives, figs, mulberries, vines, corn & pasture, villages and farms. I have had some days of superb weather, enjoying . . . cloudless skies & limpid waters: I have had another luxury . . . a double row of nightingales along the bank of the canal, in full song. . . . What a bird the nightingale would be in the climate of America! We must colonize him thither."[58]

Perhaps he pondered also whether poetry could fruitfully be cultivated on American soil, having satisfied himself during his journey "why there never was a poet North of the Alps, & why there never will be one. A poet is as much the creature of climate as an orange or palm tree."[59]

His pleasure was lessened by separation from friends at Marseilles: "My journey, after leaving you, wanted nothing but the company of Madame Cathalan and yourself, to render it perfectly agreeable. I felt the want of it peculiarly on the Canal de Languedoc, where, with society, the mode of travelling would have been charming."[60]

Inspired by delightful surroundings, Jefferson wrote to his

[58] To William Short, On the canal of Languedoc, May 21, 1787 (*William and Mary College Quarterly* [2d series], Vol. XI, No. 4 [October, 1931], 339).

[59] *Ibid.*

[60] To Stephen Cathalan, Jr., Paris, July 21, 1787 (Lipscomb and Bergh, *Writings*, VI, 176).

daughter with the same lyrical transport which had characterized his letters from Nîmes and Marseilles to Mme de Tessé and Mme de Tott: "I write you, my dear Patsy, from the canal of Languedoc, on which I am at present sailing, as I have been for a week past, cloudless skies above, limpid waters below, and on each hand, a row of nightingales in full chorus. This delightful bird had given me a rich treat before, at the fountain of Vaucluse. After visiting the tomb of Laura at Avignon,[61] I went to see this fountain—a noble one of itself, and rendered famous forever by the songs of Petrarch, who lived near it. I arrived there somewhat fatigued, and sat down by the fountain to repose myself. It gushes, of the size of a river, from a secluded valley of the mountain, the ruins of Petrarch's chateau being perched on a rock two hundred feet perpendicular above. To add to the enchantment of the scene, every tree and bush was filled with nightingales in full song." But this rhapsodical utterance was tempered with the usual paternal admonition against idleness. "We are now entering the port of Toulouse, where I quit my bark, and of course must terminate my letter. Be good and be industrious, and you will be what I shall most love in the world. Adieu, my dear child."[62]

Jefferson arrived at Bordeaux on May 24, and left on the twenty-eighth. Noticing that strawberries and peas were in season at Bordeaux as well as at Agen and Castres, he indulged in speculations to explain the fact that "the country on the canal of Languedoc seems to have later seasons than that east and west of it." Likewise, he did not neglect his archaeological investigations, but carefully measured the bricks in a Roman circus there.[63]

What called for most attention, however, was the wine country of Bordeaux, which was examined as thoroughly as that of Burgundy had already been surveyed.

[61] "The tomb of Laura is to be seen in a church of Avignon."—Library of Congress, Shippen Papers.

[62] To Martha Jefferson, May 21, 1787 (Randolph, *Domestic Life*, 122).

[63] Lipscomb and Bergh, *Writings*, XVII, 221.

The cantons in which the most famous wines of Bordeaux are made, are Medoc down the river, Grave adjoining the city, and the parishes next above; all on the same side of the river. . . . The vineyards of first quality are all worked by their proprietors. . . .

Of red wines, there are four vineyards of the first quality, viz., 1. Chateau Margau, belonging to the Marquis d'Agicourt . . . 2. La Tour de Segur, en Saint Lambert, belonging to Monsieur Miresmenil . . . 3. Hautbrion . . . 4. Chateau de la Fite . . . The wines of the three first are not in perfection till four years old; those of De la Fite, being somewhat lighter, are good at three years. . . . Red wines of the second quality, are Rozan, Dabbadie or Lionville, la Rose, Quirouen, Durfort; . . . The third class are, Calons, Mouton, Gassie, Arboete, Pontette, de Ferme, Candale; . . . All red wines decline after a certain age, losing color, flavor, and body. Those of Bordeaux begin to decline at about seven years old.

Of white wines, those made in the canton of Grave are most esteemed at Bordeaux. The best crops are, 1. Pontac . . . 2. St. Brise . . . 3. De Carbonius, belonging to the Benedictine monks . . . Those made in the three parishes next above Grave, and more esteemed at Paris, are 1. Sauterne. The best crop belonging to M. Diquem at Bordeaux, or to M. de Salus, his son-in-law; . . . The next best crop is M. de Filotte's; . . . 2. Prignac. The best is the President du Roy's, at Bordeaux . . . 3. Barsac. The best belongs to the President Pichard. . . . Sauterne is the pleasantest; next Prignac, and lastly Barsac; but Barsac is the strongest; next Prignac and lastly Sauterne; and all stronger than Grave. There are other good crops made in the same parishes of Sauterne, Prignac, and Barsac; but none as good as these. . . . In general, the white wines keep longest. They will be in perfection till fifteen or twenty years of age. . . . They never mix the wines of first quality; but they mix the inferior ones to improve them.[64]

Leaving Bordeaux on May 28, Jefferson continued on a tour of the maritime ports of Western France. From Nantes he made a circular jaunt to L'Orient and back by way of Rennes. At Nantes he examined the condition of a quantity of military stores belonging to the United States which had been seized by order of a French court in proceedings instituted by a claimant whom Jef-

[64] *Ibid.*, XVII, 222–26.

ferson interviewed with the hope of effecting a settlement. His efforts to promote American commerce with France were indefatigable. At all the seaports he endeavored "to obtain a list of the American vessels which have come to them since the peace, in order to estimate their comparative importance to us, as well as the general amount of our commerce with this country, as far as carried on in our own bottoms."[65]

After his departure from Nantes on June 6, Jefferson traversed the château country of the Loire as far as Orléans. Between Angers and Tours, he observed: "There is very good wine made on these hills; not equal indeed to the Bordeaux of best quality, but to that of good quality, and like it. It is a great article of export from Anjou and Touraine, and probably is sold abroad, under the name of Bordeaux."[66]

The sculptor David of Angers was born the year following Jefferson's visit to that city. An American naval officer who purchased Monticello, Commodore Uriah P. Levy, had David make the statue of Jefferson which stands in the Capitol at Washington. When Lafayette saw this statue, he embraced it, crying "Mon ami, mon cher ami." A copy of the statue was presented in 1905 to the city of Angers by the Commodore's kinsman, Jefferson M. Levy, from whom the Thomas Jefferson Memorial Foundation acquired Monticello in 1923.[67]

"Being desirous of inquiring . . . into a fact stated by Voltaire . . . relative to the growth of shells unconnected with animal bodies, at the Chateau of Monsieur de la Sauvagiere, near Tours," Jefferson called on a gentleman to whom he had obtained an introduction through the efforts of the Marquis de Chastellux. M. Gentil proved to be "of all men the best to whom I could have addressed myself." He "had been in correspondence with Vol-

---

[65] To Jay, Paris, June 14, 1787 (*ibid.*, VI, 138).

[66] *Ibid.*, XVII, 231.

[67] *Réception de la statue de Thomas Jefferson troisième Président des États-unis oeuvre de David d'Angers offerte à la ville d'Angers par Hon. Jefferson M. Levy citoyen américain le samedi 16 septembre 1905;* Wilstach, *Jefferson and Monticello,* 216, 218.

taire on that very subject." Unconvinced by the affirmations of his informant, Jefferson philosophizes: "What are we to conclude? That we have not materials enough yet, to form any conclusion. The fact stated by Sauvagiere is not against any law of nature, and is therefore possible; but it is so little analogous to her habitual processes, that, if true, it would be extraordinary; that to command our belief, therefore, there should be such a suite of observations, as that their untruth would be more extraordinary than the existence of the fact they affirm. . . . One, therefore, who had rather have no opinion than a false one, will suppose this question one of those beyond the investigation of human sagacity; or wait till further and fuller observations enable him to decide it."[68]

Jefferson left Orléans on June 10, and arrived in Paris the same day, "after having travelled something upwards of a thousand leagues."[69] Speaking of his tour, he declared: "I . . . never passed three months and a half more delightfully."[70] His daughter Martha, immured in her Paris convent, had suspected as much. Lamenting that her dear papa did not write to her, she somewhat skeptically observed: "I hope your wrist is better, and I am inclined to think that your voyage is rather for your pleasure than your health; however, I hope it will answer both purposes." And again she complained: "You wrote me a long letter, as I asked you; however, it would have been much more so without so wide a margin. Adieu, my dear papa. Be assured of the tenderest affection of your loving daughter. . . . Pray answer me very soon—a long letter, without a margin." The itinerant parent explained that: "I have not been able to write to you as often as I expected, because I am generally on the road, and when I stop anywhere I am occupied in seeing what is to be seen."[71]

[68] Lipscomb and Bergh, *Writings*, XVII, 232–35.
[69] To Martha Jefferson, Marseilles, May 5, 1787 (Randolph, *Domestic Life*, 121).
[70] To John Bannister, Paris, June 19, 1787 (Lipscomb and Bergh, *Writings*, VI, 130).
[71] Martha Jefferson to Jefferson, Paris, February 8, 1787; Paris, April 9, 1787 (Randolph, *Domestic Life*, 113, 117–18); to Martha Jefferson, Toulon, April 7, 1787 (*ibid.*, 118).

CHAPTER VI

The Eternal Fogs of Europe

✿

TWO years after his journey to England, the necessity of transacting public business in conjunction with Adams again called Jefferson from his post in Paris, this time to the Netherlands. In his autobiography Jefferson relates the circumstances obliging him to make the trip. Financial difficulties confronted the American government. Under the Articles of Confederation, sufficient revenue could not be obtained from the states. "Some contributed a little, some less, & some nothing, and the last furnished an excuse for the first to do nothing also. Mr. Adams, while residing at the Hague, had a general authority to borrow what sums might be requisite for ordinary & necessary expenses. Interest on the public debt, and the maintenance of the diplomatic establishment in Europe, had been habitually provided in this way. He was now . . . soon to return to America, and had referred our bankers to me. . . . But I had no powers, no instructions, no means, and no familiarity with the subject. . . . Mr. Adams had received his appointment to the court of London while engaged at Paris, with Dr. Franklin and myself, in the negotiations under our joint commissions. He had repaired thence to London, without returning to the Hague, to take leave of that government. He thought it necessary to do so now, before he should leave Europe, and accordingly went there. I learned his departure from London by a letter from Mrs. Adams received on the very day on which he would arrive at the Hague. A consultation with him, & some provision for the future was indispensable, while we could yet avail ourselves of his powers. For when they would be gone, we should be without resource. . . . I saw that there was no time to lose, and set out for the Hague."[1]

Jefferson had long felt that it would be desirable for financial arrangements to be concluded in Holland, and that Adams was the most suitable negotiator to undertake the business. "Is there not room to do a great deal of good for us in Holland in the department of money? No one can do it as well as yourself," he wrote to his New England colleague.[2]

A later letter on the same subject was answered by Mrs. Adams. That worthy lady, besides bewailing the impossibility of living on the salary received by American diplomats, informed Jefferson that: "Mr. Adams being absent I replie to your letter this day received, that Mr. Adams has written to you upon the subject you refer to. Our time here is short and pressing. Yet short as it is Mr. Adams is obliged to set out on fryday for the Hague in order to take leave there. Owing wholy to the neglect of Congress in omitting to send him a letter of recall, tho he particularly requested it of them, & has several times since repeated the same request. A memorial would then have answered. But now it cannot be received, and he finds at this late hour that he must cross that most horrid passage twice, & make a rapid journey there & back again as it would be greatly injurious to our credit & affairs to give any reasonable cause of offence. He would be delighted to meet you there, but time is so pressing that he can not flatter himself with that hope, nor be able to stay a day after he has compleated his business yet as this letter may reach you about the day he will leave London you will consider whether there is a possibility of seeing each other at the Hague."[3]

Upon receiving this communication, Jefferson wrote to Adams: "Our affairs at Amsterdam press on my mind like a mountain. . . . I am so anxious to confer with you on this . . . &

---

[1] *Autobiography*, 123–26.

[2] To Adams, Paris, February 20, 1787 (Lipscomb and Bergh, *Writings*, VI, 96). Cf. to Madison, June 20, 1787 (*ibid.*, VI, 135.)

[3] Mrs. Adams to Jefferson, London, February 26, 1788 (Library of Congress, Jefferson Papers).

get some effectual arrangement made in time that I determine to meet you at the Hague. I will set out the moment some repairs are made to my carriage. It is promised me at about 3. aclock tomorrow; but probably they will make it night, & that I may not set out till Tuesday morning. In that case I will be at the Hague Friday night. In the meantime you will perhaps have made all your bows there. I am sensible how irksome this must be to you in the moment of your departure. But it is a great interest of the U. S. which is at stake and I am sure you will sacrifice to that your feelings and your interest. I hope to shake you by the hand within 24. hours after you receive this."[4]

This letter to Adams was sent in care of Dumas, the American agent at The Hague, to whom Jefferson explained: "Being informed that Mr. Adams was to leave London on the 29th. ult. for the Hague, I have determined to meet him there. But lest he should have finished his business & be gone before I can get there, I write the enclosed to press him to await an interview, and send it by the post which will be 24 hours before me. I take the liberty of putting it under your cover, as you will certainly know where Mr. Adams is to be found."[5]

The next day Jefferson took leave of the Comte de Montmorin, French minister of foreign affairs, and informed a number of correspondents having business with him that he would be absent from Paris.[6] On March 4 he "Set out for Amsterdam," his account book shows, and reached Peronne, after going through Bourget, Louvres, Chapelle, Senlis, Le Pont St. Maxence, Bois le duc, Gournay, le Cuvilley, le Couchy, Roye, and Fouches. The following day his route led through Fins, Bonar, Cambray, Bouchain, Valenciennes, Quievran, Quaregnon, Mons, Casteau, and Braine le compte. On the sixth he breakfasted in Brussels, passed Malines, and dined in Antwerp. The boundary between

<hr>

[4] To John Adams, Paris, March 2, 1788 (Library of Congress, Jefferson Papers).

[5] To Dumas, Paris, March 2, 1788 (*ibid.*).

[6] To Comte de Montmorin, Paris, March 3, 1788 (*ibid.*).

the "Money of France" and the "Money of Holland," carefully noted in Jefferson's account book, was then at Antwerp. The next day he was in Agtenbroek, Kruystraet, and Moerdyk. Arriving in Rotterdam on March 8, Jefferson reached The Hague the following day.

Fortunately Adams had not departed. A letter to Short describes Jefferson's course from Paris to The Hague: "After two days of prosperous journey I had a good gleam of hope of reaching this place in the night of the third day. In fact however I got on the third day only to within 8 hours land journeying of the passage of the Moerdyke. Yet this remnant employed me three days and nothing less than the omnipotence of god could have shortened this time of torture. I saw the Saturday passing over, and, in imagination, the packet sailing, and Mr. Adams on board. And it was not till Sunday my anxieties were ended by finding him here. We are setting out this morning for Amsterdam, where if we fail in the principal object, I shall at least have the solace of easing my own shoulders of the burthen.

"I was at Rotterdam the evening of the prince's birthday. The illuminations were the most splendid I had ever seen & the roar of joy the most universal I had ever heard. My journey had been little entertaining. A country of corn & pasture affords little interesting to an American who has seen in his own country so much of that, and who travels to see the country & not its towns. I am as yet totally undecided as to the time and route of my return."[7]

On March 6 Adams had presented to their High Mightinesses the Lords the States General of the United Netherlands the resolution of Congress recalling him, together with a memorial of leave-taking. Their High Mightinesses took leave of the envoy, "declaring that his person and conduct have been agreeable to their High Mightinesses," and ordered "that the usual present of a chain and medal of gold, of the value of thir-

[7] To Short, The Hague, March 10, 1788 (*ibid.*).

teen hundred florins, be transmitted to him."[8] These formalities having been completed before Jefferson arrived at the Hague, Adams was free to proceed at once to Amsterdam. There Jefferson dutifully participated in the financial negotiations which had called him thither, and reported their results to John Jay, the secretary for foreign affairs of the Congress.[9] Dutch financiers speculating in American domestic debts sought to use their power over the public credit of the infant nation in order to exact payment of a year's interest on the paper held by them. At length, however, an agreement was reached with the bankers, and on March 13 Adams entered into a notarial contract before P. G. van Hole, a notary at Amsterdam. The bonds executed by Adams assured adequate funds for two years to come.

During these negotiations, Jefferson did not neglect the opportunity to see the sights of Amsterdam, study its architecture, and note what impressed him.[10] Among the curiosities he observed were: "Joists of houses placed, not with their sides horizontally and perpendicularly, but diamond wise. . . . Windows opening so that they admit air and not rain. . . . Manner of fixing a flag staff on the mast of a vessel. . . . Dining tables letting down with single or double leaves. . . . Wind sawmills. See the plans detailed in the moolen book which I bought. . . . A lanthern over the street door, which gives light equally into the antechamber and the street. . . . A bridge on a canal turning on a swivel." On March 20 he made an excursion to Haarlem, and two days later visited Zaandam, where Peter the Great of Russia learned the trade of shipbuilding.

The hostelry which Jefferson patronized in Amsterdam was Het Wapen van Amsterdam (The Arms of Amsterdam), situ-

[8] Adams, *The Works of John Adams*, VIII, 481–83.

[9] To Jay, Amsterdam, March 13, 1788; March 16, 1788 (Lipscomb and Bergh, *Writings*, VI, 435–36, 436–41); March 29, 1788 (Library of Congress, Jefferson Papers). For an account of the financial transactions in Amsterdam, see Pieter Jan van Winter, *Het aandeel van den Amsterdamschen handel aan den opbouw van het Amerikaansche gemeenebest*, I, 182–85.

[10] Lipscomb and Bergh, *Writings*, XVII, 244 ff.

ated at the corner of the Rusland and the Kloveniersburgwal. That capacious structure, which had previously been used as a sugar refinery and for amateur theatricals, has since undergone alterations, but is still standing. It now houses a publishing firm which specializes in printing Bibles. The location is within a block of the City Hall and of the University, which in 1879 moved into an edifice erected in 1754 as an old men's home. Half a dozen years after Jefferson's visit, Het Wapen van Amsterdam was the meeting place of a secret revolutionary committee, somewhat reminiscent of the gatherings in the Apollo Room of the Raleigh Tavern at Williamsburg in which the future author of the Declaration of Independence had taken part.[11]

Among Jefferson's purchases in Holland were two boxes shipped to Paris, one of which contained ironware and the other porcelain cups for tea, coffee, and chocolate. As these were prohibited articles, the American diplomat wished them to be smuggled into the city, since their trifling value, twenty-four guilders, did not warrant obtaining a passport.[12]

The tulip fields between Leyden and Haarlem must have interested Jefferson, but he makes no reference to them in his journal. Another curious lacuna is the omission of any reference to the celebrated University at Leyden, or to the church there which the Pilgrim Fathers frequented during their sojourn in that place. When Joseph C. Cabell, Jefferson's chief collaborator in founding the University of Virginia, was in Holland, he did not fail to visit the University of Leyden.[13] Likewise, Mrs. Adams did not neglect to record her impressions of the edifice

[11] Antoine E. d'Ailly, *Historische Gids van Amsterdam*, 87, 100; W. J. Olivier, *Manuel des Étrangers à Amsterdam*, 305; Hajo Brugmans, *Opkomst en Bloei van Amsterdam*, 262; J. Brandt & Zoon to the author, August 28, 1939. In 1806, according to an English traveler, the "Arms of Amsterdam" was "the principal hotel" in the city, and one "which, in point of magnitude and accommodation, might vie with the first hotels in our own metropolis."—Sir John Carr, *A Tour through Holland*, 155.

[12] To Limozin, Amsterdam, March 27, 1788; Limozin to Jefferson, Havre, April 9, 1788 (Mass. Hist. Soc., Jefferson Papers).

[13] *Early History of the University of Virginia as Contained in the Letters of Thomas Jefferson and Joseph C. Cabell*, xxix.

where Pastor Robinson preached to his flock: "I would not omit to mention that I visited the church at Leyden, in which our fore-fathers worshipped, when they fled from hierarchical tyranny and persecution. I felt a respect and veneration upon entering the doors, like what the ancients paid to their druids."[14]

Jefferson's sojourn in Amsterdam was longer than he had anticipated. To a correspondent in England he states: "I wrote you a line just as I was taking wing from Paris to this place. I expected to have staid there a week, & have been here three already, & know not yet the term of my stay. I hope however to get away in three or four days. I intend to make my return somewhat circuitous, in order to see what I have not yet seen. This renders the moment of my arrival in Paris uncertain."[15]

One of the attractions inducing Jefferson to return by way of Germany was the hope of seeing his old friend Baron de Geismer, who had been a prisoner of war in Virginia during the Revolution. The German nobleman's petition to be exchanged or permitted to return home on parole before the death of his aged father had been warmly urged upon the Virginia delegation in Congress by Jefferson.[16] From Amsterdam Jefferson wrote the

[14] Mrs. Adams to Mrs. Cranch, London, September 12, 1786 (*Letters of Mrs. Adams*, 304). Mrs. Adams may have had in mind the old church of St. Peter, erected in 1315, in which John Robinson was buried on March 4, 1625. Robinson preached in a large house on the Klok-steeg, on the square adjoining the church. It was also in the same church that a stirring ceremony was held in June, 1940, commemorating the three hundred and sixty-fifth anniversary of the founding of the University of Leyden. The speakers on that impressive occasion urged their hearers "not to despair in the difficult times through which the country was passing, but to continue the great traditions of the University, steeped in a freedom of thought which knows no national frontiers in its pursuit of scientific truth." The Dutch national anthem was sung, and the old church rang with the solemn words "exhorting the people to resist tyranny and to place their faith in God." E. N. van Kleffens, *Juggernaut over Holland*, 177–78.

[15] To Trumbull, Amsterdam, March 27, 1788 (Library of Congress, Jefferson Papers).

[16] To Richard Henry Lee, Monticello, April 21, 1779 (Alderman Library, Lee Collection). After his return to America Jefferson undertook to make arrangements for the sale of three shares of stock owned by Baron Geismer in a copper mine in the neighborhood of Newark.—To Elisha Boudinot, Philadelphia, February 1, 1799 (Morgan Library, MS Collections). Regarding the mine, see Elizabeth L. Adams, "The Jefferson Bicentenary," *More Books, The Bulletin of the Boston Public Library*, Vol. XVIII, No. 4 (April, 1943), 153, 157.

Baron of his plans: "Having been called hither, my dear friend, by business, & being somewhat at liberty as to my return, I propose to go along the Rhine as far as Strasburg before I turn off to Paris. I shall be at Frankfort probably between the 1st & 5th of April. And if your residence is still at Hanau, I know you will meet me in Frankfort. I shall be at the Rothinhouse tavern. As I may be a little earlier there or a little later than I expect, if you will lodge there a note of your address, I will contrive to see you. This pleasure has had its share in determining my return to Paris by this route, tho' I am very apprehensive you will have removed with your court from Hanau to Cassell. In that case I must fail in the effort to see you, and be contented to preserve for you in absence those sentiments of sincere attachment & esteem with which I am, my dear sir, your affectionate friend and servant."[17]

Perhaps another incentive besides the desire to see new country and the hope of a reunion with Baron de Geismer prompted Jefferson to prefer the route through Germany. He may have wished to escape the importunities of Dumas at The Hague. That functionary was fearful lest Congress might decide to dispense with his services. Jefferson promised that if he did not see Dumas again at The Hague he would write "a letter which may answer the purpose of tranquilising your family as effectually as the interview which I had hoped to have had." Jefferson kept his word, and wrote assuring Dumas that Congress would retain him. The fears which Dumas professed for Jefferson's safety, coupled with his urgent advice to avoid the perils of the German route and enjoy the hospitality of The Hague, did not deter Jefferson from his contemplated journey. Perhaps Jefferson smiled

---

[17] To Baron de Geismer, Amsterdam, March 18, 1788 (Library of Congress, Jefferson Papers). In 1806, Frankfort was said to be "particularly celebrated for the splendor of its hotels, which are reported to be the most magnificent in Europe, particularly those called the Rothen Haus or Red House, and the . . . Roman Emperor." —Carr, *A Tour through Holland*, 291.

as he wrote Dumas from Paris announcing "my safe arrival after a very agreeable tour through Germany."[18]

After being in Holland three weeks, Jefferson informed Short: "I set out to-morrow for Utrecht, Nimuegen etc. and shall pursue the course of the Rhine as far as the roads will permit me, not exceeding Strasburg. Whenever they become impassable or too difficult, if they do become so, I shall turn off to Paris. So also if anything of importance should call for me at Paris sooner you will be so good as to address to me at Francfort & Strasburg poste restant. I will call at the post offices there and be happy to find news from you relative to yourself, my daughters and America." [19] The implication would seem to be that news of "anything of importance" at Paris would not be so gratefully received by the itinerant diplomat.

Conditions in Holland brought political reflections to Jefferson's mind. "The transition from ease and opulence to extreme poverty is remarkable on crossing the line between the Dutch and Prussian territories. The soil and climate are the same; the governments alone differ. With the poverty, the fear also of slaves is visible in the faces of the Prussian subjects."[20] The people of the Netherlands, however, had not entirely escaped the evil effects of misrule. Six months before visiting that country, Jefferson had philosophized regarding events there: "What a crowd of lessons do the present miseries of Holland teach us? Never to have an hereditary officer of any sort; never to let a citizen ally himself with kings; never to call in foreign nations to settle domestic differences; never to suppose that any nation will expose itself to war for us, etc."[21]

[18] To Dumas, Amsterdam, March 16, 1788 (Library of Congress, Jefferson Papers); to Dumas, Paris [Jefferson must have dated this letter wrongly, as he was in Amsterdam at the time], March 29, 1788 (*ibid.*); Dumas to Jefferson, The Hague, March 18, 1788 (*ibid.*); to Dumas, Paris, May 15, 1788 (Lipscomb and Bergh, *Writings*, VII, 7).

[19] To Short, Amsterdam, March 29, 1788 (*Ibid.*, VI, 446–47).

[20] *Ibid.*, XVII, 252. "On entering the Prussian dominions remark the effect of despotism on the people."—Library of Congress, Shippen Papers.

[21] To Adams, Paris, September 28, 1787 (Lipscomb and Bergh, *Writings*, VI, 322).

Jefferson left Amsterdam on March 30. After passing through Utrecht, Nijmegen, Cranenburg, Cleves, Santen, Rheinberg, and Hoogstraat, he crossed the Rhine at Essenberg "in a scow with sails" on the third day following.

Nijmegen was the point where preparations had to be made in order to outwit the "harpies who prey upon travellers" in Germany. "At this place you must bribe your horse hirer to put as few horses to your carriage as you think you can travel with. Because with whatever number of horses you arrive at the first post house in Germany, with that they will oblige you to go on through the whole empire." Jefferson thought it wise to pay "the price of four horses on condition that they would put but three to my chariot."[22]

In Germany he was fascinated by "the romantic and ruinous." At Duysberg he endeavored to locate the "remains of the encampment of Varus, in which he and his legions fell by the arms of Arminius (in the time of Tiberius, I think it was), but there was not a person to be found in Duysberg who could understand either English, French, Italian, or Latin. So I could make no inquiry."[23]

At Düsseldorf, Jefferson found "the best tavern I saw in my whole journey."[24] Likewise, he recorded that "the gallery of paintings is sublime, particularly the room of Vanderwerff."[25] His enthusiasm over this collection, which the American artist Trumbull had called to his attention, was subsequently communi-

---

[22] Library of Congress, Shippen Papers.

[23] Lipscomb and Bergh, *Writings*, XVII, 253. "Near Duysberg is the place where Varus & his legions were cut off by the Germans. I could find no body in the village however who could speak any language I spoke, & could not make them understand what I wished to see. I missed my object therefore tho' I had taken this road on purpose."—Library of Congress, Shippen Papers. Perhaps Jefferson had with him and read the moving language of Tacitus, *Annales*, I, lxi. See Chapter V, n. 48, *supra*, and Chapter VII, n. 38, *infra*.

[24] Library of Congress, Shippen Papers.

[25] Lipscomb and Bergh, *Writings*, XVII, 254. See also Bullock, *My Head and My Heart*, 91.

cated to his young compatriots, Shippen and Rutledge. On April 3, after going through Langveld, Cologne, Bonn, Remagen, and Andernach, he arrived at Coblentz, where he stayed two days at "The Wild Man" Inn. In the palace of the Elector of Treves he saw a central-heating system with "large rooms very well warmed by warm air conveyed from an oven below, through tubes which open into the rooms."[26] It was thus not altogether a novelty to Jefferson when there was brought to his attention[27] years later a contrivance with pipes and bellows "for supplying families with perfumed and salubrious air for respiration." At Cologne he had seen a stove which he later purchased.[28] On April 5 he left Coblentz, and reached Nassau. The next day, having passed by way of Nastätten, Schwalbach, Wiesbaden, Hochheim, and Hattersheim, he arrived at Frankfort-on-the-Main.

On the seventh and eighth Jefferson attended the comedy at Frankfort. The following day he reported to Short:

My old friend the Baron de Geismer met me here, on a letter I had written him from Amsterdam, & has been my cicerone. It happens to be the moment of the fair of Frankfort which is very great. Yesterday we made an excursion up the Maine to Hanau, passing the ground where the battle of Bergen was fought in the war before last. Tomorrow we shall go to the vineyards of Hocheim, & perhaps of Rudesheim & Johannesberg, where the most celebrated wines are made. . . . I met in Hanau with many acquaintances, the officers who had been stationed in Albemarle while in captivity. I have seen much good country on the Rhine, & bad whenever I got a little off of it. But what I have met with the most wonderful in nature is a set of men absolutely incorruptible by money, by fair words or foul, & that this should, of all others, be the class of postillions. This however is the real character of the German postilions whom nothing on earth can induce to go out of a walk. This has

[26] Lipscomb and Bergh, *Writings*, XVII, 259.

[27] By G. F. Saltonstall, in 1804 (Mo. Hist. Soc., Bixby Collection).

[28] To Jean Jacques Peuchen, Frankfort, April 7, 1788 (Mass. Hist. Soc., Jefferson Papers); Peuchen to Jefferson, April 25, 1788 (*ibid.*); to Peuchen, Paris, August 22, 1788 (Mo. Hist. Soc., Bixby Collection); to van Staphorsts, Francfort sur Maine, April 7, 1788 (Library of Congress, Jefferson Papers).

retarded me not a little. So that I shall be glad to be delivered over to the great jack boot. The neighborhood of this place has been to us a second mother country. It is from the Palatinate on this part of the Rhine that those swarms of germans have gone who next to the descendants of the English, form the greatest body of our people. I have been continually amused by seeing here the origin of whatever is not English among us. I have fancied myself often in the upper parts of Maryland & Pennsylvania.[29]

On April 10 Jefferson went on to Mainz, from which place he made an excursion to Hochheim. The following day he enjoyed a similar jaunt to Rüdesheim and Johansberg. On the twelfth he went through Oppenheim and Worms to Mannheim. From there he made excursions to Dossenheim, Heidelberg, Schwetzingen and to Käferthal. "The gardens at Schwetzingen show how much money may be laid out to make an ugly thing," Jefferson observed. "At the village of Kaeferthal is a plantation of rhubarb, begun in 1769, by a private company."[30]

The *Schloss* at Heidelberg impressed Jefferson. "This chateau is the most noble ruin I have ever seen, having been reduced to that state by the French in the time of Louis XIV. . . . The situation is romantic and pleasing beyond expression. It is on a great scale much like the situation of Petrarch's chateau at Vaucluse, on a small one. The climate, too, is like that of Italy. The apple, the pear, cherry, peach, apricot, and almond, are all in bloom." A fourfold echo in the garden attracted Jefferson's attention. "The famous tun of Heidelberg was new built in 1751. . . . There is no wine in it now."[31] Jefferson carefully measured the celebrated cask, and ascribed to it a capacity of 283,200 bottles.

On April 15 Jefferson left Mannheim and went as far as Karlsruhe. The next day he arrived at Strasbourg. There he doubtless followed the advice he later gave his young friends

---

[29] To Short, Frankfort-on-the-Main, April 9, 1788 (Library of Congress, Jefferson Papers, 6579, 6555).

[30] Lipscomb and Bergh, *Writings*, XVII, 273, 274.

[31] *Ibid.*, XVII, 272–73.

Shippen and Rutledge to visit "the steeple of the Cathedral which I believe is the highest in the world, and the handsomest. Go to the very top of it; but let it be the last operation of the day, as you will need a long rest after it."[32]

On the eighteenth he left Strasbourg, and three days later reached Épernay. Here he completed his study of French wines by visiting the localities where champagne is produced. In the cellar of M. D'Orsay he purchased sixty bottles remaining of the year 1783, at three florins and ten sous the bottle; sparkling wine, he observes, would have cost four. Leaving Épernay on April 23, he reached Paris the same day.

Regarding the production of champagne at Épernay, Jefferson writes: "The bulk of their grapes are purple, which they prefer for making even white wine. They press them very lightly, without treading or permitting them to ferment at all, for about an hour. . . . The last part of the juice, produced by strong pressure, is red and ordinary. They choose the bunches with as much care, to make wine of the very first quality, as if to eat. Not above one-eighth of the whole grapes will do for this purpose. . . .

"The white wines are either mousseux, sparkling or non-mousseux, still. The sparkling are little drunk in France, but are almost alone known and drunk in foreign countries. This makes so great a demand, and so certain a one, that it is the dearest by about an eighth, and therefore they endeavor to make all sparkling if they can. This is done by bottling in the spring. . . . To make the still wine, they bottle in September. This is only done when they know from some circumstance that the wine will not be sparkling. So if the spring bottling fails to make a sparkling wine, they decant it into other bottles in the fall, and it then makes the very best still wine . . . which will keep much longer than that originally made still by being bottled in September. The sparkling wines lose their briskness the older they are, but they gain

[32] Library of Congress, Shippen Papers.

in quality with age to a certain length. These wines are in perfection from two to ten years old, and will even be very good to
fifteen. 1766 was the best year ever known."[33]

Of another type of wine he says: "The vin de paille is made
in the neighborhood of Colmar, in Alsace. . . . It takes its name
from the circumstance of spreading the grapes on straw, where
they are preserved till spring, and then made into wine. The
little juice then remaining in them makes a rich, sweet wine, but
the dearest in the world, without being the best by any means.
They charge nine florins the bottle for it in the taverns of Strasburg. It is the caprice of wealth alone which continues so losing
an operation. This wine is sought because dear; while the better
wine of Frontignan is rarely seen at a good table because it is
cheap."[34]

Concerning German vineyards Jefferson was equally inquisi-
tive and well informed. At Coblentz he wrote: "The best Moselle wines are made about fifteen leagues from hence, in an excessively mountainous country. The first quality (without any
comparison) is that made on the mountain of Brownberg, adjoining to the village of Dusmond; and the best crop is that of
the Baron Breidbach Burrhesheim. . . . 2. Vialen is the second
quality . . . 3. Crach-Bispost is the third . . . 4. Selting . . . 5. Kous-
Berncastle. . . . These wines must be five or six years old before
they are quite ripe for drinking." Although Rhine wine is produced from Cologne on, "yet it is only from Rudesheim to
Hocheim that wines of the very first quality are made. The river
happens there to run due east and west, so as to give its hills on
that side a southern aspect. And even in this canton, it is only
Hocheim, Johansberg, and Rudesheim, that are considered as of
the very first quality." Johansberg, thanks to improvements in
culture introduced by the Bishop of Fulda, brings double the
price of the other two varieties, and has none of the acid of
Hochheim and other Rhenish wines. Rüdesheim wines "begin to

[33] Lipscomb and Bergh, *Writings*, XVII, 285–86.
[34] *Ibid.*, XVII, 277.

be drinkable at about five years old. The proprietors sell them old or young, according to the prices offered, and according to their own want of money. . . . They are not at all acid, and to my taste much preferable to Hocheim, though but of the same price." Markebronn, near Hagenheim, three miles above Johansberg, yields wine of the second quality. "On the road between Mayence and Oppenheim are three cantons, which are also esteemed as yielding wines of the second quality. These are Laubenheim, Bodenheim, and Nierstein." Of three kinds of grapes in use for making wine, the Riesling grape, small and delicate, grows only in one spot from Hochheim to Rüdesheim, most good wines at Rüdesheim being made from the Orleans grape. Less excellent qualities of Rhine wine are made of an inferior hard grape.[35]

After his trip to the Netherlands, Jefferson made no extensive journeys from Paris until he left for America in 1789. Early in that year he attempted to find a vessel sailing directly to the United States from France. He desired transportation "for myself, my two daughters, and two servants. I do not propose to take the whole cabbin to myself, which is a useless peice of pomp, offensive to the other passengers, if there be any, and answering no end if there be none. I should propose to pay our passages as the others."[36]

These efforts bore no fruit. As autumn approached, Jefferson declared, in a letter to John Brown Cutting, an American in London: "I am become excessively anxious about finding a passage. There is no vessel in any port of France bound to the Chesapeak & has not been an arrival from America for some weeks. Mr. Trumbull handed me a proposition from Capt. Colley to take me up at Cowes. Instead of accepting it, I proposed his coming to Havre. This would be so much more convenient to me that I had better give 20 or 30 guineas more from Havre than Cowes,

---

[35] *Ibid.*, XVII, 257–58, 264, 266, 267–68.

[36] To M. Limosin, Paris, April 12, 1789 (Library of Congress, Jefferson Papers). Cf. letters of the same date to John Bondfield, M. Vannes, and John Gallway (*ibid.*).

because of double seasickness, transportation of 50 cases of baggage, entrance & duties on it in England; but I wish now that I had said, 'if he will not come to Havre, I will go to Cowes.' If he does not come, do my dear sir help my friend Trumbull in finding me some vessel bound for the Chesapeak & which will take me in at Havre or Cowes, preferably the former. But as I shall be trying to get a passage from France at the same time, while you are trying to get me one from England, it will be necessary that your engagement for me be on condition that I be not pre-engaged. I am going this morning to Versailles to take leave, and my baggage will be packed to-day, so that after to-day I can always set off at half a day's warning." Mr. Cutting replied philosophically that "It was next to impossible to induce owners of any ship here that might be bound for Virginia to order their captain to touch at Havre. The additional compensation which they demanded in case they did touch at Havre rendered the idea inadmissible. I truly regret the double seasickness, and transportation of baggage, which is incident to your embarkation at Cowes. But unpleasant as these circumstances are they seem inevitable."[37] Consequently Jefferson availed himself of accommodations secured for him by the American artist Trumbull, who was then in England.

On September 25, 1789, Jefferson's passport was issued. The following day the Marquis de Lafayette in his own handwriting added to the document a request to all the officers of the national guard, and in general to all citizens, to let Jefferson's party pass, and to give him all assistance of which he should have need. The French foreign minister was absent when Jefferson waited on him at Versailles to take leave. Upon receiving word from Trumbull that passage had been obtained, Jefferson left Paris on September 26.

Lodging successive nights at Vernon and Bolbec, he arrived

[37] To Mr. Cutting, Paris, September 24, 1789 (in similar vein to Mr. Trumbull, Paris, September 24, 1789); John Brown Cutting to Jefferson, London, September 30, 1789 (Library of Congress, Jefferson Papers).

at Havre on the twenty-eighth and took lodgings at the Aigle d'Or. "We arrived here on Monday morning 28th. September having had no accident on the road, but an axle tree broken on the phaeton and the bad tire which Roconnier put on the chariot wheels broke in two places. We have been detained here ever since by the most tempestuous weather I have seen. . . . My baggage is now aboard."[38]

The American statesman had with him the pedestal of a bust of Lafayette for the Virginia capitol. This made up about one-tenth of his baggage, he noted in his account book, and hence that proportion of the freight from Paris to Norfolk was to be charged to the state government.

From one of the anticipated inconveniences of going home by way of England, that of paying entrance and duty on fifty cases of baggage, Jefferson was exempted. In accordance with the law of nations, orders from the Treasury were sent to the customs house at Portsmouth not to molest the effects of the returning envoy.[39]

On October 7 Jefferson wrote to Short from Havre: "The day after my arrival here the equinoctial gales commenced and have prevailed now for nine days with a fury almost unexampled. Three days ago there appeared a small abatement, we got our luggage aboard the packet and tried to get out of the harbor but it was impossible. For my comfort the weatherwise tell me these winds will continue until the change of the moon, that is near a fortnight longer. As they began the day our ship was to reach London, I presume she got to the Downs and remains there, as

[38] To Short, Havre, October 4, 1789 (*ibid.*).

[39] These orders were procured by Trumbull without Jefferson's knowledge.— Jonathan Trumbull to Jefferson, London, October 10, 1789 (Library of Congress, Jefferson Papers). At Jefferson's request Trumbull procured an additional order covering four cases.—John Brown Cutting to Jefferson, received at Cowes, October 11, 1789 (*ibid.*). Four packages were unpacked "after the usual forms: so that the treasury order has been of no service with respect to them. . . . The custom-house at Portsmouth have surely not received the order from the Treasury."—Nathaniel Cutting to Jefferson, received at Cowes, October 12, 1789 (Mass. Hist. Soc., Jefferson Papers).

the wind has been constantly up the channel. I presume many accidents have happened in the channel. Of the vessels which have endeavored to make this port in distress a ship and a brig have been stranded under the pier. I was yesterday roving thro the neighborhood of this place to try to get a pair of shepherd dogs. We walked 10. miles, clambering the cliffs in quest of the shepherds, during the most furious tempest of wind and rain I was ever in. The journey was fruitless. On our return we came on the body of a man who had that moment shot himself. His pistol had dropped at his feet, & himself fallen backward without ever moving. The shot had completely separated his whole face from the forehead to the chin & so torn it to atoms that it could not be known. The center of the head was entirely laid bare. This is the only kind of news I have for you."[40] Nevertheless the quest for shepherd dogs was not entirely unsuccessful. In his expense account book for that day Jefferson entered these items: "pd. for a chienne bergere big with pups 36#. gratuity to person who brought her 9#."

On the eighth of October he "left Havre at half before one o'clock in the morning on board the packet Anna," commanded by Captain Wright and "arrived at Cowes at half after two in the morning" on the ninth.

Doubtless the emotion expressed in Jefferson's "Farewell to France," written many years later, was surging in his heart as the French coast receded in the darkness of that early autumn night: "And here I cannot leave this great and good country without expressing my sense of it's pre-eminence of character among the nations of the earth. A more benevolent people, I have never known, nor greater warmth & devotedness in their select friendships. Their kindness and accommodation to strangers is unparalleled, and the hospitality of Paris is beyond anything I had conceived to be practicable in a large city. Their eminence too in science, the communicative dispositions of their scientific men,

[40] To Short, Havre, October 7, 1789 (Library of Congress, Jefferson Papers).

the politeness of the general manners, the ease and vivacity of their conversation, give a charm to their society to be found nowhere else. In a comparison of this with other countries we have the proof of primacy, which was given to Themistocles after the battle of Salamis. Every general voted to himself the first reward of valor, and the second to Themistocles. So ask the travelled inhabitant of any nation, In what country on earth would you rather live?—Certainly in my own, where are all my friends, my relations, and the earliest & sweetest affections and recollections of my life. Which would be your second choice? France."[41]

During the delay at Cowes awaiting favorable winds, Jefferson was out of touch with political affairs. He wrote from there to Paine: "I have no news but what is given under that name in the English papers. You know how much of these I believe."[42]

But meanwhile, with his two young daughters, he made excursions to different parts of the island when weather permitted. On October 11, his account book shows, he paid "expenses at Newport and Carybrook Castle." The description given by an English traveler, who visited the Isle of Wight the same year as the American diplomat, shows that those places must have appealed to a person with Jefferson's interest in agricultural and mechanical curiosities.

Of Newport the British author says that: "Two markets are held here every week, in which great quantities of all sorts of grain and provisions are disposed of, not only for the use of the inhabitants, but for supplying the outward bound ships . . . which . . . touch at Cowes. When I mention the market, I must not forget to notice also the farmers' daughters who resort to it with the produce of their farms, and at once grace it with the charms of their persons, and the winning affability of their behavior. There is not perhaps in the kingdom a place where so many lovely girls

---

[41] *Autobiography*, 157. Cf. to Wm. Short, Monticello, November 28, 1814 (Lipscomb and Bergh, *Writings*, XIV, 218).

[42] To T. Paine, Cowes, October 14, 1789 (Library of Congress, Jefferson Papers).

attend the market as Newport; and, at the same time, they are dressed with a degree of elegance far beyond what is usually observable in persons of their rank. . . . The appearance of these charming girls not only excited our wonder and admiration, but we found that they attracted the envy of all the farmers' daughters on the neighboring coasts."[43]

Surely Jefferson must have moralized upon the market at Newport for the edification of his daughters, whom he wished to educate for a happy and useful life in the country, scorning as a "useless bauble" a "girl of mere city education."[44]

Of Carisbrook Castle ("remarkable for the confinement of Charles the First, and also for a well of uncommon depth,"[45] as Martha Jefferson recorded) the English tourist furnishes a detailed account. He relates that the well in the castle yard was said to be three hundred feet deep, "and it has always twenty feet of water in it. The persons who show the castle, generally let down a piece of lighted paper into the well, in order to exhibit to strangers a singular effect that attends it; a stream of air rushes down into it from the mouth, with such violence, as to extinguish the flame long before it reaches the bottom.

"Another circumstance, not less extraordinary, likewise attends it; a pin of a common size being dropped into it, the sound it causes by falling on the water, though at so vast a depth, may be distinctly heard.

"The water is drawn up by an ass; who has performed this duty upwards of fourteen years. And the animal that preceded the present, officiated in the same employment (for which alone he was kept) during a much longer period; having lived forty years within the castle walls. The method used in drawing the water is by a wheel of fifteen feet diameter, in which the ass turns as a dog does a spit."[46]

[43] John Hassell, *Tour of the Isle of Wight*, I, 131-32.
[44] To Mrs. Eppes, Philadelphia, 1790 (Randolph, *Domestic Life*, 189).
[45] *Ibid.*, 150-51.
[46] Hassell, *Tour of the Isle of Wight*, II, 95-104.

These various circumstances could not have been overlooked by Jefferson, who during his tour of France two years before had at Marseilles "measured a mule, not the largest, five feet and two inches high," and had ascertained that "the fountain of Nismes is so deep that a stone was thirteen seconds descending from the surface to the bottom."[47]

From Cowes Jefferson despatched a final word to Short: "Our ship has arrived here this evening, & if the wind permits we shall sail tomorrow. We have now lost exactly three weeks by contrary winds; so that in spite of my efforts to be in readiness for a passage between the equinox & winter, we shall surely be thrown late into December & perhaps into January, for our captain tells us we cannot expect less than a nine weeks passage. The ship is of 300 tons, on her 4th. voyage, a good sailor, and we shall go the southern rout, so that we may hope for good weather until we approach the coast of America."[48] The vessel was two years old. It will thus be seen that Jefferson himself observed the standards of seaworthiness which he had prescribed on the occasion of his young daughter's voyage to Europe.

On October 22 Jefferson "embarked at noon on board the Clermont for Norfolk." The next day the vessel came to anchor off Yarmouth and then weighed anchor.[49] "We sailed on the 23d of October, 1789, in company with upwards of thirty vessels . . . detained, as we were, by contrary winds."[50] Exactly a month later Jefferson "landed at Norfolk a quarter before one p. m."

The voyage was a pleasant and rapid one, of "only 26. days from land to land. After getting clear of the eternal fogs of Europe . . . the sun broke out upon us, & gave us fine autumn weather . . . so that I have now passed the Atlantic twice without knowing

[47] Lipscomb and Bergh, *Writings*, XVII, 178, 170.

[48] To Short, Cowes, October 17, 1789 (Library of Congress, Jefferson Papers).

[49] A note by H. S. R[andall] states that this must mean Weymouth. Chinard, following Ford, says that the vessel in which Jefferson embarked was the *Montgomery* (Chinard, *Jefferson: Apostle of Americanism*, 245). That was the ship on which Trumbull sailed to New York at the same time.

[50] Randolph, *Domestic Life*, 150–51.

what a storm is." Nevertheless "our sickness in the beginning was of 3. 4. or 5. days, severe enough."[51] The captain, a native of Norfolk, was "as bold a sailor as a judicious one should be, & very obliging." In view of the fine weather, he pursued a direct course after passing the meridian of Corvo, since it would have been madness to go a thousand miles out of the way "southwardly to seek what we had in perfection, that is sunshine and tropical breezes. . . . Our ship was uncommonly swift, insomuch that we passed everything most rapidly that we came in sight of: and on the whole have had a most pleasant & prosperous voiage."[52]

On board the *Clermont* Jefferson noticed "a mahogany table with sliding leaves" which pleased him. He requested the captain of the vessel to have made for him two tables of the same design, "each table to have one drawer only, as large as the frame will admit." Some weeks later the desired articles were forwarded to Jefferson by the obliging mariner.[53]

After the passengers had debarked but before the baggage had been taken from aboard ship, a fire broke out. Jefferson was greatly concerned over the fate of his public accounts, but no damage was done to any of his belongings, thanks to the thickness of the trunks in which they were carried.[54]

A month and a day after their arrival at Norfolk, the returning diplomat and his daughters, after a leisurely journey homeward, were joyously welcomed by the household at Monticello.

[51] To Short, Lynhaven Bay, November 21, 1789 (Ford, *Writings*, V, 132).

[52] To Capt. N. Cutting, Lynhaven Bay, November 21, 1789 (Library of Congress, Jefferson Papers). Cf. to Trumbull, Norfolk, November 23, 1789 (*ibid.*).

[53] Memorandum given to Captain Colley on board the *Clermont*, November 16, 1789; Captain Colley to Jefferson, Norfolk, January 22, 1791 (Mass. Hist. Soc., Jefferson Papers).

[54] Jefferson and his daughters would have found it difficult to obtain quarters in Norfolk "but for the politeness of the gentlemen at the hotel (Lindsay's), who were kind enough to give up their own rooms for our accommodation."—Randolph, *Domestic Life*, 152. The site where Jefferson thus found lodgings was probably on Freemason Street, between Church and Cumberland. According to the Norfolk directory, published in 1801, "Lindsay, Martha, widow," living at 6 Freemason Street, is the only person of that name listed. The neighborhood of Mrs. Lindsay's house was, at that time, the most desirable in Norfolk, and "some of the houses even yet have an air of original elegance." This information was courteously supplied in a letter from Dr. W. H. T. Squires, of Norfolk, to the author, April 16, 1942.

CHAPTER VII

Charged like a Bee with Honey

✦

ALTHOUGH, as has been seen, Jefferson himself traveled only where he had occasion to go, and did not indulge in needless jaunts to remote places simply for the sake of seeing the world, he eagerly encouraged and assisted those who had the inclination to undertake adventurous expeditions.

His vicarious participation in the plans and experiences of other travelers was so extensive and so whole-hearted, especially while he was in Europe, that it must be described in some detail if a complete or adequate picture of his travel activities is to be presented. Accordingly, this chapter will be devoted to Jefferson's relations with other tourists and explorers.

At Paris in 1786 he had become acquainted with John Ledyard, of Connecticut. The New England navigator was a soldier of fortune to whom Jefferson and his circle took a liking. The American diplomat was doubtless one of the benefactors who contributed to the support of the impecunious sailor. From St. Germain, where he lived in humble quarters, Ledyard wrote to a relative: "I took a walk to Paris this morning, and saw the Marquis de la Fayette. . . . I make these trips to Paris often; sometimes to dine with this amiable Frenchman, and sometimes with our minister, who is a brother to me."[1] Describing Jefferson's guests, he said: "I find at our minister's table between fifteen and twenty Americans, inclusive of two or three ladies. It is very remarkable, that we are neither despised nor envied for our love

[1] Jared Sparks, *Memoirs of the Life and Travels of John Ledyard*, 227.

of liberty, but very often caressed. I was yesterday at Versailles. It was the feast of St. Louis, but I never feasted so ill in my life, as at the hotel where I dined, and never paid so dear for a dinner. I was too late to see the procession of the king and queen, but I was little disappointed on that account, as I had already seen those baubles."[2]

Ledyard was a man of intrepid and restless disposition, who had accompanied Captain Cook on his voyage to the Pacific. "I suggested to him," Jefferson writes in his *Autobiography*, "the enterprise of exploring the Western part of our continent, by passing thro St. Petersburg to Kamschatka, and procuring a passage thence in some of the Russian vessels to Nootka Sound, whence he might make his way across the continent to America; and I undertook to have the permission of the Empress of Russia solicited. . . . The Empress refused permission at once, considering the enterprise as entirely chimerical. But Ledyard would not relinquish it"[3] and after being expelled from Russia was last heard of by Jefferson in 1789 as "he was just then plunging into the unknown regions of Africa, probably never to emerge again."[4]

In 1792, Jefferson initiated plans for an expedition to the West by a French botanist, André Michaud, under the auspices of the American Philosophical Society. A sum amounting to $128.25 was raised to finance the venture. George Washington contributed $25.00, while Jefferson and Alexander Hamilton each gave $12.50.[5] Michaud's instructions, drafted by Jefferson, in January, 1793, directed him "to find the shortest and most

[2] *Ibid.*, 212.

[3] *Autobiography*, 103–104.

[4] To Wm. Carmichael, Paris, March 4, 1789 (Ford, *Writings*, V, 75). Cf. Lipscomb and Bergh, *Writings*, XVIII, 144: "I received a letter from him, full of sanguine hopes, dated at Cairo, the 15th of November, 1788, the day before he was to set out for the head of the Nile, on which day, however, he ended his career and life; and thus failed the first attempt to explore the western part of our northern continent."

[5] Charles M. Wilson, *Meriwether Lewis*, 71. In Jefferson's account book under date of April 28, 1793, we find: "pd. ¼ of my subscription for Michaud's journey to Pacific sea 12.5." Curtis says a thousand guineas were raised (*The True Jefferson*, 370).

convenient route of communication between the United States and the Pacific Ocean, within the temperate latitudes, and to learn such particulars as can be obtained of the country through which it passes, its productions, inhabitants, and other interesting circumstances."[6] When he had proceeded as far as Kentucky, Michaud was recalled by instructions from the French Minister in Philadelphia.

A decade elapsed before Jefferson's project advanced toward fruition. While president, he sent his private secretary, Captain Meriwether Lewis, and William Clark, brother of General George Rogers Clark, on their celebrated expedition westward to the Pacific. The object of this mission was to explore the Missouri River and find "the most direct and practicable water communication across the continent for the purposes of commerce."[7] Jefferson likewise is said to have encouraged Lieutenant Zebulon Montgomery Pike in the explorations which led to the discovery of Pike's Peak.[8]

Jefferson was desirous of fostering not only the exploration of western territory, but its commercial development as well. "I experience great satisfaction," he wrote from Paris, "at seeing my country proceed to facilitate the intercommunications of its several parts, by opening rivers, canals, and roads. How much more rational is this disposal of public money, than that of waging war."[9]

In keeping with this policy, Jefferson during his presidency signed on March 29, 1806, the act providing for construction of the National Pike, a highway to connect the newly admitted state of Ohio with the Atlantic seaboard. In connection with the building of this road, many problems arose to which he was obliged

[6] Lipscomb and Bergh, *Writings*, XVII, 335.

[7] *Ibid.*, XVIII, 149.

[8] Curtis, *The True Jefferson*, 371.

[9] To James Ross, Paris, May 8, 1786 (Lipscomb and Bergh, *Writings*, V, 320). Cf. to Mr. Mills, Monticello, September 25, 1822 (photostat in New York Public Library); and to David B. Warden, Monticello, June 6, 1817, in the *Mississippi Valley Historical Review*, XXVIII, No. 2 (September, 1941), 239.

to devote considerable attention. Not until April 9, 1807, did Pennsylvania give its assent to the project, as required by the act of Congress. Even then the Pennsylvania legislature appended a proviso urging that the route recommended by the federal commissioners be changed so as to pass through the county seats of Fayette and Washington counties. Writing to Secretary of the Treasury Gallatin, himself an inhabitant of western Pennsylvania, Jefferson criticized the legislature of that state for attempting to dictate "the direction of a road made at the national expense and for national purposes." He threatened to adopt, if need be, a route "which shall not enter the State of Pennsylvania" at all.[10] Rivalry between various localities also produced friction. However, all these obstacles were eventually overcome, and the road was completed. It was one of the first great "internal improvements" undertaken by the federal government.

Jefferson's advice and letters of introduction smoothed the path of fellow countrymen visiting Europe. His counsel and hospitality did much to enhance their enjoyment of Paris.[11] He welcomed them to his home and entered into their plans with zest. Not only did he outline itineraries for them, and bring them into contact with his European friends, but also on occasion he supplied them with funds.[12] He was particularly attentive to American students desiring to make their sojourn abroad as instructive as possible.

[10] To Gallatin, Washington, April 22, 1808 (Lipscomb and Bergh, *Writings*, XII, 31-32). See also to Thos. Moore, Monticello, April 14, 1807, in the Library of Congress, Jefferson Papers; to Gallatin, Monticello, April 21, 1807, in Lipscomb and Bergh, *Writings*, XI, 194-95; and to Kerr, Moore, and Williams, Monticello, August 6, 1808, in *ibid.*, XII, 117.

[11] Jefferson gave a Fourth of July banquet in 1788 for the American gentlemen in Paris. A year later (shortly before his departure from France) he was presented with an address, as a testimonial of his services as envoy by a group of his fellow countrymen (Shepperson, *John Paradise and Lucy Ludwell*, 312, 382; Short to Shippen, Paris, July 11, 1788 [Library of Congress, Wm. Short Papers]).

[12] Kimball, *Thomas Jefferson, Architect*, 39; Randall, *Life of Jefferson*, I, 547. For an instance of financial aid to stranded countrymen, see Daniel and Thomas Fitzhugh to Jefferson, Havre, November 7, 1785; to Limozin, Paris, November 11, 1785; to Daniel and Thomas Fitzhugh, Paris, November 11, 1785 (Mass. Hist. Soc., Jefferson Collection). It may have been a letter of credit which Jefferson himself

Charles Bulfinch, noted American architect, writes in his auto-biography: "At Paris I tarried some time to view its buildings & other objects of curiosity, to which I was introduced by letters from the Marquis de La Fayette & Mr. Jefferson, then minister there."[13]

Jefferson likewise persuaded the painter Trumbull to stay and study at Paris. That artist in his reminiscences recounts that he became acquainted with Jefferson while the American states-man was in London. "He had a taste for the fine arts. . . . He encouraged me to persevere in this pursuit, and kindly invited me to come to Paris, to see and study the fine arts there, and to make his house my home during my stay.

"I now availed myself of this invitation, and went to his house, at the Grille de Chaillot, where I was most kindly re-ceived by him. . . . I employed myself, with untiring industry, in examining and studying whatever had relation to the arts. . . . Mr. Jefferson joined our party almost daily; and here com-menced his acquaintance with Mrs. Cosway."[14]

That lady, of Italian blood, was the wife of a London artist whose miniatures were in vogue and who had been invited by the Duke of Orléans to paint the duchess and her children. Jef-ferson grew quite fond of the Cosways, and learned "how impru-dent it is to place your affections, without reserve, on objects you must so soon lose, & whose loss when it comes must cost you such severe pangs." When they left Paris in the fall of 1786, Jeffer-son wrote a delicate and charming letter to Mrs. Cosway, em-bodying a lengthy dialogue which "took place between my Head

---

returned to a Boston merchant "with as many thanks for this mark of your confidence as if I had had occasion to make use of it" in Europe.—To Thomas Russell, New York, June 13, 1790 (Hist. Soc. of Pa., Society Collection). Jefferson wrote letters of introduction for two of Mr. Russell's sons visiting Europe.—To Cathalan, Paris, January 18, 1789; to Short, Philadelphia, May 14, 1791 (Mass. Hist. Soc., Jeffer-son Papers).

[13] Ellen Susan Bulfinch, *The Life and Letters of Charles Bulfinch*, 42.

[14] Trumbull, *Autobiography*, 118; to Col. Humphreys, Paris, August 14, 1786 (Lipscomb and Bergh, *Writings*, V, 400–401); to Thevenard, Paris, May 5, 1786 (Ford [ed.], *Jefferson Correspondence in Collections of Bixby*, 18).

& my Heart" while he was "seated by my fireside, solitary & sad" after "having performed the last sad office of handing you into your carriage at the pavillon de St. Denis, and seen the wheels get actually into motion."[15]

Just as he had sealed this letter, the first written with his left hand after the injury to his right wrist, he received a letter of good length, dated Antwerp, with Mrs. Cosway's name at the bottom. "I prepared myself for a feast. I read two or three sentences; looked again at the signature to see if I had not mistaken it. It was visibly yours. Read a sentence or two more. Diable! Spelt your name distinctly. There was not a letter of it omitted. Began to read again. In fine after reading a little & examining the signature, alternately, half a dozen times, I found that your name was to four lines only, instead of four pages. I thank you for the four lines however because they prove you think of me little indeed, but better a little than none. To shew how much I think of you, I send you the enclosed letter of three sheets of paper, being a history of the evening I parted with you."[16]

The letter dated Antwerp was from Trumbull. Mrs. Cosway had written a postscript in Italian expressing the hope of soon hearing of Jefferson's good health. Trumbull announced that the Cosways were in Antwerp, and urged Jefferson not to set out on his contemplated tour of French seaports until his wrist improved. The artist described his voyage from Paris to Metz, Épernay

---

[15] To Maria Cosway, Paris, October 12, 1786 (Ford, *Writings*, IV, 311–23). See also Shepperson, *John Paradise and Lucy Ludwell*, 190, 378, 413. For a biography of the Cosways, see George C. Williamson, *Richard Cosway R. A.* Concerning Jefferson's relations with Mrs. Cosway, see Marie G. Kimball, "Jefferson's Farewell to Romance," *Virginia Quarterly Review*, Vol. IV, No. 3 (July, 1928), 402–19, and Bullock, *My Head and My Heart*.

George Hadfield, Maria's brother, came from England to be assistant architect of the Capitol at Washington (Charles Henry Hart, "Life Portraits of Thomas Jefferson," *McClure's Magazine*, Vol. XI, No. 1 [May, 1898], 47). It seems improbable that neither Richard nor Maria Cosway executed portraits of Jefferson during their association in Paris, but none are known to exist. Likewise, no portraits of Mrs. Jefferson have survived (*ibid.*, 48), and very few documents in her handwriting have been preserved (Marie Kimball, *Jefferson: The Road to Glory*, 171).

[16] To Maria Cosway, Paris, October 13, 1786 (Ford, *Writings*, IV, 323–24).

(where he saw the cellars containing champagne), Frankfort, the Palatinate, Worms, Oppenheim, and Mayence. At Cologne he was obliged by bad weather to leave the boat for Andernach. "Dusseldorf is a pleasant little town, remarkable for nothing but the Electoral palace and Gallery—but such a gallery as it is would well repay the trouble of a much longer and less pleasant journey. The works of Rubens which are the finest part of the collection are wonderful—much beyond all that I had imagined. But an attempt at description would be ridiculous." After three days spent there, Trumbull went to Aix, Liege, Louvain, Bruxelles, and Antwerp. He planned to visit The Hague and London.[17]

In reply Jefferson wrote: "I duly received your favor dated Antwerp, and . . . I was much entertained by it. It revived my inclination to travel, an inclination which has always been uppermost. My first wish was to see the places you described; my second to see in preference Italy, Greece &c but god knows when I may be able to see either, or if ever." Not knowing Mrs. Cosway's address, Jefferson put his letter containing the dialogue between head and heart under cover to Trumbull. At the same time Trumbull was requested to procure a private means of conveyance for communications sent to Jefferson, since, as the diplomat explained, "all letters directed to me are read in the postoffices both of London and Paris."[18]

During Trumbull's stay in Paris, not all of his time was spent in studying art. His diary mentions several pleasure excursions with Jefferson. One Sunday he "went with Mr. Jefferson and others to see the ceremony of crowning the *rosière* of Sarennes, a village near St. Cloud, four miles from Chaillot. Every year the most amiable, industrious and virtuous poor girl of the parish is elected" and receives a crown of roses from the hands of a little

[17] Trumbull to Jefferson, Antwerp, October 9, 1786 (Library of Congress, Jefferson Papers).
[18] To Trumbull, Paris, October 13, 1786 (*ibid.*). On August 9, 1789 during a trip to England, Gouverneur Morris delivered a letter from Jefferson to Mrs. Cosway.

girl in the church, where her parents, the people of the village, and others assemble to witness the ceremony. A benediction is bestowed by the bishop, and a legacy of 300 livres from a clergyman is awarded to the fortunate beneficiary. Trumbull returned to Paris on foot. Two days later the painter "dined, in company with Mr. Jefferson" at Passy, as guest of the Abbés Chalut and Arnond, with whom the American diplomat was quite friendly. It was a fast day, but "the luxury of the table in soups, fish and fruits" seemed to the New England artist "characteristic of the opulent clergy of the time." After dinner a visit was paid to Madame de Corny, one of Jefferson's most congenial companions in Paris.[19]

Trumbull again visited Paris in the autumn of 1787. At that time he "painted the portrait of Mr. Jefferson in the original small Declaration of Independence, Major General Ross in the small sortie from Gibraltar, and the French officers in the Surrender of Lord Cornwallis, at Yorktown in Virginia. I regard these as the best of my small portraits; they were painted from the life, in Mr. Jefferson's house."[20]

A year later Trumbull wrote from London, advising Jefferson of the shipment of a box containing harness and saddles, books and writing paper, "& a little case with two pictures, one of which I hope you will do me the honor to accept, & the other I beg you to be so good as offer to Miss Jefferson:—I almost despair of its meeting her approbation, but it is all I can do until I have the happiness to see you again:—You would have recd. both long since, but for the vexation I have had with my larger pic-

---

[19] Trumbull, *Autobiography*, 101, 116.

[20] *Ibid.*, 150–51. For a discussion and reproduction of Trumbull's miniature portrait of Jefferson now in the Metropolitan Museum of Art in New York, see Harry B. Wehle, *American Miniatures 1730–1850*, 14, plate XI; and the comment in Theodore Bolton and Harry L. Binsse, "Trumbull, 'Historiographer' of the Revolution," *Antiquarian*, Vol. XVII, No. 1 (July, 1931), 54. See also Bowen, *Centennial Celebration*, 486, and opposite page 21. For a reproduction of the head of Jefferson in the small Declaration of Independence, owned by Yale University, see *ibid.*, opposite page 23.

ture,—which has left me little spirits to attend to anything else."[21]

Trumbull procured passage to Norfolk for Jefferson in 1789, and himself sailed at the same time on the *Montgomery*, bound for New York. Jefferson had urged him to remain in Europe, and promised him the post of secretary at Paris, if William Short concluded to return to America. But Trumbull decided that his prospects would be better at home, and that his European study had been sufficient.[22]

When John Rutledge, Jr., and Thomas Lee Shippen made a tour of Europe in 1788, Jefferson was consulted regarding their journey. Presumably codifying his own practices as a traveler, he prepared for their benefit some notes which he describes as hastily scribbled and undigested. "I am ashamed of them; but I will pay willingly that price, if they may, on a single occasion, be useful to you," he wrote to Rutledge.[23] He promised the young men letters of introduction to friends in Europe.[24] These[25] he later sent in duplicate, not knowing whether the travelers intended to stay together or take separate routes. It was Jefferson's own habit to travel by himself. "I . . . think one travels more usefully when alone, because he reflects more."[26]

During the summer of 1788, Shippen and Rutledge visited Bruges, Ghent, Brussels, Mechlin, Antwerp, Rotterdam, Delft,

---

[21] Trumbull to Jefferson, London, December 19, 1788 (Morgan Library, MS Collections). Short had suggested this gift for Jefferson's daughter.—Short to Trumbull, Paris, September 10, 1788 (Library of Congress, Wm. Short Papers). See also Bullock, *My Head and My Heart*, 99.

[22] Trumbull, *Autobiography*, 154–57, 169–72.

[23] To John Rutledge, Jr., Paris, June 19, 1788 (Lipscomb and Bergh, *Writings*, VII, 50). Cf. to T. Lee Shippen, Paris, June 19, 1788 (*ibid.*, VII, 52).

[24] To T. Lee Shippen, Paris, June 19, 1788 (*ibid.*, VII, 53). Jefferson wrote similar letters in 1815 for Dr. Benjamin Smith Barton of Philadelphia, who was obliged to go abroad for the benefit of his health.—To Dr. Barton, Monticello, March 7, 1817 (*More Books, The Bulletin of the Boston Public Library*, Vol. XVIII, No. 4 [April, 1943], 160).

[25] To Sasserno, Paris, July 13, 1788; and to Febbroni, Paris, July 13, 1788 (Mass. Hist. Soc., Jefferson Papers).

[26] To John Bannister, Paris, June 19, 1787 (Randolph, *Domestic Life*, 130).

The Hague, Amsterdam, Utrecht, Nimuegen, Spa, Düsseldorf, Coblentz, Aix, Cologne, Frankfort, Strasbourg, Basel, Bern, and Geneva.

The young travelers profited by Jefferson's advice. "At Dusseldorf I examined the gallery of paintings which you so judiciously recommended to my attention with infinite delight," Shippen reported. Closeted there during an entire morning, he left in the afternoon because the attendant's fair companion "did not seem quite satisfied that I should admire on canvas with so much enthusiasm what I might have found alive on her cheek more worthy of admiration." A visit to four costly palaces belonging to the Elector of the Palatinate evoked reflections on the impropriety of permitting concentration of wealth in the hands of absentee owners. To one with Jefferson's agrarian interests, it must have given satisfaction to learn that the young Americans met a person by the name of Hüpsch who presented them with four treatises of his own composition on manure, destroying insects, inoculating cattle, and other agricultural topics.

"At Coblentz we found the Wild man a very civil one to us," wrote Shippen regarding their stay at the inn which Jefferson had patronized the year before. The landlord, belatedly receiving payment for a map which Jefferson had procured during his visit there, praised the American statesman as the best man in the world for remembering the debt.[27]

Jefferson himself diligently observed the maxim he laid down for Shippen and Rutledge that a traveler should buy a map immediately upon arriving at a town. Jefferson's collection of maps

[27] Shippen to Jefferson, Strasburgh, July 31, 1788; Rutledge to Jefferson, Strasburg, August 1, 1788 (Library of Congress, Jefferson Papers). In his travel notes for Shippen and Rutledge Jefferson had written: "The Wildman ou l'Homme sauvage. A very good tavern. The tavern keeper furnished me with the carte des postes d'Allemagne. I paid his bill without examining it. When I looked into it, after my departure I found he had forgot to insert the map, & I had no sure opportunity of sending him the price. Please pay him for me with this apology, and I shall reimburse it with thankfulness. He is very obliging. He accompanied me to a gentleman well acquainted with the vineyards & wines of the Moselle about which I wished to inform myself. He will recollect me from that circumstance."—Library of Congress, Shippen Papers.

was consulted when the city of Washington was laid out by Major Pierre Charles L'Enfant. To the Frenchman Jefferson wrote: "In compliance with your request I have examined my papers and found the plans of Frankfort-on-the-Mayne, Carlsruhe, Amsterdam, Strasburg, Paris, Orleans, Bordeaux, Lyons, Montpelier, Marseilles, Turin and Milan, which I send in a roll by this post. They are on large and accurate scales, having been procured by me when in those respective cities myself."[28]

Jefferson's European friends took great delight in welcoming his compatriots. At Frankfort, Baron Geismer entertained Shippen and Rutledge. "He . . . overwhelmed me with civilities and by his attentions, rendered Frankfort so dear to me that I left it with much regret. . . . He said much of the friendship which you shewed him whilst he was a prisoner in Virginia and seem'd happy in having an opportunity of being kind to one of your friends," wrote Rutledge to Jefferson.[29]

Shippen spoke of Geismer's hospitality in similar terms: "It would have been impossible for a man to receive a long absent and much beloved brother with more cordiality or friendship than I experienced from that gentleman. He introduced me to ye Court of Hesse Cassel as his friend, shewed me everything that was to be seen in or near Hainault, and behaved in every respect with the greatest possible attention and amiability. It was not among the least of his recommendations to me that he loved and respected you as he often assured me he did without bounds. There was not in short, a thing which he did, or a word which he said which did not prove him worthy of that friendship which you honored him with and a valuable acquaintance. His senti-

[28] To L'Enfant, Philadelphia, April 10, 1791 (Elizabeth S. Kite, *L'Enfant and Washington*, 48). On the same day Jefferson wrote to President Washington that "While in Europe I selected about a dozen or two of the handsomest fronts of private buildings of which I have the plates. Perhaps it might decide the taste of the new town, were these to be engraved here, and distributed gratis among the inhabitants of Georgetown."—John C. Fitzpatrick (ed.), *The Writings of George Washington*, XXXI, 295.

[29] Rutledge to Jefferson, Strasburgh, August 1, 1788 (Library of Congress, Jefferson Papers).

ments do a like honor to his head and his heart, and his conduct seems to have always been in unison with them. How he has been able in a military life & under a despotic government to preserve his principles so pure, so free and so liberal, is alike surprizing and honorable to his character."[30]

At Geneva Shippen received word from home obliging him to curtail his tour. Deciding to proceed with Rutledge as far as Milan before turning back, he inquired of Jefferson regarding the most direct route from that place to London. Jefferson replied: "I am very sorry you are obliged to abridge your tour. With respect to your route from Milan to London, on which you were pleased to consult me, I would certainly prefer Genoa, thence along the coast to Nice, (absolutely by land, in defiance of all the persuasions you will be exposed to go by water), thence to Toulon and Marseilles. There it will depend on your time, whether you will go by Nismes, the canal of Languedoc (in the post boat), Bordeaux, Paris and Calais, or whether you must come on directly from Marseilles to Paris and Calais. But even in the latter case, make the small deviation to Nismes, to see the most perfect remains of antiquity which exist on earth. My absence from Paris becomes more doubtful than it was. I had hoped to go to Champagne to see the vintage. I am not certain now that my business will permit it."[31]

On September 16, 1788, William Short, Jefferson's secretary in Paris, set out to join Shippen and Rutledge. He went by way of Villejuif, Fontainebleau, Fossard, Auxerre, Vitteaux, Dijon, Beaune, Chalons, and Villefranche, to Chateau de l'Aye. Jefferson had been entertained there the preceding year, and Short was likewise a welcome guest. They drank and made Short drink so often to Jefferson's health, that the young Virginian was deeply impressed with the sincerity of his hosts, "the more so as we were in a plain kind of dining room as different from a salle

[30] Shippen to Jefferson, Geneva, September 22, 1788 (*ibid.*).

[31] To Shippen, Paris, September 29, 1788 (Lipscomb and Bergh, *Writings*, VII, 153–54).

à manger in Paris, as the table of some of our Albemarle friends is from that of a rich financier in Philadelphia."[32]

Proceeding through Lyon, Geneva, and Turin, Short arrived in Milan October 22, only to learn that Shippen had left two hours before. In Milan, Short and Rutledge enjoyed the courtesies of Count del Vermi and Count Castiglioni. The latter took them to dine and spend the night at Montbello, seat of his brother's father-in-law, nine miles from Milan, adjacent to Lake Como. The Count's brother, Short remarked, was a person as much attached to American plants as the Count to Americans themselves.[33]

After a week in Milan, Short left for Bergamo in company with Rutledge. There he was taken ill, and recuperated at the seat of Count Barziza, in the neighborhood of Bergamo. Meanwhile Rutledge went back to Milan. Towards the end of November the travelers left Bergamo for Venice; thence made their way to Ferrara by water, thence on to Bologna, Pietro del Castello, Forli, Rimini, Pesaro, Ancona, Loretto, Tolentino, Sena, Foligno, Spoleto, and Terni. They arrived in Rome three days before Christmas. Here they witnessed "the great ceremony of Christmas mass performed by the Pope in all his pomp surrounded by his cardinals." Several inches of snow fell shortly before New Year's Day.[34]

Rutledge's rapture in Rome was unbounded: "I have not words which can express my admiration of Rome and everything in it, indeed every thing seems like enchantment. . . . As yet I have seen little of Rome but have seen enough to persuade me that of all places in this world it is the most agreeable and charming."[35]

Short extracted lessons in political philosophy from the ruins

[32] Short to Jefferson, Lyons, October 2, 1788 (Library of Congress, Jefferson Papers).

[33] Short to Jefferson, Milan, October 28, 1788 (*ibid.*).

[34] Short to Jefferson, Rome, December 31, 1788 (*ibid.*).

[35] Rutledge to Jefferson, Rome, December 31, 1788 (*ibid.*).

A VIEW from MR COSWAY's BREAKFAST-ROOM PALL MALL,

WITH THE PORTRAIT OF M.^{RS} COSWAY.

The Landscape Painted by Wm Hodges R.A and the Portrait by C.^d Cosway R.A.

& engraved by W. Birch Enamel Painter

Publish'd Feby 1. 1789 by Wm Birch. Hampstead Heath. & sold by T. Thornton, Southampton Str.^t Cov.^t Garden.

Maria Cosway

*Paris, as seen from the house
of the Abbés Chassi and Arnout at Passy
(From a sketch by Trumbull)*

he surveyed. "The remains of antiquity here speak much in favor of free government," he asserted. Under the Republic useful public works were constructed, he observed, while under the Empire ostentatious monuments were erected, magnificent structures without the slightest practical utility.

Engaging a tutor in architecture, the young Americans found that that science was more difficult than they had anticipated. They did not pursue its study to the exclusion of social diversions. Mme de Tessé's letter of introduction to Cardinal de Bernis secured them many attentions. On one occasion Short suffered from a headache caused by intemperate dancing at a ball for the princess of Saxe.[36]

Moreover, excursions from Rome to other celebrated spots provided additional enjoyments. "I procured at Naples according to your request the mould for making macaroni," Short informed Jefferson. "I went to see the macaroni made." Likewise they made a pilgrimage along the route of Horace's journey to Brindisi and visited the tomb of Vergil, where Jefferson had instructed Short to "tug well at the laurel which shall be shown you," in order to detect the "roguery" practiced by the guides on credulous tourists. They were at Vesuvius, Herculaneum, and Pompeii. "Here we drank what is called lachrymae Christi wine, as we had done Falernian on the other side of Naples. . . . They are both rather good than otherwise, but remarkable more for their name than anything else."[37]

The reports from his young compatriots describing their experiences in the classical country doubtless afforded the busy

[36] Short to Jefferson, Rome, January 14, 1789; Short to Jefferson, Rome, December 31, 1788; Shippen to Jefferson, London, March 16, 1789 (*ibid.*). A similar letter of introduction was procured by Jefferson for Benjamin Huger of South Carolina, who was also given a letter to Fabbroni at Florence.—To Huger, Paris, July 26, 1789; to Fabbroni, Paris, July 26, 1789 (Mass. Hist. Soc., Jefferson Papers). Cf. to Mrs. Kinloch, Paris, July 1, 1789 (*ibid.*).

[37] Short to Jefferson, Rome, February 11, 1789 (Library of Congress, Jefferson Papers); to Short, Paris, September 20, 1788 (Lipscomb and Bergh, *Writings*, VII, 148); Short to Jefferson, Rome, February 17, 1789 (Library of Congress, Jefferson Papers).

American plenipotentiary a considerable measure of vicarious adventure. "The present letter will probably reach you amidst the classical enjoiments of Rome," he remarked to Short. "I feel myself kindle at the reflection, to make that journey: but circumstances will oblige me to postpone it at least."[38]

In the summer of 1787, Jefferson had not seen much of Italy. "Milan was the spot at which I turned my back on Rome and Naples. It was a moment of conflict between duty which urged my return, & inclination urging me forwards. I do not despair altogether of finding yet some favorable interval when I may be able to go on to those renowned places."[39]

Jefferson was fully aware of the attractions of the Italian metropolis. Regarding the education of two young Virginians whose health required them to seek a more favorable climate than that of Edinburgh, he said: "I should not hesitate to prefer Rome, where all the advantages may be obtained which can at Geneva, and where moreover there is a genial climate like their native one, classical ground to tread on which will occasion them to derive new instruction and new delight from every page of the Latin poets & historians, articles & processes of culture adapted to the temperature of their own country, and lessons in painting, sculpture & architecture constantly before their eyes and which no other place can offer."[40]

[38] To William Short, Paris, December 8, 1788 (*William and Mary College Quarterly* [2d series], Vol. XII, No. 2 [April, 1932], 146). Jefferson advised Shippen and Rutledge that "it gives infinite pleasure to apply one's classical reading on the spot." He recommended that, before entering Italy, the tourists buy Addison's travels and the latest edition of the "Guide pour le voyage d'Italie en poste." He also urged frequenting the theaters, public walks and public markets, since "at these you see the inhabitants from high to low."—Library of Congress, Shippen Papers.

[39] To Gaudenzio Clerici, Paris, August 15, 1787 (Library of Congress, Jefferson Papers).

[40] To Mr. Elder, Paris, November 25, 1785 (Mass. Hist. Soc., Jefferson Papers). Late in life Jefferson wrote to the father of a young American studying in Europe: "I believe were I twenty years younger, instead of writing, I should meet him there and take with him his classical voyage to Rome, Naples and Athens. I wish him all the happiness and information, and they will be very great, which he will derive from it."—To Elisha Ticknor, December 12, 1816 (*ibid.*, quoted in Orie W. Long, *Thomas Jefferson and George Ticknor, A Chapter in American Scholarship*, 20).

Early in March, Short and Rutledge left Rome. "Had I had more time I should have enjoyed Rome still more—there are many things here that deserve to be studied as well as seen—but I have been obliged to content myself with superficial views only," said Short, before his departure.

Rutledge seems to have had a fondness for Milan. "Rutledge insists on going to spend a fortnight at Milan. If he agrees to stay two days only I will go with him," Short wrote to Jefferson.[41]

At Florence, Rutledge and Short were welcomed by Giovanni Fabbroni. Jefferson had given them a letter of introduction to him. Fabbroni, besides being assistant director of the Royal Museum, was secretary of the Royal Academy of Agriculture and author of a volume of reflections on agriculture. A copy of his brother's treatise on fermentation of wines was given to Short to be delivered to Jefferson.[42]

When the travelers left Florence, they proceeded by way of Marseilles, Aix, Avignon, Orange, Pont St. Esprit, Nismes, Montpellier, to Beziers, where they took the post boat along the Canal of Languedoc. They stopped a day at Castelnaudari to see the reservoir of St. Feriol. "But we did not go to Escamase because we learned that it was nothing more than a vault under which the water passed—nor to Lampy because it would have required more than the day." Likewise they did not go to Cette, but continued by water, past Toulouse, to Bordeaux. They were heeding implicitly, it seems, Jefferson's advice to Rutledge that "there is nothing in France so well worth your seeing as the canal & country of Languedoc, and the wine country of Bordeaux."[43]

Rutledge had contemplated going to Spain from Bordeaux, pursuant to Jefferson's counsel. Just as he pressed Ledyard, Mi-

[41] Short to Jefferson, Rome, February 25, 1789 (Library of Congress, Jefferson Papers).

[42] Giovanni Fabbroni to Jefferson, Firenze, July 9, 1785; Jean Fabbroni to Jefferson, Florence, March 25, 1789; Jefferson to Fabbroni, Paris, May 24, 1787 (Mass. Hist. Soc., Jefferson Papers).

[43] Short to Jefferson, Toulouse, April 20, 1789; to J. Rutledge, Jr., Paris, March 25, 1789 (Library of Congress, Jefferson Papers).

chaud, Pike, and Lewis and Clark to explore the West, so Jefferson had urged Shippen and Rutledge to push on to Constantinople if they found it safe to travel in Turkey. Likewise he exhorted Rutledge to visit Spain and Portugal because an acquaintance with those countries, on account of their American possessions, would prove valuable to one in public life. "By a letter which your father did me the honor of writing me on the 6th. of April," Jefferson informed the young man, "he approves of my proposition of your going to Madrid & Lisbon rather than increasing your tour & stay in the Northern parts of Europe. If this meets your own ideas, you should not turn off from the route you have hitherto had in view, till you get to Bordeaux. Our connections with the Spaniards and Portuguese must become every day more and more interesting, and I should think the knowledge of their language, manners, and situation, might eventually and even probably become more useful to yourself & country than that of any other place you will have seen. The womb of time is big with events to take place between us & them, and a little knowledge of them will give you a great advantage over those who have none at all."[44]

Accordingly Rutledge, although his itinerary remained problematical, requested Jefferson to procure him letters of introduction. The American plenipotentiary thereupon forwarded letters recommending his young fellow countryman to Carmichael and Count d'Aranda at Madrid, and to Mr. Gueldermestre, the Dutch consul at Lisbon.[45]

Nevertheless, as the moment of separation from his traveling

[44] To J. Rutledge, Jr., Paris, July 13, 1788 (*ibid.*). Cf. to John Rutledge, Jr., Paris, June 19, 1788, and to Shippen, July 13, 1788 (Lipscomb and Bergh, *Writings*, VII, 50, 64).

[45] To John Rutledge, Jr., Paris, March 25, 1789; to Rutledge, April 17, 1789; to Carmichael, Paris, March 25, 1789; to the Count d'Aranda, Paris, March 25, 1789 (Library of Congress, Jefferson Papers). Jefferson also procured permission for the Americans to inspect French fortifications. "I wrote to the Count d'Estaing to obtain a permit for yourself and Mr. Rutledge to see Toulon minutely. I now enclose his letter for the Commandant."—To Wm. Short, Paris, March 16, 1789 (*William and Mary College Quarterly* [2d series], XII, No. 2 [April, 1932], 152).

companion at Bordeaux approached, Rutledge's determination to visit Spain faltered. "Rutledge will probably come on to Paris with me, he seems already sick of a Spanish journey," declared Short. A week later Rutledge himself, writing to thank Jefferson for the letters of introduction, announced his decision to abandon the undertaking: "I fear, Sir, you will think me very capricious when I inform you that I have defer'd going into Spain and Portugal, & shall proceed with Mr. Short to Paris. In giving up seeing those countries, I have been determined, by my desire to see you before you sail for America, by the advanced state of the season, the accounts I have received of the danger there is in travelling thro' Spain in summer, & because I wish to be quietly settled in some place, for two or three months, that I may digest all I have seen for these last twelve months."[46]

In spite of the fact that Jefferson's proposals with respect to visiting Constantinople and Spain did not bear fruit, the young Americans made a very interesting and profitable tour, doubtless justifying Jefferson's declaration to Rutledge's father that: "He is likely to be as much improved by his tour as any person can be, and to return home, charged, like a bee, with the honey gathered on it." To Shippen's father likewise Jefferson wrote: "He will thus have seen the best part of the Netherlands, Germany, Italy, & France, & return satisfied that no part of the earth equals his own country. He will return charged, like a bee, with the honey of wisdom, a blessing to his country & honour & comfort to his friends."[47]

The Decalogue for Tourists which Jefferson hastily composed for the use of his two compatriots deserves quotation at length:

[46] Short to Jefferson, Toulouse, April 20, 1789; Rutledge to Jefferson, Bordeaux, April 27, 1789 (Library of Congress, Jefferson Papers).

[47] To Governor Rutledge, Paris, July 12, 1788 (*ibid.*); to Dr. Wm. Shippen, Paris, May 8, 1788 (Library of Congress, Shippen Papers). When Shippen and Rutledge parted company, "we wept undissembled involuntary tears on the occasion."— T. L. Shippen to Wm. Shippen, London, December 5, 1788 (*ibid.*).

Traveling Notes for Mr. Rutledge and Mr. Shippen, June 3, 1788.[48]
General Observations.

On arriving at a town, the first thing is to buy the plan of the town, and the book noting its curiosities. Walk round the ramparts when there are any, go to the top of a steeple to have a view of the town and its environs.

When you are doubting whether a thing is worth the trouble of going to see, recollect that you will never again be so near it, that you may repent the not having seen it, but can never repent having seen it. But there is an opposite extreme, too, that is, the seeing too much. A judicious selection is to be aimed at, taking care that the indolence of the moment have no influence in the decision. Take care particularly not to let the porters of churches, cabinets, etc., lead you through all the little details of their profession, which will load the memory with trifles, fatigue the attention, and waste that and your time. It is difficult to confine these people to the few objects worth seeing and remembering. They wish for your money, and suppose you give it the more willingly the more they detail to you.

When one calls in the taverns for the *vin du pays,* they give what is natural and unadulterated and cheap; when *vin etrangere* is called for, it only gives a pretext for charging an extravagant price for an unwholesome stuff, very often of their own brewery. The people you will naturally see the most of will be tavern keepers, *valets de place* and postilions. These are the hackneyed rascals of every country. Of course they must never be considered when we calculate the national character.[49]

---

[48] These are quoted as published in Lipscomb and Bergh, *Writings,* XVII, 290–93, and constitute part of the second of five small folios written in Jefferson's fine hand. The remaining portion of these notes, like a guidebook, deals with particular places, giving Jefferson's recommendations of hotels and objects of interest. Thus, at San Remo he found "the auberge de la Poste a very good one. The rooms look into a handsome garden, and there are Palm trees under the windows." At Nice, he writes, "I lodged at the Hotel de York. It is a fine English tavern, very agreeably situated, & the mistress a friendly agreeable woman."—Library of Congress, Shippen Papers. Jefferson's advice to Rutledge and Shippen should be compared with that given in Lord Chesterfield's *Letters to his Son,* Nos. LXXXV, XCVI, CXLVIII; CXI (Juvenile Section).

[49] When Professor C. D. Ebeling in 1795 was preparing his *Biography and History of North America,* Jefferson advised him that Mr. Morse and Mr. Webster were good authorities for anything relating to the eastern states, but unreliable in their information about the South. "They both I believe took a single journey through the Southern parts, merely to acquire the right of being considered as eyewitnesses. But to pass once along a public road thro' a country & in one direction

Objects of Attention for an American.

1. Agriculture. Everything belonging to this art, and whatever has a near relation to it. Useful or agreeable animals which might be transported to America. Species of plants for the farmer's garden, according to the climate of the different States.

2. Mechanical arts, so far as they respect things necessary in America, and inconvenient to be transported thither ready-made, such as forges, stone-quarries, boats, bridges (very especially) etc., etc.

3. Lighter mechanical arts, and manufactures. Some of these will be worth a superficial view; but circumstances rendering it impossible that America should become a manufacturing country during the time of any man now living, it would be a waste of attention to examine these minutely.

4. Gardens. Peculiarly worth the attention of an American, because it is the country of all others where the noblest gardens may be made without expense. We have only to cut out the superabundant plants.

5. Architecture. Worth great attention. As we double our numbers every twenty years, we must double our houses. Besides, we build of such perishable materials that one-half of our houses must be rebuilt in every space of twenty years, so that in that time houses are to be built for three-fourths of our inhabitants. It is, then, among the most important arts; and it is desirable to introduce taste into an art which shows so much.

6. Painting. Statuary. Too expensive for the state of wealth among us. It would be useless therefore, and preposterous, for us to make ourselves connoisseurs in those arts. They are worth seeing, but not studying.

7. Politics of each country, well worth studying so far as respects internal affairs. Examine their influence on the happiness of the people. Take every possible occasion for entering into the houses of the labourers and especially at the moment of their repast; see what they eat, how they are clothed, whether they are obliged to work too hard; whether the government or their landlord takes from them an unjust proportion of their labour; on what footing stands the property they call their own, their personal liberty, etc., etc.

8. Courts. To be seen as you would see the Tower of London or

only, to put up at it's taverns, and get into conversation with the idle, drunken individuals who pass their time lounging in these taverns, is not the way to know a country, it's inhabitants, or manners. To generalize a whole nation from these specimens is not the sort of information which Professor Ebeling would wish to compose *his work* from."—Ford, *Writings*, VII, 44.

menagerie of Versailles with their lions, tigers, hyaenas, and other beasts of prey, standing in the same relation to their fellows. A slight acquaintance with them will suffice to show you that under the most imposing exterior, they are the weakest and worst part of mankind. Their manners, could you ape them, would not make you beloved in your own country, nor would they improve it could you introduce them there to the exclusion of that honest simplicity now prevailing in America, and worthy of being cherished.

Biographers of Jefferson have sought to make apologies for the "utilitarian preoccupations" which dominated him while traveling, and which are clearly manifested in the passages just quoted. Chinard calls this memorandum a "damning document," which "has to be read to be believed," which evinces a "puritanical distrust of purely æsthetic enjoyments." He points out too that Jefferson in his notebooks did not speak of the cathedrals at Milan or Cologne; that he was interested in the canal at Carcassonne and "the carp caught there," but did not mention the walls. Randall exculpates his hero by saying: "That he records nothing, does not prove that he felt nothing."

Chinard doubtless hits upon the correct explanation when he goes on to say that Jefferson in these memoranda "noted information for which he foresaw some further use, interesting knowledge which could be utilized at Monticello or for the benefit of his fellow countrymen. . . . All this required exactness and precision and could scarcely be trusted to memory. Pleasant impressions of travel, on the contrary, could always be evoked through the imagination and would lose very little of their charm and value with time. . . . Furthermore there was in these purely æsthetic pleasures something really too personal to be indulged in, at least in writing."[50]

It is preposterous to suppose that Jefferson could have failed to see the cathedral at Cologne. It would be superfluous for him to have recorded that fact. But unless one made a note of it at the

[50] Chinard, *Jefferson: Apostle of Americanism*, 164, 165, 166, 169; Randall, *Life of Jefferson*, I, 450.

time, one might easily forget that "there are about two hundred and fifty Catholic churches in the city."[51]

Jefferson himself states that in visiting English country seats and gardens: "My inquiries were directed chiefly to such practical things as might enable me to estimate the expense of making and maintaining a garden in that style." A similar purpose may be presumed in the case of all his memoranda made while traveling. In his journal he "was . . . recording useful facts to carry home to his countrymen."[52] Thoroughness such as this in gathering information enabled him to return to his native land, as he hoped other American tourists would return, "charged like a bee with honey."

[51] Lipscomb and Bergh, *Writings*, XVII, 225.
[52] *Ibid.*, XVII, 237; Randall, *Life of Jefferson*, I, 467.

CHAPTER VIII

Cumbrous Trappings of Rank

✦

WHEN Jefferson, returning to the United States, landed at Norfolk on November 23, 1789, he had been absent abroad for more than five years. It was his intention, after the marriage of his daughter Martha and the settlement of his personal business, to return to Paris.[1] But he had not yet reached Monticello when at Eppington he received a letter from President Washington tendering him a cabinet post in the administration of the new government under the Constitution. With some reluctance, Jefferson found himself writing letters of adieu to the diplomats and ladies of his acquaintance at the French capital and instructing William Short what to do about breaking up housekeeping on the Champs Elysées and shipping Jefferson's furniture and books to America.

To take up his new duties as secretary of state, Jefferson left Monticello on March 1, 1790, and a week later set out from Richmond for New York. He arrived on the twenty-first, and took lodgings at the City Tavern until he could find a house. That famous hostelry, built in 1700 and torn down in 1850, occupied the block between Cedar and Thames Streets, on Broadway, next to Trinity Church. Writing to his daughter Martha he said: "I

---

[1] "Patsy's age requiring now that she should return to her own country, other considerations that Polly should accompany her, and not choosing to trust them to any care but my own during such a voyage, I have asked from Congress leave of absence for 5. or 6. months of the coming year, during which I propose to accompany them to Virginia, to be of what service I can there in the arrangement of my own affairs, & to return to this place."—To Francis Eppes, Paris, December 15, 1788 (Huntington Library, MS Collections).

saw in Philadelphia your friends Mrs. Trist and Miss Rittenhouse. Both complained of your not writing. In Baltimore I
enquired after Mrs. Buchanan and Miss Holliday. The latter is
lately turned Methodist, the former was married the evening I
was there to a Mr. Turnbull of Petersburg in Virginia. Of course
you will see her there. I find it difficult to procure a tolerable
house here. It seems it is a practice to let all the houses the 1st. of
February, & to enter into them the 1st. of May. Of course I was
too late to engage one, at least in the Broadway, where all my
business lies. I have taken an indifferent one nearly opposite Mrs.
Elsworth's, which may give me time to look about me & provide
a better before the arrival of my furniture."[2] His books and
papers "had been left in Paris and Virginia; and this place yields
fewer resources in the way of books than could have been imagined," he wrote from New York.[3]

Jefferson's house was located at 57 Maiden Lane. He moved
in on June 1, having rented it on March 29 from Robert and
Peter Bruce "for a year @ £ 100."[4] Across the back of the building he erected a many-windowed gallery, supported on posts,
for his library. The drawing has been preserved where he
sketched the plans for this alteration.[5] There now stands at 57
Maiden Lane an office building occupied by the Home Insurance Company, which in 1921 marked the site of Jefferson's residence by a plaque.

In June, Jefferson and a group of friends spent a three days'
fishing trip, very probably on Hamilton's sloop, off Sandy Hook.

[2] To Martha Jefferson Randolph, New York, April 4, 1790 (Morgan Library,
MS Collections).

[3] To David Rittenhouse, New York, June 12, 1790 (Lipscomb and Bergh,
Writings, XIX, 73).

[4] Randall, *Life of Jefferson*, I, 560; Albert Ulmann, *A Landmark History of
New York*, 278.

[5] To Wm. T. Franklin, New York, July 16, 1790 (Ford, *Writings*, V, 210–
11); Kimball, *Thomas Jefferson, Architect*, 150, 151. New York houses, Jefferson
observed, have the chimneys at the ends of the house, instead of at the point where
the partition into rooms is located, as is the practice in Philadelphia, and it is therefore practicable to vary the size of the rooms in a New York house by simply moving the partition.

Regarding this outing Jefferson wrote to his daughter Martha: "I am going tomorrow on a sailing party of three or four days with the President. Should we meet sea enough to make me sick I shall hope it will carry off the remains of my headache."[6]

In August, Jefferson accompanied the President on a visit to Rhode Island. That state, belatedly admitted to the Union, welcomed the Father of his Country with the zealous contrition of a returning prodigal. The inhabitants greeted their chief executive with extraordinary manifestations of sincere enthusiasm and respect. Leaving New York on the fifteenth, aboard the packet *Hancock*, commanded by Captain Brown, the party sailed through Long Island Sound. Arriving at Newport on the morning of the seventeenth, they were conducted to their lodgings at Mrs. Almy's house on Thames Street near Mary Street by the clergy and leading citizens of the place, who greeted them at the dock. Later they took a walk around the town and the heights above it; after which a banquet was held in the town hall. About eighty persons were present, and the affair cost $210, although nearly every family in the community had contributed some part of the food or tableware. After a toast to the town of Newport, President Washington withdrew, and a toast to "the man we love," proposed by Judge Henry Marchant, was drunk by the company standing. Later in the evening, again taking a walk, the President stopped to drink a glass of wine with Judge Marchant before returning to his lodgings. The next morning the Judge was so agitated that he was unable to read an address presented on behalf of the town by the committee of which he was chairman. He was obliged to hand it to another member of the committee, Colonel Henry Sherburne, who read it very composedly. After the presentation of several other addresses by religious and fraternal groups, the President and his entourage

---

[6] Stephen Decatur, *The Private Affairs of George Washington*, 133; Isaac Newton Phelps Stokes, *The Iconography of Manhattan Island*, V, 1268; William S. Baker, *Washington after the Revolution*, 183; to Martha Jefferson Randolph, New York, June 6, 1790 (Morgan Library, MS Collections).

sailed from Newport at a very early hour on the morning of the eighteenth.[7]

That afternoon they arrived at Providence after a tedious passage of seven hours, and were zealously welcomed by Governor Arthur Fenner, who jumped aboard the packet as soon as it got to the wharf. The visitors were escorted to their lodgings at the Golden Ball Inn, later known as Mansion House. This hostelry on Benefit Street was kept by Abner Daggett. The procession to the tavern was conducted with more solemnity and formality than that at Newport, there being troops and music. A printed program was issued, designating the order of precedence to be observed by the marchers. Meanwhile the populace fired salutes, rang bells, and paraded the streets. A Providence newspaper reported that "All Ages Classes and Sexes, were full of Sensibility on this Joyful Occasion.—The brilliant Appearance of the Ladies from the Windows was politely noticed by the President, and gave Animation to the Scene.—On the Presidents arrival at Mr Daggets, another federal Salute took Place, and after three Cheers the People retired."[8]

Preparations for the event had been made in advance. Two days earlier the town meeting had resolved "to cause the Windows in the Market House to be immediately mended." The inhabitants were directed "to clean the Streets against their respective Houses and Dwellings." In order that the President might be received "in a Manner Suitable to his high dignity" it was voted "to procure the necessary Powder for the Occasion and in Case the State will not pay for the same this Town will."

The college edifice was illuminated in the evening. Upon

---

[7] Maud L. Stevens, "Washington and Newport," *Bulletin of the Newport Historical Society*, No. 84 (July, 1932), 12–16; Albert Matthews (ed.), "Journal of William Loughton Smith," in Massachusetts Historical Society *Proceedings*, LI (1918), 36–37. Jefferson had lodged at Mrs. Almy's in June, 1784.

[8] The quotations in this and the two following paragraphs are from Howard W. Preston, "Washington's Visits to Providence," in Rhode Island Historical Society *Collections*, Vol. XIX, No. 4 (October, 1926), 109–15. See also Matthews, "Journal of William Loughton Smith," 37; Richard M. Bayles, *History of Providence County*, I, 191; and William R. Staples, *Annals of the Town of Providence*, 354.

learning that the students had prepared this spectacle in his honor, the President went to see it, although the weather was rainy and it was his practice not to go out at night. In the course of a long walk the next morning "which completely fatigued the company which formed his escort," the President with his companions visited the college library and museum, went on board an Indiaman of 900 tons on the stocks, and stopped to drink wine and punch at the homes of several prominent citizens. Later "an elegant Entertainment was served in the Court-House for upwards of Two Hundred Persons." Thirteen toasts were drunk, with discharges of cannon. President Washington toasted the city and went immediately on board ship. The crowd which had accompanied the party to the wharf returned to Governor Fenner's, "and after three Cheers dispersed in good order."

The cruise terminated at New York on the afternoon of the twenty-first. Jefferson informed his daughter Martha: "I . . . returned yesterday, after a very pleasant sail of two days going and two days returning thro' the Sound. We visited Newport and Providence, where the President was received with great cordiality."[9] As the expenses of this trip were borne by the President, Jefferson's account book does not shed any light on details of the visit. The accounts of Tobias Lear, Washington's secretary, however, show that on the twenty-third he paid the sum of £ 24-6-9 for the President's expenses to Rhode Island, and the following day paid Captain Brown hire of vessel to and from Rhode Island £ 43-4-0.[10]

These were not the only excursions made by Jefferson from New York to points of interest in the vicinity. On July 10, his

[9] To Martha Jefferson Randolph, New York, August 22, 1790 (Morgan Library, MS Collections).

[10] Decatur, *The Private Affairs of Washington*, 148–49. See also Stokes, *Manhattan Island*, V, 1272; Baker, *Washington after the Revolution*, 190–93; and John C. Fitzpatrick (ed.), *The Writings of George Washington*, XXXI, 93–94. All the foregoing say the trip began August 15 and ended on the twenty-second. According to Griswold (*The Republican Court*, 227–28), the dates were August 14 and 21. Matthews ("Journal of William Loughton Smith," 34, 36, 39) gives August 15 and 21, as does Jefferson's account book.

account book records an outlay for "grease for wheels going to Fort Washington" and on the following day "expences at Hellgate." On the seventeenth of July he crossed the Brooklyn ferry, spent the next day visiting Jamaica and Flushing, and returned by the same route.

The first of September Jefferson left New York, and proceeded by way of Princeton, Trenton, Philadelphia, Wilmington, Chestertown, Annapolis, Georgetown, Alexandria, Mt. Vernon, Dumfries, and Fredericksburg to Monticello, where he arrived on the nineteenth. Traveling with Madison, he was accompanied during part of this trip by Thomas Lee Shippen. That young man, whose tour of Europe two years previously had brought him into close association with Jefferson, was now on his way to Stratford to visit his kinsmen of the Lee family. In a letter to his father, written from Alexandria on September 15, 1790, he thus described his enjoyable experiences: "I arrived here late the night before yesterday, and yesterday I was so engrossed by the Lees who abound here, that I could not find time to write to you. My journey was a delightful one from Chestertown to Georgetown, whether spoken of for the excellence of the society, my fare, the weather, or the roads. For I overtook, as I told you I expected I should, my two valuable friends Messrs. Jefferson and Madison. At Rock Hall, 12 miles from Chestertown, we waited all that day for want of a vessel to take us over, and I never knew two men more agreeable than they were. We talked and dined and strolled and rowed ourselves in boats, and feasted on delicious crabs." The following day Shippen wrote to his father from Mount Vernon: "My having joined those charming men, Jefferson and Madison, though it gave me infinite pleasure, cost me money, so that when I arrived here I found that I was by thirty dollars poorer than when I left you. This, added to the necessity which I find still exists of giving money to servants, and much money too, occasions that of my asking you the favour of a bill for $50, or a bank note of that amount, to me here."[11]

[11] Edmund Jennings Lee, *Lee of Virginia*, 117, 119. In the spring of 1791

Jefferson left Monticello for Philadelphia on November 8, 1790, the temporary seat of government having been transferred to that place. He traveled by way of Mt. Vernon, Baltimore, Head of Elk, and Chester, reaching Philadelphia on November 21. There he again was faced with the problem of obtaining comfortable living quarters.

On the thirtieth Jefferson's French furniture arrived. He paid $544.53 for freight from Havre to Philadelphia. Two months later, however, he informed William Short that "not more than half of it is as yet opened, as I am in a house not yet finished."[12] There were eighty-six packing cases, the contents of which were carefully listed in an invoice covering thirteen pages. The cases had been plumbed at Paris, and were not to be opened at Havre, but a mob there suspected them to be the property of certain execrated passengers who had sailed on the *Citoyen* a few days before, and insisted on making an examination. Though the municipal authorities could not prevent the populace from opening the packages, the national guard presided to keep order during the proceedings. Two marble pedestals and three busts were completely unpacked, being suspected from their weight to contain money. Books and wearing apparel were found in other boxes inspected. After viewing the contents of eight packages, the crowd was satisfied and the ringleaders disappeared. The American diplomat's belongings, undamaged, were put on board the *Henrietta* and shipped to Philadelphia.

Fifteen of the packing cases contained books. The titles of books purchased by Jefferson while abroad were entered by him in a notebook now in the possession of the Massachusetts His-

---

Shippen married the widow of John Banister, Jr., another young American student who corresponded with Jefferson in Europe.—*Ibid.*, 126. See Chapter VII, *supra*.

[12] To Wm. Short, Philadelphia, January 24, 1791 (*William and Mary College Quarterly* [2d series], Vol. XIII, No. 2 [April, 1933], 98). See also Randall, *Life of Jefferson*, II, 14. Jefferson had not anticipated delay from this cause. "I shall not be housekeeping till I recieve [*sic*] my furniture from France, but that may be hourly expected."—To Francis Eppes, Monticello, October 31, 1790 (Huntington Library, MS Collections).

Trumbull's miniature of Jefferson,
made at Jefferson's home
in Paris in 1787

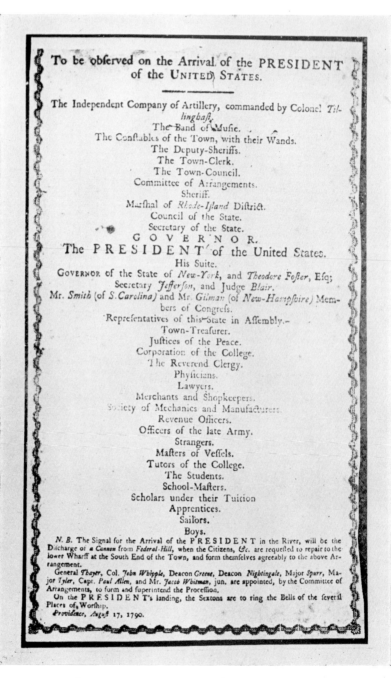

To be observed on the Arrival of the PRESIDENT of the UNITED STATES.

The Independent Company of Artillery, commanded by Colonel *Tillinghast.*
The Band of Music.
The Constables of the Town, with their Wands.
The Deputy-Sheriffs.
The Town-Clerk.
The Town-Council.
Committee of Arrangements.
Sheriff.
Marshal of *Rhode-Island* District.
Council of the State.
Secretary of the State.
GOVERNOR.
The PRESIDENT of the United States.
His Suite.
GOVERNOR of the State of *New-York,* and *Theodore Foster,* Esq;
Secretary *Jefferson,* and Judge *Blair.*
Mr. *Smith* (of *S. Carolina)* and Mr. *Gilman* (of *New-Hampshire)* Members of Congress.
Representatives of this State in Assembly.—
Town-Treasurer.
Justices of the Peace.
Corporation of the College.
The Reverend Clergy.
Physicians.
Lawyers.
Merchants and Shopkeepers.
Society of Mechanics and Manufacturers.
Revenue Officers.
Officers of the late Army.
Strangers.
Masters of Vessels.
Tutors of the College.
The Students.
School-Masters.
Scholars under their Tuition
Apprentices.
Sailors.
Boys.

N. B. The Signal for the Arrival of the PRESIDENT in the River, will be the Discharge of *a Cannon* from *Federal-Hill,* when the Citizens, &c. are requested to repair to the lower Wharff at the South End of the Town, and form themselves agreeably to the above Arrangement.

General *Thayer,* Col. *John Whipple,* Deacon *Greene,* Deacon *Nightingale,* Major *Spurr,* Major *Tyler,* Capt. *Paul Allen,* and Mr. *Jacob Whitman,* jun. are appointed, by the Committee of Arrangements, to form and superintend the Procession.

On the PRESIDENT's landing, the Sextons are to ring the Bells of the several Places of Worship.

Providence, August 17, 1790.

Order of procession on arrival in Providence

torical Society.[13] In 1814, after the Capitol at Washington had been burned by British troops, Jefferson sold his library to the government, receiving for it $23,950. The books, worth probably twice that sum, became the nucleus of the Library of Congress.[14] In its Rare Book Room such of them as survived a subsequent fire in 1851 are now treasured items. For a long time the library continued to follow the system of classification adopted by Jefferson in the catalog he made of his books.[15] In offering his collection to the nation, Jefferson related that: "While residing

[13] Of the works on architecture owned by Jefferson, about thirty were acquired while he was abroad.—Kimball, *Thomas Jefferson, Architect*, 91 ff. It is difficult to determine which volumes were acquired during this period. At the beginning of the notebook Jefferson wrote " V This mark denotes the books I have. Those unmarked I mean to procure. 1783. Mar. 6. 2640 vols." The handwriting and color of ink indicate that the original list was written on the left-hand pages of the book, the titles on the right-hand pages being added later and including volumes published long after 1783. (Sometimes the later additions were inserted on the left-hand pages.) The titles were divided into forty-six chapters, embracing three main headings: history, philosophy, and fine arts. The approximate number of pages devoted to various topics follows: history, 38; natural philosophy, 23; ethics (including international law) and religion, 20; law, 35; politics, 19; mathematics, 4; geography, 16; fine arts, 57.

Jefferson's interest in "revolutions" is noteworthy. Among the titles listed are: "Tableau des revolns d'Allemagne par de B.," "Revolution des Provinces unis de Mandrillon," "Revolns de Hongrie," "The revolt of Ali Bey. by S. L. Kosmopolitos," "Revolutions de Maroc. par Bathwaite," "Revolutions d'Angleterre par le P. d'Orleans," "Histoire de la revoln de l'Amerique septentrionale par Chas et Le Brun," "Ramsay's history of the American revolution," "Coup d'oeil sur les revolutions et sur la reforme de la medicine. par Cabanis," "Rivoluzioni del teatro musicale Italiano. dal Arteaga."

Other interesting titles are: "Le Philadelphien á Geneve," "Ray's American Tars in Tripoli," "Philips's grandeur of the law," "The laws of honour," "Goldsmith's Crimes of cabinets," "Vater on the peopling of America," "Histoire des troubles d'Amerique. par Sonle's," "Catalogus Graduatorum Collegii Yalensis," "La Forest, l'art de soigner les pieds," "Cutbush on the health of soldiers & sailors," "Baynard on cold Bathing," "Pringle on the diseases of the army," "Kirkpatrick on the putrefaction of dead bodies," "Bland's military discipline," "Adye's Bombardier & pocket gunner," "Rules for the government of an army," "Hoyle's games," "Fessenden's Science of sanctity," "The whole duty of man," "The Power of religion on the mind by Lindley Murray," "Bentham's Panopticon." Works on agriculture, gardening, shorthand, cookery, and other "technical arts" are numerous. Cookbooks in Latin as well as French are listed. The annotation "given by the author" appears after several titles.

[14] While president, Jefferson had helped to obtain books for the use of Congress. See his letters to Short, George W. Erving, and Mr. Duane, Washington, July 16, 1802, and the list of books, dated July 19, 1802 (Mo. Hist. Soc., Bixby Collection).

[15] Of 6,487 volumes 2,000 escaped destruction. The system of classification now

in Paris, I devoted every afternoon I was disengaged, for a summer or two, in examining all the principal bookstores, turning over every book with my own hand, and putting by everything which related to America, and indeed whatever was rare and valuable in every science. Besides this, I had standing orders during the whole time I was in Europe, on its principal book-marts, particularly Amsterdam, Frankfort, Madrid and London, for such works relating to America as could not be found in Paris."[16]

Not all the furniture of the Hôtel de Langeac was sent to America by Short. Some common things in ordinary wood were left in Paris: the book cases and secretaire, two or three tables, ten chairs, and five dumb-waiters. In the shipment there were fifty-nine chairs. Jefferson had asked Abigail Adams for advice on the proper mode of packing these. A few of them are said to be still in the hands of Jefferson's descendants. The "6 sophas with gold leaf" and "44 chairs gold leaf" listed among Jefferson's household goods in an inventory of his taxable property in Albemarle County, made in 1815, probably came in the shipment from France.

In addition to his chairs, Jefferson brought back to the United States sofas, tables, beds, commodes, chiffoniers, mirrors, paintings, statuary, curtains, and draperies. These included "six large blue damask curtains, eight medium size of the same, a drapery in two parts," six crimson curtains, and eight cords with crimson tassels. There were also twenty-two bellpulls and "a bundle of mixed chintz"; as well as a piece of *toile de Jouy*, a material of which Jefferson was particularly fond. In an undated memorandum he computed the price of various fabrics. "Toile de Jouy is 35 pouces (37.38 inches) wide & 5 f 15 the aune, which is 10 sous the square pied." Cotton toile was 6⅓ sous the square foot, taffeta 1 franc, damask 37 sous.[17] In choosing crimson as well as

---

in use was adopted in 1898 (Randolph G. Adams, "Thomas Jefferson, Librarian," in *Three Americanists*, 88, 94).

[16] To Samuel H. Smith, Monticello, September 21, 1814 (Ford, *Writings*, IX, 486).

[17] Library of Congress, Jefferson Papers, 41568.

blue curtains, Jefferson seems to have followed both the old and the new in fashion; for the French aristocracy clung to crimson or golden yellow damask, while the class of bankers and bourgeoisie preferred sky blue. Eleven pairs of these "foreign curtains" were still in use at Monticello in 1815.

So far as is known, Jefferson was the first American to import French furniture on so extensive a scale. Some thirty years later President Monroe furnished the rebuilt White House at a total expense of $50,000, of which $18,417 was spent for furniture from France. Jefferson's Paris acquisitions were not used by him in the White House, but were taken to Monticello when he left Philadelphia at the conclusion of his service as secretary of state. "What has become of Jefferson's French furniture is something no one knows. A few isolated pieces are preserved among the statesman's descendants; but that Jefferson ever owned so large a body of French things, so many delicate, gilded chairs with gay damask covering, beds with upholstery of blue silk, commodes and tables with decorations of ormolu, had never been suspected. Ten years before his death, many of them still stood at Monticello; but, in the inventory of his effects made shortly after that event, no sofas or chairs with gold are mentioned. Whether they were inherited by his grandsons and granddaughters, or whether they were bought by the neighbors and friends who wandered up the steep slopes of Monticello that July day, in 1827, when many of Jefferson's things were sold, has never been revealed." Perhaps most of them wore out, like the frayed leather chairs, worn through, with the hair sticking out in all directions, which caught the attention of a young New England visitor at Monticello in 1814.[18]

The dwelling in Philadelphia where Jefferson installed his imported belongings was rented by him from Thomas Leiper for $100 quarterly. Later the rent was increased.[19] On January

[18] Marie Kimball, "Thomas Jefferson's French Furniture," *Antiques*, Vol. XV, No. 2 (February, 1929), 128; Francis Calley Gray, *Jefferson in 1814*, 68.
[19] To Thomas Lieper, Philadelphia, August 24, 1791; December 16, 1792 (Mass. Hist. Soc., Jefferson Papers).

3, 1793, he records paying "Thos Lieper half year's rent due this day £ 125-0-0 = D. 333.33." The house was located, according to Clement Biddle's Philadelphia directory for 1791, at 274 High Street. That thoroughfare, according to the same authority, was 100 feet wide, and commonly called Market Street. The Department of State occupied a three-story brick building at 307 High Street, that is to say, on the northwest corner of Eighth Street and Market. Jefferson's residence was on the south side of Market Street, the fourth house west of Eighth. The distinguished jurist James Wilson lived there after Jefferson. This "very large four story house" at 806 Market Street "was once occupied as the Washington Museum, and afterwards as Barrett's Gymnasium." It was still standing in 1867, but was razed to make room for the building erected in 1900 by Gimbel Brothers.[20]

During the winter of 1790 the house was gradually prepared for occupancy by Jefferson. Early in December the Secretary of State wrote to his younger daughter: "We have already had two or three snows here. The workmen are so slow in finishing the house I have rented here, that I know not when I shall have it ready, except one room which they promise me this week, and which will be my bedroom, study, dining-room, and parlor."[21] On December 11, 1790, he "entd. into possn of the 2. rooms of 3d. story"; on the seventeenth he "took possn of stable"; on the nineteenth he "took possn of bedroom"; on the twenty-fourth "took kitchen"; and on January 9, 1791 he "took possn drawg room & parlour. begin to dine at home." Two days later "Billy's wife begins to wash for me @ £ 20 a year."

Jefferson's domestic arrangements were devised with a view

[20] Jackson, *Market Street*, 141; Jackson, *Literary Landmarks of Philadelphia*, 187; Jackson, *Philadelphia*, III, 788; John T. Scharf and Thompson Westcott, *History of Philadelphia*, I, 462; Thompson Westcott, *A History of Philadelphia*, III, Chap. CCCVI; G. A. Lough, controller of Gimbel Brothers, to the author, September 29, 1938.

[21] To Maria Jefferson, Philadelphia, December 7, 1790 (Randall, *Life of Jefferson*, II, 14).

to comfort and convenience. His bed, invisible by day, was installed in a recess between the library and the breakfast room, so that if he awoke before breakfast time he could get out of bed on the side where his books were. On the south side of the house he built a veranda which was very pleasant in the summer.[22]

The plans of Leiper's house thus had to be altered considerably in order to meet Jefferson's requirements. The additions were a book room, a stable, and a garden house. He was to occupy the room over the kitchen, "which must therefore be well finished." In order to install an alcove bed, he found it essential that the door of this room be located in the northeast corner. At the end of his bedroom he desired an additional room, fourteen feet wide, supported on pillars like the gallery of his New York house, to be built across the whole lot, and even into the next adjoining lot if possible. "As it is to be a book room, length becomes important and you can not give it length by running it lengthwise of the tenement instead of across, for then it would front west." Jefferson wished a larger dining room, twenty-six by fourteen feet, with an antechamber of fourteen feet. Moreover, "I shall want stables for five horses, and carriage room for three carriages. No seats at the street door to collect lounging servants. I expect of course a reasonable addition to the rent for the additional book room. To take a house, built on my own plan, for ten years, would be wedding myself to the seat of government longer than I would chuse."[23]

A unique garden house was also contemplated by Jefferson, "that I might have a place to retire and write in where and when I wished to be unseen and undisturbed even by my servants, and for this purpose it was to have a sky light and no lateral windows. . . . When I returned from Virginia I found the garden house

---

[22] Scharf and Westcott, *History of Philadelphia*, I, 462.

[23] To Carstairs, New York, July 25, 1790 (Kimball, *Thomas Jefferson, Architect*, 151). Jefferson was willing to pay additional rent for the stable and book room, and requested his landlord to make a definite proposition, on the basis of which Jefferson could then decide whether to stay or not. To Lieper, Philadelphia, August 16, 1791 (Huntington Library, MS Collections).

made with a window-door at each end, no sky light, and a set of joists which were in the way. This rendered it absolutely useless for my purpose." Consequently he refused to finish it, as Leiper wished him to, towards the end of his tenancy.[24]

Jefferson had planned to take two houses adjoining each other, when the government moved to Philadelphia, in order "to assign the lower floor of both to my public offices, and the first floor and both gardens entirely to my own use." It would thus be possible to increase the length of his book room, while keeping within the budget. "There has never been paid more than 80 £ for an office for my department, and therefore I must endeavor to get one at that price." When seeking to obtain lodgings for Monroe, he informed the latter: "I can accomodate you myself with a stable & coach house without any expense, as I happen to have two on hand; and indeed, in my new one I have had stalls enough prepared for 6 horses, which are 2 more than I keep."[25]

Jefferson's tastes had become more exacting since his contact with European standards of refinement. The north-lighted galleries for books, the alcove bedroom, and the proposed garden house lighted only from above, were innovations based upon his observations abroad. In addition to his imported furniture and books, he ordered French wallpaper, doubtless for use in his Market Street abode.

In his personal attire Jefferson manifested a similar liking for European elegance. Soon after establishing himself in Philadelphia, he instructed his tailor: "If either now or at any time hence you can find a superfine French cloth, of the very dark blue which you know I wear, I will be obliged to you to make and send me a coat of it. Furnish me also if you please a pair of black

---

[24] To Thomas Leiper, Philadelphia, December 16, 1792 (Kimball, *Thomas Jefferson, Architect*, 152; Mass. Hist. Soc., Jefferson Papers, 1028–29). Jefferson had also complained that Carstairs was making no chimney in the book room.—To Leiper, New York, May 19, 1791 (Mass. Hist. Soc., Jefferson Papers).

[25] To Wm. T. Franklin, New York, July 16, 1790 (Ford, *Writings*, V, 210–11); Kimball, *Thomas Jefferson, Architect*, 151; to James Monroe, Philadelphia, July 10, 1791 (Ford, *Writings*, V, 351).

silk & a pair of black satin breeches."[26] Of his appearance a Philadelphia lady at whose home he was a frequent visitor writes: "He had resided at the Court of France, and upon his return appeared in somewhat of its costume, and wore a suit of silk, ruffles, and an elegant topaz ring; but he soon adopted a more republican garb, and was reproached with going to the other extreme as a bait for popularity."[27]

This "Jeffersonian simplicity" attained its height when as president he wore slippers down at the heels and clothing indicative of studied slovenliness the day the bumptious British minister, Mr. Merry, made his first official call. It was likewise Jefferson's opposition which kept the justices of the United States Supreme Court from imitating the English custom of wearing wigs as part of their apparel while on the bench.[28]

Jefferson also relished gastronomic delicacies to which he had become accustomed while abroad. It is said that he "introduced into America French cooks, finger-bowls, and other fashions which had met with his approval in Paris. . . . He was served by butlers and footmen in livery, and was fastidious about his table china and plate."[29] His establishment numbered four or five male hired servants (as well as his daughter's maid) and was presided over by his French steward, Petit, who had served him in Paris.[30]

[26] To Mr. Bache, Philadelphia, August 14, 1791 (Mass. Hist. Soc., Jefferson Papers).

[27] Deborah Norris Logan, *Memoir of Dr. George Logan of Stenton*, 50. Shortly after his retirement as president, Jefferson requested his grandson in Philadelphia to send to Monticello "a half dozen pounds of scented hair powder," remarking that: "None is to be had here, and it is almost a necessary of life with me."—To Thomas Jefferson Randolph, Monticello, May 6, 1809 (Mass. Hist. Soc., Jefferson Papers [quoted in Bernard Mayo, *Jefferson Himself*, 288]).

[28] Charles Warren, *The Supreme Court in United States History*, I, 48.

[29] Curtis, *The True Jefferson*, 191–92.

[30] Randolph, *Domestic Life*, 206–207. His Paris establishment numbered six male servants, one female, and Petit. One of his servants there was called "Sans-sens" (Account Book, November 23, 1785). On one occasion in Philadelphia a disagreement arose, and Jefferson made it plain that Francis, the coachman, must remove his wife from the house if she could not get along with Petit.—To Mr. Taylor, Monticello, August 13, 1792; to M. Adrian Petit, Monticello, August 13, 1792 (Mass. Hist. Soc., Jefferson Papers); Petit to Jefferson, July 28, 1792 (Mo. Hist. Soc., Bixby Collection).

Petit agreed, after some hesitancy, to follow Jefferson to Philadelphia,[31] and was instructed to "bring a stock of macaroni, Parmesan cheese, figs of Marseilles, Brugnoles, raisins, almonds, mustard, vinaigre d'Estragon, other good vinegar, oil and anchovies."[32]

During his travels in Europe Jefferson made it a point to sample the foods and fruits of the localities through which he passed. In Holland he first tasted waffles and promptly bought a waffle iron. In Southern France he compared the oranges obtained in the various towns he visited. Ortolans also attracted his attention; and the nourishment supplied by the olive tree he believed to be a blessing to the poor. The introduction of a new variety of rice he considered as one of his greatest public services. Before the Revolution he tried to cultivate wine grapes in Virginia; to renew the experiment he bought vines at Hochheim and Rüdesheim during his tour of vineyards along the Rhine. He is said to have been the first to use vanilla and macaroni in the United States. His recipes for "Nouilly à maccaroni," meringues, macaroons, ice cream, biscuit de Savoye, Blanc manger, wine jellies, pêches à l'eau-de-vie, making coffee, and preserving green beans for winter are still available to housewives.[33]

In the White House as well as in his Philadelphia establishment, the southern statesman had a French steward and French cooks. Patrick Henry denounced him on the stump as one who had "abjured his native victuals."[34] His table was famous. No

---

[31] Randolph, *Domestic Life*, 206; to Martha Jefferson Randolph, Philadelphia, May 8, 1791 (Morgan Library, MS Collections); to Short, Philadelphia, January 24, 1791 (*William and Mary College Quarterly* [2d series], Vol. XIII, No. 2 [April, 1933], 98); March 16, 1791 (*ibid.*, 102); Petit to Jefferson, Paris, August 3, 1790 (Mo. Hist. Soc., Bixby Collection).

[32] *William and Mary College Quarterly* (2d series), Vol. XII, No. 4 (October, 1932), 293. Cf. to Cathalan, Paris, November 13, 1787 (Mass. Hist. Soc., Jefferson Papers).

[33] Library of Congress, Jefferson Papers, 41864, 41868, 41869, 41870.

[34] Curtis, *The True Jefferson*, 202, 213–14. In later life Jefferson wrote: "I envy M. Chaumont nothing but his French cook and cuisine. These are luxuries which can neither be forgotten nor possessed in our country."—To Wm. Short, Monticello, November 24, 1821 (Lipscomb and Bergh, *Writings*, XVIII, 316).

president ever surpassed him in the art of entertaining. A New England Federalist, Senator Plumer, said after enjoying Jefferson's hospitality: "I wish his French politics were as good as his French wines."[35] Another visitor marvelled when balls of ice cream in warm pastry were served at the White House. John Adams had given large dinners at frequent intervals; Jefferson gathered a group of about a dozen at his table every day. The guests were invited with a view to forming a congenial company, and the host was a model of tact. The diners were always seated at a round or oval table where they could all see one another, and the conversation was a general "meeting of minds." Everyone could speak freely, and no restraint because of the presence of servants was felt, since the use of dumb-waiters enabled the guests to serve themselves.

A dinner party given by Jefferson in 1793 at Philadelphia, however, was the scene of a quarrel between the artist Trumbull and Senator Giles of Virginia. Trumbull had recently caused the Senator to lose face in the presence of a lady by making him admit that he had not read a book which he was severely criticising. At Jefferson's house, therefore, Giles was in a hostile frame of mind towards Trumbull and engaged in a savage dispute with him, attacking Christianity. Curiously enough, it was David Franks, a Jewish banker, who came to Trumbull's support in meeting the onslaughts of Giles. Trumbull in an account of the incident records that he declared to Giles when the latter frankly avowed his own skeptical views on religion: " 'Sir, I would not trust such a man with the honor of a wife, a sister, or a daughter—with my own purse or reputation, or with any thing which I thought valuable. Our acquaintance, sir, is at an end.' I rose and left the company, and never after spoke to Mr. Giles." The host had smiled continually during the altercation, and "from this time my acquaintance with Mr. Jefferson became cold and distant."[36]

[35] Adams, *History of U. S. during Administration of Jefferson*, II, 364.
[36] Trumbull, *Autobiography*, 170, 172.

In the vicinity of Philadelphia, Jefferson found a number of congenial friends. One of these was Judge Richard Peters, who lived at Belmont, on the outskirts of the city. Inviting Jefferson to call there, he lamented: "My strawberries are gone and I have no Temptations to offer you. Come then from disinterested Motives when you wish for a little Country Air and you will get it here. Should it create an Apetite I will give you something to eat. I do not esteem you as Men do many things for your Scarcity. If this could make you more valuable than you are there would be no end to the Calculation." Writing to Judge Peters a few days later, Jefferson announced his intention to visit Belmont in the course of "my afternoon excursions: that being the part of the day which business and long habit have allotted to exercise with me. . . . Call on me in your turn, whenever you come to town: and if it should be about the hour of three, I shall rejoice the more. You will find a bad dinner, a good glass of wine, and a host thankful for your favour, and desirous of encouraging repetitions of it without number, form or ceremony. When Madison returns you will often find him here without notice & always with it: and if you complain again of not seeing him, it will be that the place of rendesvous does not enjoy your favour."[37]

President Washington often sought recreation in the vivacious company of Judge Peters. The jurist had quite a reputation for wit. Upon his adoption into an Indian tribe he had been given the name "Tegohtias" or "Talking Bird." During Lafayette's visit to America in 1824 Judge Peters punctured the eloquence of a young orator who professed that his generation intended "should our country be attacked, to tread in the shoes of our forefathers," by exclaiming "No, no, that you never can do, because your fathers fought barefooted." During the Judge's

---

[37] Richard Peters to Jefferson, Belmont, June 26, 1791 (Ford [ed.], *Jefferson Correspondence in Collections of Bixby*, 47–48); to Richard Peters, June 30, 1791 (Ford, *Writings*, V, 347–48). See also Peters to Jefferson, Belmont, June 20, 1790, in Ford's *Jefferson Correspondence in Collections of Bixby*, 40–42; and Jefferson to Peters, New York, June 13, 1790 (Hist. Soc. of Pa., Peters MSS., Vol. IX). Jefferson regarded Judge Peters as "an excellent farmer."—*Garden Book*, 203.

lifetime Belmont was a seat of elegant hospitality, and the leading statesmen of the period were often entertained there. Lansdowne, the country estate of Mrs. Bingham, the leader of Philadelphia society, likewise was visited by Washington and Jefferson.[38]

The splendid library and hemlock trees at Stenton, the mansion of Dr. George Logan, constituted another attraction which frequently gave delight to Jefferson. Stenton is located on Eighteenth Street, between Courtland and Wyoming, near Wayne Junction. The mansion, built in 1728, is regarded as an outstanding example of early American architecture, and is maintained through the efforts of the Colonial Dames. In 1777 General Washington made his headquarters there on his way to the battle of Brandywine.[39]

Beneath the venerable trees surrounding the Logan house momentous conversations between Jefferson and Genêt, the erratic envoy of the French Republic, took place without formality. Indeed, Stenton was often the scene of friendly gatherings. As the Quaker physician's widow, Deborah Norris Logan, records: "My husband's friendship with Thomas Jefferson began soon after the formation of the federal government. When that gentleman was Secretary of State he used frequently to visit us in a social and intimate manner, sometimes with small parties whose company was agreeable to one another and sometimes alone. His conversation was very pleasing. . . . He abounded in anecdotes of great interest."[40]

Jefferson found frequent opportunities for "Madison, Monroe and himself to enjoy a canter together along the banks of the Schuylkill. It was oftener a walk than a ride. Once it was a 'wade.' 'What say you,' he writes to Madison, during a rainy week in

[38] Thompson Westcott, *The Historic Mansions and Buildings of Philadelphia*, 391–93, 347.

[39] Charles Francis Jenkins, *Washington in Germantown*, ix.

[40] *Memoir of Dr. George Logan*, 53, 50. It was Jefferson's opinion that Dr. Logan was "the best farmer in Pensylva. both in theory & practice."—*Garden Book*, 199.

April, 1791, 'to taking a wade into the country by noon? It will
be pleasant above head at least, and the party will finish by dining here.' "[41]

Among the lodgers at the Fifth Street boarding house patronized by Madison was Colonel Beckwith, an English agent with
whom Hamilton was intimate. In order to draw his fellow Virginian into a more suitable circle, Jefferson invited Madison "to
come & take a bed and plate with me. I have 4. rooms of which
any one is at your service. . . . To me it will be a relief from a solitude of which I have too much: and it will lessen your repug-
nance to be assured it will not increase my expenses an atom.
When I get my library open you will often find convenience in
being close at hand to it."[42]

In 1791 Madison accompanied Jefferson on a lengthy jaunt
through New York and New England. Jefferson left Philadelphia on May 17 and returned on June 19. He traveled 920 miles,
of which 256 were by water. Political opponents declared that
this journey was not just a hunting and fishing trip, but was mo-
tivated by the desire to cement the unwieldy and scattered groups
of anti-Federalists into a party organization capable of concerted
action.

Hamilton's son wrote that "Jefferson and Madison left Philadelphia for New York; where they arrived on the nineteenth of
May, seventeen hundred ninety-one; and after frequent inter-
views with Chancellor Livingston and Burr, they made a visit to
Clinton under the pretext of a botanical excursion to Albany,
thence extended their journey to Vermont; and, having sown a
few tares in Connecticut, returned to the seat of government."
While the Virginians were "journeying to the east for the purpose of extending the opposition to his administration," says the
same writer, President Washington was making a tour of the
Southern states "in order to give it strength." Beckwith be-

[41] James Parton, *Life of Thomas Jefferson*, 400; to Madison, Philadelphia,
March 13, 1791 (Mass. Hist. Soc., Jefferson Papers).
[42] To Madison, Philadelphia, March 13, 1791 (*ibid.*).

lieved that this expedition to New England had been undertaken for the purpose of agitating an anti-British policy, and he imagined that his own personal exertions in that territory before Jefferson and Madison arrived had been successful in frustrating their objects.[43]

There is no evidence to be found that the tour was undertaken for any ulterior purpose. But it is not probable that Jefferson would fail to take advantage of any opportunity to further his political projects.[44]

Madison proceeded to New York by himself, at which place Jefferson addressed him on May 9: "I shall propose to you when we tack about from the extremity of our journey, instead of coming back the same way, to cross over through Vermont to Connecticut river & down that to New-haven, then through Long Island to N. Y. & so to Philada. Be this however as you will." Madison promptly acquiesced: "I do not foresee any objection to the route you propose. . . . Health, recreation & curiosity being my objects, I can never be out of my way."[45]

As a lesson in geography, Jefferson had already announced his itinerary in a letter to his young daughter Mary. Upon returning, he admonished her: "I hope you have received the letter I wrote you from Lake George, and that you have well fixed in your mind the geography of that lake, and of the whole of my

---

[43] John C. Hamilton, *History of the Republic of the United States as Traced in the Writings of Alexander Hamilton and His Contemporaries*, IV, 506.

[44] Samuel Flagg Bemis, *Jay's Treaty: A Study in Commerce and Diplomacy*, 83; Bowers, *Jefferson and Hamilton*, 79; Saul K. Padover, *Jefferson*, 199. In any event, before his departure Jefferson called a meeting of a committee of the American Philosophical Society appointed to study the Hessian fly. "Th. Jefferson presents his respects to the gentlemen of the committee on the Hessian fly, and prays their attendance at the Hall of the Philosophical society tomorrow (Friday) at half after seven P. M. . . . He leaves town on Sunday for a month, to set out on a journey which will carry him through N. York & the whole of Long island, where this animal has raged much. He is therefore anxious to take with him the decision of the committee and particularly prays of Dr. Barton to have his queries prepared to present to them." —To Dr. Benjamin S. Barton, Philadelphia, May 12, 1791 (*More Books, The Bulletin of the Boston Public Library*, XVIII, No. 4 [April, 1943], 156–57).

[45] Jefferson to James Madison, Philadelphia, May 9, 1791 (Library of Congress, Madison Papers); Madison to Jefferson, New York, May 12, 1791 (*Writings of James Madison*, V, 51).

tour, so as to be able to give me a good account of it when I shall see you." From Monticello she replied: "My dear Papa— I have received both your letters, that from Lake George and of June the 26th. I am very much obliged to you for them, and think the bark that you wrote on prettier than paper."[46]

From Lake Champlain Jefferson's married daughter, Martha, likewise received a letter written on birch bark: "I wrote to Maria yesterday while sailing on Lake George, and the same kind of leisure is afforded me to-day to write to you. Lake George is, without comparison, the most beautiful water I ever saw; formed by a contour of mountains into a basin thirty-five miles long, and from two to four miles broad, finely interspersed with islands, its water limpid as crystal, and the mountain sides covered with rich groves of thuja, silver fir, white pine, aspen and paper birch down to the water-edge; here and there precipices of rock to checker the scene and save it from monotony. An abundance of speckled trout, salmon trout, bass, and other fish, with which it is stored, have added to our other amusements, the sport of taking them. Lake Champlain, though much larger, is a far less pleasant water. It is muddy, turbulent, and yields little game. After penetrating into it about twenty-five miles, we have been obliged by a head wind and high sea to return, having spent a day and a half in sailing on it. . . . Our journey has hitherto been prosperous and pleasant, except as to the weather, which has been as sultry hot through the whole as could be found in Carolina or Georgia. I suspect, indeed, that the heats of Northern climates may be more powerful than those of Southern ones in proportion as they are shorter. . . . On the whole, I find nothing anywhere else, in point of climate, which Virginia need envy to any part of the world. . . . When we consider how much climate contributes to the happiness of our condition . . . we have reason to value highly the accident of birth in such a one as that of Virginia."[47]

[46] To Mary Jefferson, Philadelphia, May 8, 1791; to Mary Jefferson, Philadelphia, June 26, 1791; Mary Jefferson to Jefferson, Monticello, July 10, 1791 (Randolph, *Domestic Life*, 199–200, 204, 205).

[47] To Martha Jefferson Randolph, Lake Champlain, May 31, 1791 (Ford, *Writings*, V, 337–38).

At Bennington, Vermont, Jefferson's progress was halted by a law prohibiting travel on Sunday. He took advantage of the enforced delay by writing to his son-in-law and to President Washington. To the latter he said: "In my last letter from Philadelphia I mentioned that Mr. Madison and myself were about to take a trip up the North River as far as circumstances should permit. The levelness of the roads led us quite on to Lake George where taking boat we went through that and about 25. miles to Lake Champlain. Returning then to Saratoga, we concluded to cross over thro' Vermont to Connecticut river and go down that instead of the north river which we had already seen. And we are so far on the rout. On the course of the rout we have had opportunities of visiting Stillwater, Saratoga, Forts Wm. Henry & George, Ticonderoga, Crown point, & the scene of Genl. Starke's victory. . . . We encounter the Green mountains tomorrow, with cavalry in part disabled, so as to render our progress a little uncertain. I presume however I shall be in Philadelphia in a fortnight."[48] To the former he likewise recounted his visit to the places "which have been scenes of blood from a very early part of our history. We are more pleased however with the botanical objects which continually presented themselves." The statesmen felt no scruples, however, against shooting red squirrels when occasion offered.[49]

In the course of his letter to President Washington, Jefferson discussed an incident which had caused alarm along the Canadian frontier. An English vessel had stationed itself south of its usual post at Point au Fer to visit for customs purposes ships passing to and from Canada. This "exercise of power further within our jurisdiction" than was customary "became the subject of notice & clamor with our citizens." In turn, the establishment of a custom house at Albany, nearly opposite to Point au Fer gave concern to the British.

Jefferson also informed himself about Canadian internal

[48] To George Washington, Bennington, June 5, 1791 (*ibid.*, V, 339-40).
[49] To T. M. Randolph, Bennington, June 5, 1791 (*ibid.*, V, 340).

politics. "On enquiring into the dispositions in Canada on the subject of the projected form of government there, we learn, that they are divided into two parties; the English who desire something like an English constitution & so modelled as to oblige the French to chuse a certain proportion of English representatives, & the French who wish a continuance of the French laws, moderated by some engraftments from the English code. The judge of their common pleas heads the former party, & Chief Justice secretly guides the latter."[50] Doubtless it was these investigations which caused Mr. Beckwith to suppose that Jefferson's tour had the purpose of fomenting anti-English sentiment.

Jefferson's visit to Vermont gave him an opportunity to observe at first hand the manner in which sugar maple trees were there cultivated and utilized in the production of sugar. Since he was eager to promote that industry in Virginia, he wished to have seeds of the New England sugar maple tree sent to him at Monticello. On Long Island a few days later he visited the establishment of a Flushing Landing nurseryman, whose entire stock of sugar maples (as well as specimens of four other varieties of trees) Jefferson undertook to purchase. On returning to Philadelphia he ordered from a catalog twenty-eight additional items, including ten kinds of roses.[51]

Both travelers found their trip enjoyable and beneficial. Madison wrote to his father: "The tour I lately made with Mr. Jefferson . . . was a very agreeable one, and carried us thro an interesting country new to us both." Jefferson informed his daughter Martha: "I wrote to each of you once during my journey, from which I returned four days ago, having enjoyed through the whole of it very perfect health. I am in hopes the relaxation it gave me from business has freed me from the almost constant headache with which I had been persecuted during

---

[50] To George Washington, Bennington, June 5, 1791 (*ibid.*, V, 339–40).

[51] Joseph Fay to Jefferson, Bennington, August 9, 1791; to William Prince, Philadelphia, July 6, 1791; to James Brown, Philadelphia, November 28, 1791 (Mass. Hist. Soc., Jefferson Papers). See also *Garden Book*, 166–69.

Market Street, Philadelphia, in 1799
Jefferson's residence is in the right foreground
(From an engraving by Thomas Birch)

Stenton, the home of Dr. Logan, near Philadelphia

the whole winter and spring. Having been entirely free of it while travelling, proves it to have been occasioned by the drudgery of business." In later years the wedding trip of one of his grandchildren, Ellen Randolph, duplicated Jefferson's journey except that it terminated at Boston, her new home.[52]

To endure the virulence of partisan antipathy in Philadelphia was painful to Jefferson, and he longed for the tranquil felicity of country life at Monticello in the midst of family and friends. "Party animosities here," he wrote, "have raised a wall of separation between those who differ in political sentiments. They must love misery indeed who would rather at the sight of an honest man feel the torment of hatred and aversion than the benign spasms of benevolence and esteem."[53] According to one historian, "There is a tradition to this day in Philadelphia that so strongly ran the class feeling against Jefferson that Logan, Thomson, and Rittenhouse were his only social equals who did not exclude him from the hospitality of their homes."[54]

Early in 1793 he wished to resign as secretary of state, but was prevailed upon to postpone the date of his retirement. Meanwhile, he "permitted my house to be rented after the middle of March" and "sold such of my furniture as would not suit Monticello." He wrote his daughter Martha: "I have given up my house here, and taken a small one in the country, on the banks of the Schuylkill, to serve me while I stay. We are packing all our superfluous furniture, and shall be sending it by water to Richmond when the season becomes favorable. My books, too, except a very few, will be packed and go with the other things; so that I shall put it out of my own power to return to the city again to keep house, and it would be impossible to carry on business in the

---

[52] James Madison to James Madison, Sr., New York, July 2, 1791 (*Writings of James Madison*, VI, 53); to Martha Jefferson Randolph, Philadelphia, June 23, 1791 (Randolph, *Domestic Life*, 203); to Ellen W. Coolidge, Monticello, August 27, 1825 (*The Jefferson Papers, Collections of the Massachusetts Historical Society* [seventh series], I, 353).

[53] To Mrs. Church, October, 1792 (Ford, *Writings*, VI, 116).

[54] *Ibid.*

winter at a country residence. Though this points out an ultimate term of stay here, yet my mind is looking to a much shorter one."[55]

On the last day of March he informed Madison: "I . . . shall in the course of the week get on the banks of the Schuylkill."[56] On the previous day he had paid "portage of 12. loads of furniture to warehouse." On April 6 he paid "portage 7. loads of books to the country" and "8 loads of furniture to water side." On the eighth, his account book records "portage of looking glasses to water side," and on the ninth, "portage 2 loads of books to country" and "furniture to waterside."

On April 11 he addressed a parting word to the landlord of his Market Street dwelling: "According to an arrangement with Mr Wilson, who was to succeed me in your house, I have continued in it till now. We have at length got every thing out of it except an article which will be taken away to-day or tomorrow. The coachman's wife also who happened to lay in on Sunday last, has Mr Wilson's permission to remain till she can safely remove. I have had every repair made which according to the information of the workmen ought to be made by the tenant, & have employed, where I could do it, the very workmen who built the house, taking it for granted that they would make a point of restoring things to the best state. They have all finished except the plaisterer who had some nail holes to fill in two rooms this morning. I shall be obliged to you to visit the house, and drop me a line if you think I have put it into a proper state, in which case I shall immediately give you an order for the rent. If the note is lodged at my office I shall get it at whatever hour I may happen to come to town."[57]

Jefferson's architectural impulse was insatiable. He even

[55] To Martha Jefferson Randolph, Philadelphia, January 26, 1793; March 10, 1793 (Randolph, *Domestic Life*, 215, 220).

[56] To Madison, Philadelphia, March 31, 1793 (Ford, *Writings*, VI, 210).

[57] To Mr. Leiper, Philadelphia, April 11, 1793 (Library of Congress, Jefferson Papers). Jefferson's lease expired on March 9.—To Leiper, Philadelphia, December 9, 1792 (Mass. Hist. Soc., Jefferson Papers).

"proposed to add a projecting salon à la français" to the simple three-room cottage where he spent the summer of 1793. That rustic dwelling stood on the banks of the Schuylkill, near Gray's Ferry. The site of the house is located on the east side of the river at a point between Thirty-sixth and Thirty-seventh Streets and Reed and Dickinson Streets. It was opposite Dr. Say's residence. The property afterwards was owned by General Harmer. When Jefferson occupied it he paid "Moses Coxe rent 100 D." on January 2, 1794.[58]

Jefferson's younger daughter, Mary, was with him. To her sister Martha he wrote: "I will endeavor to prevail on her to write, & perhaps may succeed, as the day is too wet to admit her saunters on the banks of the Schuylkill, where she passes every Sunday with me. We are in sight of Bartram's & Gray's gardens, but have the river between them & us." A little later he said: "She passes two or three days in the week with me under the trees, for I never go into the house but at the hour of bed. I never before knew the full value of trees. My house is entirely embosomed in high plane-trees, with good grass below; and under them I breakfast, dine, write, read, and receive my company. What would I not give that the trees planted nearest round the house at Monticello were full-grown."[59]

One of Jefferson's callers under the plane trees was President Washington, who urged him to remain as secretary of state. But in anticipation of his final visit to Philadelphia in that capacity, Jefferson communicated his plans to Madison: "I break up my house the last of Septemb. Shall leave my carriage & horses in Virginia & return in the stage, not to have the embarrassment

---

[58] To Mr. Eppes, Philadelphia, April 3, 1793 (*ibid.*); Kimball, *Thomas Jefferson, Architect*, 150; Jackson, *Philadelphia*, III, 788.

[59] To Martha Jefferson Randolph, Philadelphia, May 26, 1793 (Ford, *Writings*, VI, 267); to Martha Jefferson Randolph, July 7, 1793 (Randolph, *Domestic Life*, 222). Jefferson later visited Monticello "for the purpose of planting trees, in order that they may be growing during my absence."—To John W. Eppes, Washington, February 21, 1803 (Huntington Library, MS Collections).

of ploughing them through the mud in January. I shall take private lodgings on my return."[60]

An epidemic of yellow fever raged in Philadelphia that summer. Among the sufferers were Hamilton and his wife. Jefferson would have left early in September, but for the fact that he had announced that he was not going until the beginning of October and did not wish "to exhibit the appearance of panic. Besides that I think there might serious ills proceed from there not being a single member of the administration in place." But when he found, on going to town, that he "had but one clerk left, and the business could not be carried on," he determined to set out for Virginia as soon as he could dispatch his accumulated correspondence. He decided also "to remove my office into the country so as to have no further occasion to go into the town."[61]

He left for Monticello on September 17, informing his landlord on that day: "I have had my furniture packed, so as to be out of the way if you would chuse to occupy the house in order to secure yourself against the prevailing infection. I have been obliged to place my boxes of furniture in the passage below and above stairs, and to leave 4. or 5. trunks piled on one another in one of the rooms. I would have put them in the room below ground but on account of the damp . . . I have also left a pipe of wine in the small cellar. I am sorry that these things will be somewhat in the way, there are between 2. & 3. dozen chairs not packed, which may be useful to the family, & save the trouble of bringing chairs. The same circumstance of infection has put it out of my power to have workmen from town to mend 5. or 6. broken panes of glass, fill up screw holes made by the clock, cover with tin a small hole made in the trap door for the bell wire of the clock, & plain out a scratch in the passage floor made in moving a heavy box of books. These are all the repairs I know of

<hr>

[60] To Madison, August 25, 1793 (Ford, *Writings*, VI, 398).

[61] To Madison, September 8, 1793 (*ibid.*, VI, 419); to George Washington, Schuylkill, September 15, 1793 (*ibid.*, VI, 428); to Martha Jefferson Randolph, Schuylkill, September 8, 1793 (Morgan Library, MS Collections).

which should have been made by me, & if you will be so good as to have them done & make a bill, I will pay them with my rent on my return. I leave a servant to finish packing my furniture so soon as I can get 2. or 3. more boxes from town. I shall be happy if my early departure shall be an accommodation to you, as it is certainly a moment when refuge in the country is desirable."[62]

In the winter of 1793 Congress met in Germantown, because of the plague in Philadelphia. After an expensive journey by stage, Jefferson procured lodgings at the King of Prussia Tavern, whose landlord was named Bockius. The site is now 5516–18–20 Germantown Avenue. In the middle of November Jefferson moved to a house belonging to Matthew Clarkson, the mayor of Philadelphia. This dwelling stood at 5275–7 Germantown Avenue. As the epidemic subsided, Jefferson returned to the city on November 30. He informed Martha: "This place being entirely clear of all infection, the members of Congress are coming into it without fear. The President moved in yesterday, as did I also. I have got comfortably lodged at the corner of 7th. & Market street." He reported to a representative from Maryland that uncontaminated quarters could be had at "Francis's hotel near the Indian Queen."[63]

Jefferson's resignation as secretary of state took effect at the end of the year. Laying aside for a time the "cumbrous trappings of rank," he left Philadelphia as a private citizen on January 5, 1794.

[62] To ———, Schuylkill, September 17, 1793 (Mass. Hist. Soc., Jefferson Papers).

[63] To Martha Jefferson Randolph, Philadelphia, December 1, 1793 (Morgan Library, MS Collections); to John F. Mercer, December 7, 1793 (Jenkins, *Washington*, 233).

CHAPTER IX

Turmoil, Bustle, and Splendor

"THE motion of my blood no longer keeps time with the tumult of the world," Jefferson had told friends who exhorted him to continue in public life; yet it was only three years later that "the pomp, the turmoil, the bustle, and splendor of office" again claimed him.[1] He returned to Philadelphia in 1797 as vice president. His election to that office he viewed with satisfaction, because "it will give me philosophical evenings in the winter, and rural days in summer."[2] He was thinking, perhaps, of his plane trees on the banks of the Schuylkill and of the hemlocks at Stenton. He did not find his duties exacting. His political opponents were in power, and did not welcome his counsel. All that was required of him was to preside over debates in the Senate. This task he performed with impartiality and distinction. "Jefferson's Manual," the compilation of parliamentary practice which he prepared in that connection, is still recognized as authoritative by Congress. In the fall of 1797 his younger daughter Mary was married, and his loneliness in the midst of partisan enmity was intensified. It was quite natural that Jefferson maintained no independent establishment at Philadelphia while he was vice president,[3] but stayed at the hotel of John Francis, and spent as much time as he could in Virginia.

[1] To Madison, June 9, 1793 (Randolph, *Domestic Life*, 218); *ibid.*, 326.

[2] To Dr. Rush, Monticello, January 22, 1797 (Lipscomb and Bergh, *Writings*, IX, 374).

[3] At this time Jefferson also disposed of his carriage. "I am happy to have it in my power to make you & Maria [a] present of my chariot, which is in possession of Quarrier at Richmond. It has a harness. I believe it is the best piece of work that

Jefferson's choice of lodgings was made with an eye to his comfort and convenience. Declining an invitation to live elsewhere, he wrote to John Barnes: "I thank you sincerely for the very kind offer of accommodations at your house. But I could not consent to displace you so inconveniently, from the apartments you occupy yourself. Besides which, having hitherto lodged with Mr. Francis, and with himself and Mrs. Francis being very obliging, it would be painful to leave them. I am there also nearer to the Statehouse & Philosophical halls."[4]

Francis's hotel was located at 13 South Fourth Street. The proprietor, an elderly Frenchman, in 1796 told Thomas Twining, a young Englishman who sought lodging there, that it was "not a public tavern, but a private house for the reception of members of Congress." The proprietor's wife, however, a tall, young, handsome American woman, reminded him that there was a small spare room available until the next day, when there would be a vacant room next to that of President Adams. The Indian Queen, which was also one of Jefferson's stopping places in Philadelphia, was kept by James Thompson, at 15 South Fourth Street, on the west side of the street, north of Chestnut. "Dunwoody's Tavern" was another which Jefferson patronized.[5]

During the time Jefferson was in Philadelphia as vice president, the rancor engendered by party strife reached its height. "Men who have been intimate all their lives, cross the streets to

---

has crossed the ocean. I find I shall have no occasion for such after this year. It may be useful to you & Maria. It will require some caution to get it clear of a considerable expense of storage. Quarrier was to have a certain percent on it if sold, in lieu of storage. You must therefore tell him you have given me 400. dollars for it and that he is to draw on me for the per cent agreed on. I forget what it was. I inclose you a letter to him which makes the storage a matter of account merely between him and me. The wheels of the carriage were originally heavy & bad. I am in hopes they will hold out to carry you to Monticello, where I will have a set of good ones made for you."—To J. W. Eppes, Philadelphia, February 18, 1798 (Huntington Library, MS Collections). See also to Mary Jefferson Eppes, Philadelphia, April 1, 1798 (*ibid.*).

[4] To John Barnes, Monticello, November 23, 1798 (*ibid.*).

[5] This establishment, known as the Spread Eagle Inn, was then kept by John Dunwoody at 715 Market Street [between Seventh and Eighth Streets] (Jackson, *Market Street*, 127).

avoid meeting, and turn their heads another way, lest they should be obliged to touch their hats," Jefferson declared. "I never was more home-sick or heart-sick. The life of this place is peculiarly hateful to me, and nothing but a sense of duty and respect to the public could keep me here a moment."[6] He found refuge in intellectual diversions. "Abandoning the rich, and declining their dinners and parties, and associating entirely with the class of science, of whom there is a valuable society here," he frequented the rooms of the Philosophical Society, of which he had been chosen as president on January 6, 1797, to succeed Rittenhouse. In accepting the honor, he professed as his sole qualification for the post "an ardent desire to see knowledge so disseminated through the mass of mankind that it may at last reach the extremes of society, beggars and kings." He held this office until 1814, although after his removal from Philadelphia he could not concern himself so actively with the work of the society.[7]

Likewise "in the evenings of 1798–99" Jefferson enjoyed "delightful conversations" with Dr. Benjamin Rush, in which "the Christian religion was sometimes our topic" and which "served as an anodyne to the afflictions of the crisis through which our country was then laboring." To the end of his life Jefferson remembered those days of torment, and asserted: "No person who was not a witness of the scenes of that gloomy period, can form any idea of the afflicting persecutions and personal indignities we had to brook. They saved our country however."[8]

Jefferson's political antagonists in the Federalist party were intent on bringing about war between the United States and

[6] To Edward Rutledge, Philadelphia, June 24, 1797 (Lipscomb and Bergh, *Writings*, IX, 411); to John W. Eppes, Philadelphia, May 6, 1798 (Randall, *Life of Jefferson*, II, 385).

[7] To Martha Jefferson Randolph, February 11, 1800 (*ibid.*, II, 535); Nicholas Biddle, *Eulogium on Thomas Jefferson*, 29. See also Gilbert Chinard, "Jefferson and the American Philosophical Society," *Proceedings* of the American Philosophical Society, Vol. LXXXVII, No. 3 (July, 1943), 263–76; and to Robert Patterson, Monticello, November 23, 1814 (Lipscomb and Bergh, *Writings*, XIV, 210–11).

[8] To Dr. Benjamin Rush, Monticello, April 21, 1803 (*ibid.*, X, 379); Ford, *Writings*, X, 369.

France. Much to their dismay, President Adams, boldly disregarding their desires, decided, notwithstanding the "XYZ" affair, to appoint an envoy to negotiate the settlement of pending differences with the French government, provided assurance was given by France that the American mission would be properly received.

While the war fever was raging, Dr. Logan, Jefferson's Quaker friend at Stenton, quietly left on June 17, 1798, for Europe. He carried a letter of recommendation from Jefferson.[9] His purpose in going abroad was to ascertain in France whether the attitude of that government was really such as to necessitate war with America.

The Federalists were furious. At the instigation of Timothy Pickering (whose own intercourse with the British minister in 1808 violated the law he sponsored), they passed in Congress a rather fruitless statute, since known as the "Logan Act" of January 30, 1799, making punishable the conduct of "every citizen of the United States . . . who, without the permission or authority of the Government, directly or indirectly commences or carries on any verbal or written correspondence or intercourse with any foreign government, or any officer or agent thereof, with an intent to influence the measures or conduct of any foreign government, or of any officer or agent thereof, in relation to any disputes or controversies with the United States, or to defeat the measures of the Government of the United States."[10] This law did not prevent a similar visit to England by the undaunted Quaker physician before the War of 1812.

[9] This letter of June 4, 1798, was written by Jefferson as a private citizen. The French translation, unlike the original, adds his official title "vice-President des Etats Unis de l'Amerique." In a similar certificate dated June 11, 1798, Chief Justice Thomas McKean of Pennsylvania included his title (Hist. Soc. of Pa., Logan Papers, Vol. V).

[10] Adams, *History of U. S. during Administration of Jefferson*, IV, 236. This law, curiously enough, was invoked twice during Jefferson's administration, but without effect.—Jefferson to Attorney General Levi Lincoln, June 24, 1804 (Library of Congress, Jefferson Papers); Lincoln to Jefferson, June 25, 1804 (*ibid.*); Adams, *History of U. S. during Administration of Jefferson*, II, 259. Cf. Charles Warren, *Odd Byways in American History*, 172–75.

While Dr. Logan was in France, his wife was treated as if her husband, in seeking to avert war, had been a traitor to his country. A friendly Federalist warned her that the government planned to search the house for treasonable papers, and advised her to destroy them. She replied that she "had nothing to secrete," and that the Federalist sleuths would accomplish nothing by their efforts except to insult an honorable man.[11]

In the Federalist newspaper, *Porcupine's Gazette,* for July 21, 1798, an item appeared seeking to implicate Jefferson in the treasonable conspiracy and concealment of the incriminating documents: "It is said, that Jefferson, went to his friend Doctor Logan's farm, and spent three days there, soon after the Doctor's departure for France. Quere: What did he do there? Was it to arrange the Doctor's *valuable manuscripts?*"

Mrs. Logan's account of Jefferson's visit reveals the extent of Federalist machinations: "Soon after the departure of my husband I received a visit from Thomas Jefferson, then Vice-President of the United States, who told me that he had been greatly concerned for me on account of the obloquy and abuse which had been so freely bestowed on Dr. Logan's character, and advised me to evince my thorough consciousness of his innocence and honour by showing myself in Philadelphia as one not afraid or ashamed to meet the public eye. He said he could not have believed it possible that the utmost bitterness of party spirit could have invented, or have given credit to, such unfounded calumnies. That he was himself dogged and watched in the most extraordinary manner; and he apologized for the lateness of his visit (for we were at tea when he arrived) by saying that, in order to elude the curiosity of his spies, he had not taken the direct road, but had come by a circuitous route by the Falls of Schuylkill along one of the lanes to Germantown, and passing by the house and gate, had come in by the entrance on the York Road (an excess of caution which seemed to me to be quite unavailing, for his Federal inspectors did not impute an iota less of evil designs to him, for

[11] *Memoir of Dr. George Logan,* 59.

all his care to avoid suspicion). He spoke of the temper of the times and of the late acts of the Legislature with a sort of despair, but said he thought even the shadow of our liberties must be gone if they attempted anything that would injure me. This was the only time I saw him during my husband's absence."[12]

Jefferson and his friends believed that the government intended to prosecute him under the ill-famed Sedition Act as a result of the Logan affair. He felt certain that his correspondence was regularly read by the Federalist postmasters to discover seditious language.[13]

But in spite of all the efforts of his enemies, Jefferson's party triumphed at the polls in 1800. That same year the national capital was moved to Washington. Jefferson arrived there on November 27. On March 4, 1801, he became the third president of the United States. Of the "revolution" in American politics which his victory signified, he wrote to a friend who had shared his labors in establishing the Republic: "The storm through which we have passed, has been tremendous indeed. The tough sides of our Argosie have been thoroughly tried. Her strength has stood the waves into which she was steered, with a view to sink her. We shall put her on her republican tack, & she will now show by the beauty of her motion the skill of her builders."[14]

When Jefferson arrived in Washington, he took lodgings at the boarding house of Conrad & McMun, on New Jersey Avenue, where the New House Office Building now stands. This establishment was one of the best in the town. It was situated "on the south side of Capitol hill and commanded an extensive and beautiful view. It was on the top of the hill, the precipitous sides of which were covered with grass, shrubs and trees in their wild uncultivated state. Between the foot of the hill and the broad

---

[12] *Ibid.*, 75–76.

[13] Randall, *Life of Jefferson*, II, 413. Cf. Zechariah Chafee, Jr., *Free Speech in the United States*, 513.

[14] To John Dickinson, Washington, March 6, 1801 (Ford, *Writings*, VIII, 7).

Potomac extended a wide plain through which the Tiber wound its way."[15]

Payments of $218.90, $259.50, and $250.67 for the three months he spent there before he was inaugurated as president and moved into the "President's House" show that the cost of living was high in Washington then as now, for Jefferson's accommodations were nothing exceptional. "He had a separate drawing-room for the reception of his visitors; in all other respects he lived on a perfect equality with his fellow boarders.... Far from taking precedence over other members of Congress, he always placed himself at the lowest end of the table. Mrs. Brown, the wife of the senator from Kentucky, suggested that a seat should be offered him at the upper end, near the fire, if not on account of his rank as vice-President, at least as the oldest man in the company. But the idea was rejected by his democratic friends, and he occupied during the whole winter the lowest and coldest seat at a long table at which a company of more than thirty sat down. Even on the day of his inauguration when he entered the dining-room no other seat was offered him by the gentlemen. Mrs. Brown from an impulse which she said she could not resist, offered him her seat, but he smilingly declined it, and took his usual place at the bottom of the table. She said she felt indignant and for a moment almost hated the leveling principle of democracy, though her husband was a zealous democrat."[16]

As chief executive, Jefferson again had a household establish-

[15] Margaret Bayard Smith, *The First Forty Years of Washington Society*, 9, 10. To a prominent political figure Jefferson wrote: "If you can be contented with a bad tavern dinner, I should be happy if you would come and dine with our mess tomorrow, if convenient to you, or the next day, and if you could come half an hour before dinner, I would be alone that we might have some conversation; say at half after two."—To Charles Pinckney, Washington, March 6, 1801 (Ford, *Writings*, VIII, 6–7).

[16] Smith, *Washington Society*, 12. Perhaps because existing establishments did not sufficiently cater to Jefferson's partisans, a proposal was made during his first administration to open "a House of entertainment on Capitol Hill, for the reception and deliberation of the friends of" the administration. This was to be called the National Coffee House & Hotel, and was "to be in readiness on the day Congress shall convene."—Richard Willson to Jefferson, Washington, August 22, 1803 (Mo. Hist. Soc., Bixby Collection).

ment of his own besides the one at Monticello.[17] "Thomas Jefferson was the first President of the United States actually to live in the White House. The Adamses, to be sure, had moved in, a few months before the close of their administration, and Mrs. Adams had written her famous description of what a President's mansion should not be; but Jefferson . . . may really be said to have been its first occupant. It was he who selected those elaborate and forgotten furnishings, of which hitherto so little has been known, and it was he who transformed an unfinished, barnlike structure into the most sumptuous house of the time."[18]

Here his daughters visited him (their husbands both being members of Congress), and he found greater happiness in his public life than during previous years. His official duties were much more onerous, however, and his excursions to Monticello briefer, though more frequent, than before.[19] Within less than a month after his inauguration, Jefferson was endeavoring to find the best road from Washington to Monticello, and planning the best route for the construction of future highways.[20] In Wash-

[17] Here again Jefferson had a French *maître d'hôtel.*—To M. La Tombe, Washington, February 22, 1801; March 5, 1801; March 19, 1801; July 29, 1801 (Mass. Hist. Soc., Jefferson Papers). Cf. to d'Yrujo, Washington, March 19, 1801 (Mo. Hist. Soc., Bixby Collection). He urged Rapin to impress upon his successor LeMaire "that while I wish to have every thing good in it's kind, I am a great enemy to waste and useless extravagance, and see them with real pain."—To Rapin, Monticello, August 14, 1801 (Mass. Hist. Soc., Jefferson Papers). He later advised LeMaire not to hire a servant who stood too much on etiquette. "I like servants who do every thing they are wanted to do."—To LeMaire, Monticello, May 14, 1802 (*ibid.*).

[18] Marie Kimball, "The Original Furnishings of the White House," *Antiques,* Vol. XV, No. 6 (June, 1929), 481. Among the imported articles of elegance purchased for the White House during Jefferson's administration is the large oval gilt-leaf mirror with an eagle at the top, now in the possession of Mr. J. F. Biggs at "Pratt's Castle" in Richmond.

[19] While head of the Department of State, he spent at home a total of 197 days; as vice president, 876; as president, 831.—Wilstach, *Jefferson and Monticello,* 79, 89–92.

[20] He set out on horseback resolving to find the shortest and most level route between Washington and Slate Run Church. To Colo. Little, Washington, March 31, 1801 (Mo. Hist. Soc., Bixby Collection). His investigations yielded satisfactory results. "Thos. Jefferson presents his compliments to Mr. Milledge and encloses him an itinerary from hence to Mr. Randolph's with a strong recommendation to him, to let no man's persuasion induce him to vary the route in any part. Mr. J. after

ington he kept "one Chariot, two Phaetons and one Gig." For a license permitting him to use those vehicles, the city collected a tax of $32 annually.[21]

Rather than stop over at places where only disagreeable quarters were available, Jefferson would occasionally travel all day through the rain. Sometimes in wet weather his "water proof coat was a perfect protection."[22] Likewise, thanks to his "palisse," while traveling in winter, he "felt no more sensation of cold than if" he "had been in a warm bed."[23]

The hardship was not always negligible. Writing from Washington in 1802 to his daughter Martha, he recounted: "I arrived here last night after the most fatiguing journey I have experienced for a great many years. I got well enough to Orange C.H. the first day. The 2d. there was a constant heavy drizzle through the whole day, sufficient to soak my outer great coat twice, and the roads very dirty and in places deep. The third the roads became as deep as at any season, & as laborious to the horse. Castor got into ill temper and refused to draw, and we had a vast deal of trouble and fatigue with him and obliged to give him up at last. I was from day light to sunset getting from Fauquier C.H. to Colo. Wren's, where I left John with the carriage, mounted my horse and arrived here at 9. aclock in the night more

---

near 30 years travelling and trying every road, having by little and little learned this particular route, which he believes no other person is acquainted with, and having found it, from his own experience, to be the shortest that exists and by far the best."—To John Milledge, Washington, April 30, 1802 (*Virginia Magazine of History and Biography*, Vol. XLVIII, No. 2 [April, 1940], 97).

[21] License dated May 7, 1805; tax bill dated February 20, 1806; tax receipt dated February 28, 1806 (Mo. Hist. Soc., Bixby Collection).

[22] To Martha Jefferson Randolph, Washington, June 3, 1802 (Morgan Library, MS Collections). See also to Martha Jefferson Randolph, Washington, October 7, 1804; October 13, 1805 (*ibid.*).

[23] To Martha Jefferson Randolph, Philadelphia, December 27, 1798 (*ibid.*). Writing to his son-in-law several years later, Jefferson said: "Patsy thinks her cough better since the journey. To me it appears very bad. When the carriage comes for them, a spare cloak or two should come as far as Mr. Strode's. They will have mine to that place. I hoped to send them by the stage, and without them they would have suffered, as they moved early and the mornings were cold."—To T. M. Randolph, Washington, November 25, 1802 (Huntington Library, MS Collections).

sore & fatigued than I ever remember to have been with a journey. With the circuitous route I was obliged to take it made about 55. miles, of as deep & laborious road as could be travelled. A night's sleep has a little rested me, but I am yet extremely the worse for my labour. I hope a day or two more will entirely relieve me. Certainly I shall never again so far forget my age as to undertake such another day of fatigue."[24]

Five years later he again met with misfortune: "My journey to this place was not as free from accident as usual. I was near losing Castor in the Rapidan, by his lying down in the river, where . . . he was nearly drowned before the servants, jumping into the water, could lift his head out and cut him loose from the carriage. This was followed by the loss of my travelling money, I imagine as happened on the sopha in the morning I left Monticello, when it was given me again by one of the children. Two days after my arrival here I was taken with the influenza."[25]

On March 11, 1809, when his successor, James Madison, had been inaugurated as president, Jefferson left Washington for the last time. After a fatiguing journey, in the course of which he encountered a disagreeable snow storm lasting eight hours and was obliged to spend the last three days on horseback, he arrived at Monticello on the fifteenth. Thereafter, he never made any lengthy trips away from home. However, it was his custom to make frequent visits to Poplar Forest, his plantation in Bedford County, on the confines of Campbell County, near Lynchburg. Here he built a simply furnished home which served as a rustic retreat where he could enjoy the society of his family and escape the throng of visitors at Monticello.[26]

[24] To Martha Jefferson Randolph, Washington, May 14, 1802 (Morgan Library, MS Collections).

[25] To Martha Jefferson Randolph, Washington, October 12, 1807 (*ibid.*). On another occasion Jefferson caught a cold while traveling.—To Martha Jefferson Randolph, Philadelphia, April 5, 1798 (Huntington Library, MS Collections). A few months later he wrote: "I was taken on my journey with sore eyes, and have continued so ill with them, & still am, as to be unable to do business almost entirely. Nevertheless my anxiety for an account of payments I have to make in Philadelphia obliges me to address you."—To John Barnes, Monticello, July 27, 1798 (*ibid.*).

[26] Randall, *Life of Jefferson*, I, 352, 363; III, 341–45; Paul Wilstach, "Thomas

His father-in-law had left an old-fashioned house near the road, but Jefferson preferred to live in a more secluded spot near the center of the estate at Poplar Forest. He constructed there a remarkable little octagonal dwelling. It had a central chamber surrounded by octagonal rooms except on the north side, where an entrance hall divided the octagonal space into two hexagonal rooms.

Describing this "most excellent house," which "could not be valued at less than 10,000 D.," and which was located "in a part of the country which I really consider as the most desirable in this state, for soil, climate and convenience to market," Jefferson said: "It is an Octagon of 50. f. diameter, of brick, well built, will be plaistered this fall, when nothing will be wanting to finish it compleatly but the cornices and some of the doors. When finished, it will be the best dwelling house in the state, except that of Monticello; perhaps preferable to that, as more proportioned to the faculties of a private citizen."[27]

Jefferson's Secret Home," *Country Life*, Vol. LIII, No. 6 (April, 1928), 41–43. A list dated February 11, 1815, of taxable property in Bedford and Campbell counties shows that Jefferson had there 3,790 acres of land, a dwelling house valued at over $500, and less than $200 worth of furniture other than beds and bedding. There were forty-six slaves twelve years and up; twelve slaves under nine years; twelve horses and colts; thirty-nine cattle; four book-cases with mahogany sashes; three parts of dining tables, mahogany; and four Pembroke tables, say tea tables, mahogany (Mo. Hist. Soc. Bixby Collection). A few years earlier, Jefferson had thus described his situation at Poplar Forest: "I write to you from a place ninety miles from Monticello, near the New London of this State, which I visit three or four times a year, and stay from a fortnight to a month at a time. I have fixed myself comfortably, keep some books here, bring others occasionally, am in the solitude of a hermit, and quite at leisure to attend to my absent friends."—To Benjamin Rush, Poplar Forest, August 17, 1811 (Lipscomb and Bergh, *Writings*, XIII, 74). Ten years later he wrote: "I was just returned from Poplar Forest, which I have visited four times this year. I have an excellent house there, inferior only to Monticello, am comfortably fixed and attended, have a few good neighbors, and pass my time there in a tranquillity and retirement much adapted to my age and indolence."—To Wm. Short, Monticello, November 24, 1821 (*ibid.*, XVIII, 314). In 1781 Jefferson had sought refuge at Poplar Forest during the British invasion of Virginia.—To ———, Monticello, May 15, 1826 (*ibid.*, XVI, 180). Apparently his first visit there was in 1773.—*Garden Book*, 42.

27 To John Wayles Eppes, Monticello, July 16, 1814; September 18, 1812 (Norma B. Cuthbert, "Poplar Forest: Jefferson's Legacy to His Grandson," *The Huntington Library Quarterly*, Vol. VI, No. 3 [May, 1943], 348, 344).

Jefferson's house on the Schuylkill
(From a water color by David J. Kennedy)

*Poplar Forest, Jefferson's octagonal house on his
plantation in Bedford County, Virginia
(From a painting by Helen M. McGehee)*

Jefferson seems to have visited Poplar Forest as early as 1773. While confined there in 1781 by injuries received in falling from a horse, he worked at the task of writing his *Notes on Virginia*. Seldom did he mention Poplar Forest, it seems, except to intimate friends or neighbors from that place; secrecy and silence served to keep intruders from disturbing his repose. The only conspicuous guest known to have been entertained by Jefferson at Poplar Forest was General Andrew Jackson.

While writing to Monticello for warmer clothing during the winter of 1815, Jefferson recorded that: "I am this moment interrupted by a croud of curious people come to see the house." Later he added a postscript to his letter: "I was most agreeably surprised to find that the party whom I thought to be merely curious visitants were General Jackson and his suite, who passing on to Lynchburg did me the favor to call." That military hero was on his way to Washington after his triumph at the battle of New Orleans, receiving everywhere the nation's plaudits. At Lynchburg a banquet was held in his honor, at which Jefferson was present and proposed a toast.[28]

Though defeated by General Jackson at New Orleans, England had succeeded in bringing about the overthrow of Napoleon. The Corsican was banished to Saint Helena, and not permitted to seek refuge in the United States. But when Jefferson arrived to superintend operations at Poplar Forest soon after the Battle of Waterloo, the populace believed that he was making preparations to receive the exiled French Emperor. "The story of the neighborhood immediately was that I had brought a croud of workmen to get ready my house in a hurry for Bonaparte. Were there such people only as the believers in this, patriotism would be a ridiculous passion," Jefferson exclaimed.[29]

[28] To Martha Jefferson Randolph, Poplar Forest, November 4, 1815 (Morgan Library, MS Collections); James Parton, *Life of Andrew Jackson*, II, 334. Cf. Marquis James, *Andrew Jackson: Portrait of a President*, 415; and John S. Bassett, *The Life of Andrew Jackson*, I, 329.

[29] To Martha Jefferson Randolph, Poplar Forest, August 31, 1815 (Morgan Library, MS Collections).

That same summer he planned to travel on horseback to Natural Bridge, after attending Buckingham court, where he was to be a witness in a will case.[30] The distance from Poplar Forest to Natural Bridge, by Petit's Gap, was twenty-nine miles. It was probably at this time that Francis Walker Gilmer visited that locality, in the course of a scientific excursion with Jefferson and another scholarly friend, the Abbé Joseph Francisco Correa de Serra, a Portuguese diplomat.[31] Gilmer's observations on the geological formation of the Natural Bridge of Virginia were communicated to the American Philosophical Society not long afterwards. The trip was made, according to reports, in a vehicle much resembling a mill hopper, and the travelers, in addition to measuring the elevation of the Peaks of Otter, explored the countryside, making geological and botanical investigations. "At home in every science, botany is their favorite," Jefferson wrote regarding his companions, who proceeded on a tour farther south after having accompanied him to Poplar Forest.[32]

Two years later Jefferson spent several days "engaged from sunrise to sunset with a surveyor" in making the rounds of his property lines at Poplar Forest. Such a survey had never before been made; and Jefferson found that as a consequence of his inattentiveness a neighbor by the name of Cobbs "has cleared one half of his field on my land, and been cultivating it for 20. years chiefly in corn." The trespassing farmer had also cut down the

[30] To Martha Jefferson Randolph, Poplar Forest, August 31, 1815; Montpelier, August 13, 1815 (*ibid.*). Jefferson remarked that: "I do not know that my evidence can be of any importance; but if it be thought so, I could not attend without being subpoenaed; because the testimony of a person volunteering in a case is not received with the same confidence as when he attends in obedience to a summons."— To Lilburne Jefferson, Monticello, August 19, 1815 (Mo. Hist. Soc., Bixby Collection). Regarding the litigation and Jefferson's deposition dated September 15, 1815, see Bernard Mayo, *Thomas Jefferson and His Unknown Brother Randolph*, 10.

[31] Richard B. Davis, *Francis Walker Gilmer: Life and Learning in Jefferson's Virginia*, 275.

[32] *Ibid.*, 89. Of Correa, Jefferson said on another occasion: "He is perhaps the most learned man in the world, not merely in books, but in men & things. And a more amiable & interesting one I have never seen."—Jefferson to Samuel Brown, Monticello, April 28, 1814 (*Garden Book*, 533).

trees which served as landmarks, so that it was almost impossible to determine the true location of the line.[33]

The following year Jefferson went to Rockfish Gap, where he presided over a meeting of commissioners appointed to determine, and report to the legislature, the most suitable location for the University of Virginia. He rode to Rockfish Gap from Monticello on horseback, a distance of twenty-eight miles. Because of infirmity, he thought it well not to make the entire journey in a single day.[34] There had been talk of postponing the meeting because of inadequate accommodations, but Jefferson had opposed adjournment "as long as we can get bread and water and a floor to lie on at the Gap."[35] He was pleased with the arrangements made for the comfort of the commissioners, as well as with the results of their deliberations. The site favored by Jefferson, at Central College near Charlottesville and Monticello, was approved by a preponderant majority. He wrote to his daughter: "All our members, except 3 who came not at all arrived on Saturday morning so that we got to work by 10. aclock, and finished yesterday evening. We are detained till this morning for fair copies of our report. Staunton had 2. votes, Lexington 3. the Central college 16. I have never seen business done with so much order, & harmony, nor an abler nor pleasanter society. We have been well served, too. Excellent rooms, every one his bed, a table altho' not elegant, yet plentiful and satisfactory."[36]

From Rockfish Gap Jefferson accompanied Judge Archibald Stuart to Staunton, and from that place proceeded on horseback

[33] To Martha Jefferson Randolph, Poplar Forest, November 29, 1817 (Morgan Library, MS Collections). Jefferson had previously contemplated selling part of his Poplar Forest lands because of financial exigencies.—To Charles Clay, Monticello, December 15, 1809 (copy of the letter in the possession of Mr. George F. Scheer, Jr., of Richmond, Va., furnished to the author, August 20, 1940.)

[34] Three years later Jefferson wrote that on a visit to Natural Bridge he was "six days successively on horseback from breakfast to sunset."—To Wm. Short, Monticello, November 24, 1821 (Lipscomb and Bergh, *Writings*, XVIII, 315).

[35] Honeywell, *Jefferson*, 73.

[36] To Martha Jefferson Randolph, Rockfish Gap, August 4, 1818 (Morgan Library, MS Collections).

to Warm Springs, a health resort. He found "the table very well kept by Mr. Fry, and every thing else well. Venison is plenty, and vegetables not wanting." However, he complained that there was "but little gay company here at this time, and I rather expect to pass a dull time."[37]

His discontent did not diminish as the days passed. "Having been now here a week & continued to bathe 3 times a day, a quarter of an hour at a time, I continue well, as I was when I came. Having no symptom to judge by at what time I may presume the seeds of my rheumatism eradicated, and desirous to prevent the necessity of ever coming here a 2d time, I believe I shall yeild to the general advice of a three weeks course. But so dull a place, and so distressing an ennui I never before knew. I have visited the rock on the high mountain, the hot springs, and yesterday the falling spring, 15. miles from here; so that there remains no other excursion to enliven the two remaining weeks. . . . Yesterday we were reduced to a single lady (Miss Allstone) but there came in 4. more in the evening. . . . Yesterday too Genl. Breckenridge left us, who had accompanied me from the Rockfish gap, and who has been my guide and guardian and fellow-lodger in the same cabin. We were constantly together, and I feel his loss most sensibly. . . . I have contracted more intimacy with Colo. Allstone than with any other now remaining. He is the father of Mr. Allstone who married Burr's daughter."[38] A week later Jefferson remarked "a greater proportion of ladies than formerly; but all invalids, and perfectly recluse in their cabins. . . . We had been many days without venison till the day before yesterday, in the course of which 8. deer were brought in. . . . I do not know what may be the effect of this course of bathing on my constitution." On the whole Jefferson's stay at Warm Springs was probably more detrimental to his health than beneficial.[39]

[37] To Martha Jefferson Randolph, Warm Springs, August 7, 1818 (*ibid.*).
[38] To Martha Jefferson Randolph, Warm Springs, August 14, 1818 (*ibid.*).
[39] To Martha Jefferson Randolph, Warm Springs, August 21, 1818 (*ibid.*);

Jefferson greatly enjoyed his visits to Poplar Forest. One of his granddaughters, who generally accompanied him, thus describes the outing: "Our journeys to and from Bedford, were almost always pleasant. The weather at the season of our visit was good of course, though we were once or twice caught by an early winter. My grandfather travelled in his own carriage, with his own horses, his faithful Burwell on horseback by his side. It took us nearly three days to make the hundred miles. We always stopped at the same country inns, where the country-people were as much pleased to see the 'Squire,' as they always called Mr. Jefferson, as they could have been to meet their own best friends. They set out for him the best they had, gave him the nicest room, and seemed to hail his passage as an event most interesting to themselves." Ford's Tavern was one of his stopping places along the way. A younger granddaughter relates: "In his journeys to Bedford, he always took two of us along with him. . . . His cheerful conversation, so agreeable and instructive, his singing as we journeyed along, made the time pass pleasantly, even travelling through the solitudes of Buckingham and Campbell counties over indifferent roads. Our cold dinner was always put up by his own hands; a pleasant spot by the roadside chosen to eat it, and he was the carver and helped us to our cold fowl and ham, and mixed the wine and water to drink with it. During those visits to Poplar Forest, he took us to see all his neighbors, and to Lynchburgh sometimes to see the place, and to make some purchase to please us in the shops."[40]

The aged statesman was keenly conscious of his solitude when at Poplar Forest unaccompanied by his granddaughters. Shut in one winter after snow had fallen seven times, he wrote: "I have wished for Anne but once since I came here, and that has been from the moment of my arrival to the present one. The weather has been such that I have seen the face of no human being for

Randall, *Jefferson*, III, 547; *Garden Book*, 581. See also to Wm. Short, Monticello, November 24, 1821, in Lipscomb and Bergh, *Writings*, XVIII, 314.

[40] Randall, *Life of Jefferson*, III, 344.

days but the servants. I am like a state prisoner. My keepers set before me at fixed hours something to eat & withdraw." He philosophized more cheerfully when they were with him: "Ellen writes to you and of course will give you the news of this place if she can muster up any. The history of our expedition to the Natural bridge she will write you of course. . . . It will not be new that we give all our love to young & old, male & female of the family, and our kisses to Septimia particularly, with gingerbread which she will prefer to them." In the same strain, though declaring that the girls spent most of the day at their studies, he wrote: "I trust to Ellen & Cornelia to communicate our love to Septimia in the form of a cake."[41]

Poplar Forest could be reached from Monticello by traveling about eighty miles, but the roads were far rougher than those over which Jefferson made his way to Bedford. It was his practice, after his retirement as president, to visit Poplar Forest several times each year. In 1821 he was there four times. Thereafter, old age rendering him more sensible to fatigue, he undertook the journey but once a year, in May. The trip in 1823 was his last, "as indeed, it appears to have been his last trip of any distance from Monticello."[42]

[41] To Martha Jefferson Randolph, Poplar Forest, February 24, 1811; August 18, 1817; August 31, 1817 (Morgan Library, MS Collections).

[42] Wilstach, *Jefferson and Monticello*, 160, 202; *Garden Book*, 608. In the fall of 1821 Jefferson was at Buckspring.

CHAPTER X

The Blessed Shores of Liberty

✷

U PPERMOST in Jefferson's mind, as he traveled, was the desire to acquire experience abroad which could be applied for the welfare of his country. "Everything he sees seems to suggest to him the question whether it can be made useful in America."[1] Hence, in his suggestions to Shippen and Rutledge, he discourages expert study of painting and sculpture, since the cultivation of those arts is too costly for American pocketbooks, but recommends paying careful attention to architecture, gardening, and agriculture, which are indispensable at home.

He busied himself constantly to introduce the culture of new plants in America. He also furnished to French friends, especially Mme de Tessé, specimens of American agriculture. Although he believed that American farmers could employ their energies more profitably than in the production of wine, Jefferson did not neglect to compile detailed information about the different sorts of wine, as he visited their localities of origin. He favored introduction of light wines in America, in order to drive out the addiction to whisky which was depraving the population. French cooking likewise won his approval.

The temperate and courteous manners of France appealed to Jefferson. He observed that "a Frenchman never said no: and it is difficult for a stranger to know when he means it."[2] To a Florentine gentleman, professor of modern languages in William and

[1] Quoted from a writer in the *Edinburgh Review*, by Randolph in *Domestic Life*, 150.
[2] To Paine, Paris, July 3, 1788 (Mass. Hist. Soc., Jefferson Papers).

Mary College, he wrote from Paris: "With respect to what are termed polite manners, without sacrificing too much the sincerity of language, I would wish my countrymen to adopt just so much of European politeness, as to be ready to make all those little sacrifices of self, which really render European manners amiable, and relieve society from the disagreeable scenes to which rudeness often subjects it. Here, it seems that a man might pass his life without encountering a single rudeness. In the pleasures of the table, they are far before us, because, with good taste, they unite temperance. They do not terminate the most sociable meals by transforming themselves into brutes. I have never yet seen a man drunk in France, even among the lowest of the people. Were I to proceed to tell you how much I enjoy their architecture, sculpture, painting, music, I should want words. It is in these arts they shine. The last of them, particularly, is an enjoyment, the deprivation of which, with us, cannot be calculated. I am almost ready to say it is the only thing which from my heart I envy them, and which in spite of all the authority of the Decalogue, I do covet. But I am running on in an estimate of things infinitely better known to you than to me, and which will only serve to convince you that I have brought with me all the prejudices of country, habit, and age."[3]

Mindful of her friend's love of music, Mrs. Adams wrote to Jefferson, after attending a performance of Handel's *Messiah* in Westminster Abbey: "It was sublime beyond description. I most sincerely wisht for your presence, as your favorite passion would have received the highest gratification. I should have sometimes fancied myself amongst a higher order of Beings if it had not been for a very troublesome female who was unfortunately seated behind me; and whose volubility not all the powers of music could still."[4]

---

[3] To Charles Bellini, Paris, September 30, 1785 (Lipscomb and Bergh, *Writings*, V, 153–54).

[4] Mrs. Adams to Jefferson, London, June 6, 1785 (Hale, *Franklin in France*, II, 347).

As a youth in Virginia Jefferson had already said that music "is the favorite passion of my soul, and fortune has cast my lot in a country where it is in a state of deplorable barbarism."[5] Perhaps he had in mind this delight of which he would be deprived on his return to America when he declared that if one travels he acquires tastes and habits which cannot be gratified at home, and is tormented all his days thereafter by memories tinged with regret and longing for past pleasures. Men of sober age are compensated for this diminution of their happiness, Jefferson believed, by the wisdom they acquire; young men, not being prepared by antecedent training to reap the benefits of travel, suffer its disadvantages all the more keenly, especially if their formative years are spent abroad under circumstances unfitting them for useful life in their own country.

These opinions were proclaimed in several notable letters written by Jefferson from Paris. Enumerating the objects to which his nephew, Peter Carr, should give his attention, Jefferson said:

Travelling. This makes men wiser, but less happy. When men of sober age travel, they gather knowledge which they may apply usefully for their country, but they are subject ever after to recollections mixed with regret, their affections are weakened by being extended over more objects, & they learn new habits which cannot be gratified when they return home. Young men who travel are exposed to all these inconveniences in a higher degree, to others still more serious, and do not acquire that wisdom for which a previous foundation is requisite by repeated & just observations at home. The glare of pomp & pleasure is analogous to the motion of their blood, it absorbs all their affection & attention, they are torn from it as from the only good in this world, and return to their home as to a place of exile & condemnation. Their eyes are forever turned back to the object they have lost, & it's recollection poisons the residue of their lives. Their first & most delicate passions are hackneyed on unworthy objects here, & they carry home only the dregs, insufficient to make themselves or anybody else happy. Add to this that a habit of idle-

[5] To ———, Williamsburg, June 8, 1778 (Ford, *Writings*, II, 158).

ness, and inability to apply themselves to business is acquired & renders them useless to themselves & their country. These observations are founded in experience. There is no place where your pursuit of knowledge will be so little obstructed by foreign objects as in your own country, nor any wherein the virtues of the heart will be less exposed to be weakened. Be good, be learned, & be industrious, & you will not want the aid of travelling to render you precious to your country, dear to your friends, happy within yourself.[6]

A vigorous philippic against education abroad was delivered by Jefferson in response to a request by John Banister, Jr., for the former's "opinion respecting the best seminary of education at this time in Europe for the elevation of youth, my father being desirous of sending over my two brothers in the spring. After every information I can gain it appears to me that Geneva is the most eligible."[7] Jefferson replied that Geneva and Rome were the most desirable localities for that purpose,[8] but that young Americans ought not to receive their upbringing in Europe at all.

Let us view the disadvantages of sending a youth to Europe. To enumerate them all would require a volume. I will select a few. If he goes to England, he learns drinking, horse-racing, and boxing. These are the peculiarities of English education. The following circumstances are common to education in that, and the other countries of Europe. He acquires a fondness for European luxury and dissipation, and a contempt for the simplicity of his own country . . . he forms foreign friendships which will never be useful to him, and loses the season of life for forming, in his own country, those friendships which, of all others, are the most faithful and permanent . . . he recollects the voluptuary dress and arts of the European

---

[6] To Peter Carr, Paris, August 10, 1787 (Lipscomb and Bergh, *Writings*, VI, 261–62). Cf. to Mrs. Trist, Paris, February 23, 1787 (Mass. Hist. Soc., Jefferson Papers). See also Shepperson, *John Paradise and Lucy Ludwell*, 230.

[7] John Banister, Jr., to Jefferson, Avignon, September 19, 1785 (Mass. Hist. Soc., Jefferson Papers). Cf. John Banister to Jefferson, February 9, 1785 (*ibid.*).

[8] Geneva and Edinburgh are recommended in a letter to Mr. M'Alister, Philadelphia, December 22, 1791 (Lipscomb and Bergh, *Writings*, VIII, 274). So in a letter to George Washington, Monticello, February 23, 1795 (*ibid.*, XIX, 109), Jefferson says: "The colleges of Geneva and Edinburgh were considered as the two eyes of Europe in matters of science, insomuch that no other pretended to any rivalship with either."

women, and pities and despises the chaste affections and simplicity of those of his own country; he retains through life a fond recollection, and a hankering after those places, which were the scenes of his first pleasures and his first connections; he returns to his own country, a foreigner, unacquainted with the practices of domestic economy, necessary to preserve him from ruin, speaking and writing his native tongue as a foreigner, and therefore unqualified to obtain those distinctions, which eloquence of the pen and tongue ensures in a free country. . . . The consequences of foreign education are alarming to me, as an American. I sin, therefore, through zeal, whenever I enter on the subject. You are sufficiently American to pardon me for it.[9]

In an earnest exhortation to his "adopted son," William Short, Jefferson reiterates his belief that for an American to spend his early years in Europe is undesirable:

Having no intelligence from America, and the affairs of Europe offering no new matter for a letter, I shall make yourself the subject of this, invited to it by your last. If I have ever been silent on this head, it has been because nobody is better qualified than yourself to form just opinions for your own guidance. But as I perceive by your letter that you are balancing in your own mind upon the questions Whether and When you shall return to America, the opinions of your friends may not be unacceptable. In the first place I must put you on your guard as to my recommendation to continue in Europe during the ensuing summer, because in that I am interested, & my interest may warp my judgment. I wrote not only to Mr. Madison, but to Mr. Jay hoping to get you named Chargé des affaires, and I pressed this at least as far as it was prudent. I now know that my letter would have to lie over for the new government, and of course that it is Genl. Washington who will decide on it. This gives me more confidence it will be complied with than I should have had if it had rested

---

[9] To John Banister, Jr., Paris, October 15, 1785 (Lipscomb and Bergh, *Writings*, V, 186–88). After receiving this letter Banister tried to dissuade his father from sending over his brothers.—Ford (ed.), *Jefferson Correspondence in Collections of Bixby*, 19; John Banister, Jr., to Jefferson, Avignon, March 11, 1786 (Mass. Hist. Soc., Jefferson Papers). In the case of Banister himself, however, Jefferson wrote that he was glad to learn of a "prospect of your visiting Italy. Such a trip will certainly furnish you pleasing reflections through life."—To Banister, Paris, September 7, 1786 (Library of Congress, Shippen Papers). Similarly, Jefferson advised that T. M. Randolph, Jr., study and travel in Europe.

with the ancient Congress. I have grounded the proposal of permitting me to return, expressly on your personal qualifications to conduct the business, and were you to go in the spring, I should think myself obliged to stay till I could consult them on some other appointment. You see then that I am interested in your continuance here till my return. The question then arises What are you to do afterwards? Here my opinion will be against my interest, for affection and the long habit of your society have rendered it necessary to me. And how much more so will it be when I shall have parted with my daughters? But I am to say what is for your interest, not what is for my own. The first question is Whether you should propose to finish your life in Europe or America? In Europe I doubt whether you can; because our government gives it's offices on it's own knolege of persons, & not on the recommendations of others. They give their diplomatic appointments with more caution too because of the distance at which they are to be exercised and the necessity which that induces of leaving to them a great latitude of discretionary power. I think therefore you must be personally known to them before you could expect a permanent diplomatic appointment in Europe. But let us suppose you could obtain one, even of the best. The best admits of no savings. They afford but a bare existence and a solitary existence too, for a married man could not live on them without abandoning all respect to character. A young man indeed may do without marriage in a great city. In the beginning it is pleasant enough; but take what course he will whether that of rambling, or of a fixed attachment, he will become miserable as he advances in years. It is then he will feel the want of that friendship which can be formed during the enthusiasm of youth alone, and formed without reproach. It is then too he will want the amusement and comfort of children. To take a middle course, and pass the first half of your life in Europe & the latter in America is still worse. The attachments and habits formed here in your youth would render the evening of life more miserable still in America than it would be here. The only resource then for a durable happiness is to return to America. If you chuse to follow business, a short apprenticeship at the bar would ensure you an early retirement on the bench; especially if you followed the assembly at the same time with the bar. If you should chuse the line of public office, you may be assured of obtaining anything in that line as soon as you should have had time to acquire those details in business which practice alone gives and that intimate knolege of your own country which is necessary to enable you to serve it to your own satisfaction. After a short course in this line, you may be anything you please either in America or Europe. For should you find yourself disposed after a while to come to Europe in a diplomatic character, your talents will place you on the foremost ground, and your former residence in Europe will give you a preference over all competitors. But I think you will never wish to return to Europe. You will then be sensible that the happiness of your own country is more tranquil, more unmixed, more permanent. You will prefer serving your country there in easy & honorable station, & in what station you please. I will not say in the first. That will never be given to virtue and talents alone but to him whom some happy hit of fortune shall have enabled to make himself generally known. If you say that public emploiment in America will not make you a fortune? Nor will it in Europe. If fortune be decisively your object, the bar offers it to you. You may shortly be without a rival there. Permit me to say so who knows you and knows the ground. This you say is drudgery? This is not a world in which heaven rains riches into every hand that will open itself. Whichever of these courses you adopt, delay is loss of time. The sooner the race is begun the sooner the prize will be obtained. I say this with a bleeding heart: for nothing can be more dreary than my situation will be when you & my daughters shall all have left me. I look forward to it with dismay, and I am relieved by the limits of my paper which turning me from it's contemplation, warns me it is time to repeat to you assurances, ever warm and ever sincere of the affectionate esteem of Dr. Sir your friend & servant   Th: Jefferson.[10]

In his reply Short acknowledged that "my happiness is to be found in America only," but felt less optimistic regarding the opportunity to amass the fortune he craved.[11]

Jefferson's old friend Charles Thomson, translator of the Bible and secretary of the Continental Congress, wrote regarding a young American: "I must beg leave to recommend to your

[10] To William Short, Paris, March 24, 1789 (Library of Congress, Jefferson Papers).

[11] Short to Jefferson, Marseilles, April 3, 1789 (*ibid.*). See also Short to Jefferson, Philadelphia, November 1, 1810 (*The Jefferson Papers, Collections of the Mass. Hist. Soc.* [seventh series], I, 145–46); January 18, 1814 (*ibid.*, 190); June 9, 1814 (*ibid.*, 196–97).

friendly notice and attention Mr Isaac Norris a near relative of Mrs. Thomson. As he is a young man of an amiable disposition & considerable fortune, I am anxious he should return as uncorrupted as he went, which I fear will not be the case with some of our young men. Mr. Jay was so obliging as to take him under his protection. And I shall esteem it as a particular favour if you will by your advice and countenance direct his pursuits so that he may avoid the temptations that will be thrown in his way and become a useful member of society."[12]

Perhaps having in mind Short's romantic attachment to a French noblewoman, Jefferson replied: "There is one danger at his age which some other instances have proved real—that of forming a connection, as is the fashion here, which he might be unwilling to shake off when it shall be proper for him to return to his own country, and which might detain him disadvantageously here. I have not the smallest intimation that he is disposed to do this, but it is difficult for young men to refuse it where beauty is a begging in every street. Indeed, from what I have seen here I know not one good purpose on earth which can be affected by a young gentleman coming here. He may learn indeed to speak the language, but put this in the scale amongst other things he will learn and evils he is sure to acquire and it will be found too light. I have always disapproved of a European education for our youth from theory; I now do it from inspection."[13]

Nevertheless, Jefferson advised T. M. Randolph, Jr., who later married Martha Jefferson, that since law, history, and politics were topics to be mastered by reading, which could be done at one place as well as another, it would be well to pursue those

[12] Charles Thomson to Jefferson, Philadelphia, June 18, 1784 (Library of Congress, Jefferson Papers). Isaac Norris's brother Joseph was the subject of a similar letter.—Thomson to Jefferson, October 26, 1784 (New York Historical Society, *Revolutionary Papers*, I [1879], 195). Benjamin Rush likewise wrote to Jefferson a letter of recommendation in behalf of Samuel Fox, a Quaker traveling to Europe.—Rush to Jefferson, Philadelphia, June 16, 1785 (Morgan Library, MS Collections).

[13] To Charles Thomson, Paris, November 11, 1784 (Ford, *Writings*, IV, 14–15); Lewis R. Harley, *The Life of Charles Thomson*, 200–202.

studies in France, where he would be learning French besides. At the same time Jefferson told the young man's father that the advantages of having traveled through the most interesting part of Europe would be cheaply purchased for the 150 or 200 guineas it would cost, even if it were necessary to deduct the amount from his son's patrimony.[14]

Perhaps the true cause of Jefferson's strictures on foreign education was his preference for rural over city life and his conviction that if young men and women are to spend their lives on a farm they ought to be so educated as to be happy there, without desires incapable of gratification except by the luxuries of a metropolis. "We do not suppose city habits are those which make people either the happiest or most useful who are to live in the country," Jefferson declared. On another occasion he said: "I am not a friend to placing young men in populous cities, because they acquire there habits and partialities which do not contribute to the happiness of their after life."[15]

Not only did Jefferson "view great cities as pestilential to the morals, the health and the liberties of man," and foresee that when ignorant "mobs" in America "get piled upon one another in large cities as in Europe, they will become corrupt as in Europe," but his firmly held convictions regarding the place of women in society were likewise outraged by what he observed abroad. Like the tourist in France in recent years, Jefferson was struck with the sight of male chambermaids: "The encroachments by the men, on the offices proper for the women, is a great derangement in the order of things. Men are shoemakers, tailors, upholsterers, house-cleaners, bed-makers; they *coiffe* the ladies, and bring them to

---

[14] To T. M. Randolph, Jr., Paris, July 6, 1787 (Lipscomb and Bergh, *Writings*, VI, 166); to the same, Paris, August 27, 1786 (Ford, *Writings*, IV, 291); to T. M. Randolph, Sr., Paris, August 11, 1787 (Lipscomb and Bergh, *Writings*, VI, 267–68). Cf. to Wm. Short, On the Canal of Languedoc, May 21, 1787 (*William and Mary College Quarterly* [2d series], Vol. XI, No. 4 [October, 1931], 339); and to Mr. Elder, Paris, November 25, 1785 (Mass. Hist. Soc., Jefferson Papers).

[15] To Mr. Peale, Monticello, August 24, 1800 (Library of Congress, Jefferson Papers); to Casper Wistar, Washington, June 21, 1807 (Lipscomb and Bergh, *Writings*, XI, 242–43).

bed; the women, therefore, to live, are obliged to undertake the offices which they abandon. They become porters, carters, reapers, sailors, lock-keepers, smiters on the anvil, cultivators of the earth, etc. Can we wonder, if such of them as have a little beauty, prefer easier courses to get their livelihood, so long as that beauty lasts?"[16]

When for the first time, on his tour through France, Jefferson saw women at hard labor, out of doors, he noted in his journal: "I observe women and children carrying heavy burdens, and laboring with the hoe. This is an unequivocal indication of extreme poverty. Men, in a civilized country, never expose their wives and children to labor above their force and sex, as long as their own labor can protect them from it." The phenomenon recurring, Jefferson again philosophizes about it: "It is an honorable circumstance for man, that the first moment he is at his ease, he allots the internal employments to his female partner, and takes the external on himself. And this circumstance, or its reverse, is a pretty good indication that a people are, or are not at their ease. Among the Indians, this indication fails from a particular cause; every Indian man is a soldier or warrior, and the whole body of warriors constitute a standing army, always employed in war or hunting. To support that army, there remain no laborers but the women. Here, then, is so heavy a military establishment, that the civil part of the nation is reduced to women only. But this is a barbarous perversion of the natural destination of the two sexes."[17]

On another occasion, in the neighborhood of Nancy, noticing the trinkets worn by French and German working women, Jefferson thus mused regarding the foibles of the fair sex: "The women here, as in Germany, do all sorts of work. While one con-

[16] To Benjamin Rush, Monticello, September 23, 1800 (*ibid.*, X, 173); Ford, *Writings*, III, 269; to Madison, Paris, December 20, 1787 (*ibid.*, IV, 479–80); Lipscomb and Bergh, *Writings*, XVII, 211.

[17] *Ibid.*, XVII, 154, 280. For similar views regarding woman's sphere, see Countess Barziza, née Lucy Paradise, to Jefferson, Bergamo, March 3, 1789 (Mass. Hist. Soc., Jefferson Papers). Cf. Xenophon, *Oeconomicus*, VII, 3, 22–23.

siders them as useful and rational companions, one cannot forget that they are also objects of our pleasures; nor can they ever forget it. While employed in dirt and drudgery, some tag of a ribbon, some ring, or bit of bracelet, earbob or necklace, or something of that kind, will show that the desire of pleasing is never suspended in them. . . . Women are formed by nature for attentions, not for hard labor. A woman never forgets one of the numerous train of little offices which belong to her. A man forgets often."[18]

Woman's happiness, Jefferson assures Mrs. Bingham, the vivacious leader of Philadelphia society, is to be found in the nursery, in "the tender and tranquil amusements of domestic life," and not in the bustling pleasures of existence at Paris. Mrs. Bingham replied with spirit that, after all, life in Paris would not be unattractive, and that the ladies of the French capital occupied a position of considerable importance. "The women of France interfere with the politics of the country, and often give a decided turn to the fate of empires. Either by the gentle art of persuasion, or the commanding force of superior attractions and address, they have obtained that rank and consideration in society which the sex are entitled to, and which they in vain contend for in other countries. We are therefore bound to admire and revere them for asserting our privileges, as much as the friends of the liberties of mankind reverence the successful struggles of the American patriots."[19]

Perhaps alarmed by these heretical sentiments, Jefferson communicated to Mrs. Bingham, at a moment when political excitement was at a high pitch both in France and America, his conviction that "our good ladies, I trust, have been too wise to wrinkle their foreheads with politics. They are contented to soothe and calm the minds of their husbands returning ruffled from political debate." To another fair compatriot he exclaimed: "The

[18] Lipscomb and Bergh, *Writings*, XVII, 279–80.
[19] To Mrs. Bingham, Paris, February 7, 1787 (Randolph, *Domestic Life*, 97); Mrs. Bingham to Jefferson, June 1, 1787 (*ibid.*, 99).

tender breasts of ladies were not formed for political convulsions; and the French ladies miscalculate much their own happiness when they wander from the field of their influence into that of politicks." The political activities of French women horrified Jefferson, and Mrs. Bingham's doctrines were somewhat unacceptable to one who as president wrote to his secretary of the treasury regarding an applicant for a position: "The appointment of a woman to office is an innovation for which the public is not prepared, nor am I."[20]

In the matter of home life and political organization Jefferson was convinced that American conditions were far preferable to those prevailing in Europe, and should be preserved from contamination by foreign influence and example. In France, he thought, the condition of mankind was deplorable: the humble suffered from misery and oppression; the great from the emptiness and vanity of their existence.

"Intrigues of love occupy the younger, and those of ambition, the elder part of the great. Conjugal love having no existence among them, domestic happiness, of which that is the basis, is utterly unknown. In lieu of this are substituted pursuits which nourish and invigorate all our bad passions, and which offer only moments of ecstasy, amidst days and months of restlessness and torment. Much, very much inferior, this, to the tranquil, permanent felicity with which domestic society in America blesses most of its inhabitants." And again: "Their manners may be the best calculated for happiness to a people in their situation, but I am convinced they fall short of effecting a happiness so temperate, so uniform, and so lasting, as is generally enjoyed with us. The domestic bonds here are entirely done away, and where can their compensation be found? Perhaps they may catch some moments

---

[20] To Mrs. Bingham, Paris, May 11, 1788 (Ford, *Writings*, V, 9); to Angelica Church, Paris, September 21, 1788 (Ford [ed.], *Jefferson Correspondence in Collections of Bixby*, 35); to Gallatin, Washington, January 13, 1807 (Ford, *Writings*, IX, 7). For Jefferson's horror at the political activity of French women, see also letter to George Washington, Paris, December 14, 1788 in Lipscomb and Bergh, *Writings*, VII, 228.

of transport above the level of the ordinary tranquil joy we experience, but they are separated by long intervals, during which all the passions are at sea without rudder or compass. Yet, fallacious as the pursuits of happiness are, they seem on the whole to furnish the most effectual abstraction from a contemplation of the hardness of their government. Indeed, it is difficult to conceive how so good a people, with so good a King, so well-disposed rulers in general, so genial a climate, so fertile a soil, should be rendered so ineffectual for producing human happiness by one single curse—that of a bad form of government. But it is a fact. In spite of the mildness of their governors, the people are ground to powder by the vices of the form of government. Of twenty millions of people supposed to be in France, I am of opinion there are nineteen millions more wretched, more accursed, in every circumstance of human existence, than the most conspicuously wretched individual of the whole United States."[21]

The educative effect of observing these conditions at first hand was so impressive that, in spite of the danger that young and impressionable minds might be seduced into preferring the "profusion and servitude"[22] of Europe to the simplicity and liberty of the New World, Jefferson urged his countrymen to come and see for themselves.

To Monroe he wrote: "I sincerely wish you may find it convenient to come here; the pleasure of the trip will be less than you expect, but the utility greater. It will make you adore your own country, its soil, its climate, its equality, liberty, laws, people, and manners. My God! how little do my countrymen know what precious blessings they are in possession of, and which no other people on earth enjoy. I confess I had no idea of it myself. I will venture to say no man now living, will ever see an instance of an American removing to settle in Europe, and continuing

---

[21] To Charles Bellini, Paris, September 30, 1785 (*ibid.*, V, 153); to Mrs. Trist, August 18, 1785 (*ibid.*, V, 80–81). Cf. to George Washington, Paris, November 14, 1786 (*ibid.*, VI, 4).

[22] To Samuel Kercheval, Monticello, July 12, 1816 (*ibid.*, XV, 39).

there. Come, then, and see the proofs of this, and on your return add your testimony to that of every thinking American, in order to satisfy your countrymen how much it is their interest to preserve, uninfected by contagion, those peculiarities in their governments and manners, to which they are indebted for those blessings."[23]

James Madison received an elaborate disquisition on political organization: "Societies exist under three forms sufficiently distinguishable. 1. Without government, as among our Indians. 2. Under governments wherein the will of every one has a just influence, as is the case in England in a slight degree, and in our states, in a great one. 3. Under governments of force; as is the case in all other monarchies and in most of the other republics. To have an idea of the curse of existence under these last, they must be seen. It is a government of wolves over sheep."[24]

Example was felt by Jefferson to be the most effective argument. "The best schools for republicanism are London, Versailles, Madrid, Vienna, Berlin, &c," he asserted. "If any of our countrymen wish a king, send them to Europe. They will come back good republicans." The comparison of American governments, in spite of defects in federal or state constitutions, with those of Europe is "like a comparison of heaven & hell. England, like the earth, may be allowed to take the intermediate station. And yet I hear there are people among you who think the experience of our governments has already proved that republican governments will not answer. Send those gentry here to count the blessings of monarchy." The best "medicine for monarchists" is to study the habits of royalty. The effect of Jefferson's own observation was reflected in a letter to George Washington: "I was much an enemy to monarchies before I came to Europe. I am ten thousand times more so, since I have seen what they are."[25]

[23] To James Monroe, Paris, June 17, 1785 (*ibid.*, V, 21). Cf. to Wm. Rutledge, Paris, February 2, 1788 (*ibid.*, VI, 418).

[24] To James Madison, Paris, January 30, 1787 (Ford, *Writings*, IV, 362).

[25] To Governor Rutledge, Paris, August 6, 1787 (Lipscomb and Bergh, *Writings*, VI, 252); to Dr. David Ramsay, Paris, August 4, 1787 (*ibid.*, VI, 226); to

These lessons which Jefferson learned as a traveler guided his policies when he became president of the United States.[26] In his administration he stressed the need of "a wise and frugal government, which shall . . . not take from the mouth of labor the bread it has earned." It was his earnest desire that never in America should it come to pass "that, after leaving to labor the smallest part of its earnings on which it can subsist, government shall itself consume the residue of what it was instituted to guard."[27] After his retirement he thus recapitulated his endeavors: "Having seen the people of other nations bowed down to the earth under the wars and prodigalities of their rulers, I have cherished their opposites, peace, economy, and riddance of public debt, believing that these were the highroad to public as well as to private prosperity and happiness."[28]

Discussing French politics in 1789 Jefferson declared: "I have so much confidence on the good sense of man, and his qualification for self-government, that I am never afraid of the issue where reason is left free to exert her force; and I will agree to be stoned as a false prophet if all does not end well in this country. Nor will it end with this country. Here is but the first chapter of the history of European liberty."[29]

The true home of human freedom and happiness, however, regardless of the outcome of European struggles, was to be found in the Western Hemisphere. A new civilization, based on

Joseph Jones, Paris, August 14, 1787 (*ibid.*, VI, 274); to Mme de Tessé, December 8, 1813 (Ford, *Writings*, IX, 437); to General Washington, Paris, May 2, 1788 (Lipscomb and Bergh, *Writings*, VI, 454). Cf. to Benjamin Hawkins, Paris, August 4, 1787 (*ibid.*, VI, 232).

[26] Samuel Flagg Bemis, *American Secretaries of State and Their Diplomacy*, II, 9.

[27] First Inaugural Address, March 4, 1801 (Lipscomb and Bergh, *Writings*, III, 321); First Annual Message, December 8, 1801 (*ibid.*, III, 333). Cf. Claude G. Bowers, *Jefferson in Power*, 88.

[28] To Henry Middleton, Monticello, January 8, 1813 (Lipscomb and Bergh, *Writings*, XIII, 202).

[29] To Count Diodati, Paris, August 3, 1789 (Mass. Hist. Soc., Jefferson Papers).

"cherishment of the people," Jefferson believed, was destined to arise in America:

> The doctrines of Europe were, that men in numerous associations cannot be restrained within the limits of order and justice, but by forces physical and moral, wielded over them by authorities independent of their will. Hence their organization of kings, hereditary nobles, and priests. Still further to constrain the brute force of the people, they deem it necessary to keep them down by hard labor, poverty and ignorance and to take from them, as from bees, so much of their earnings, as that unremitting labor shall be necessary to obtain a sufficient surplus barely to sustain a scanty and miserable life. And these earnings they apply to maintain their privileged orders in splendor and idleness, to fascinate the eyes of the people, and excite in them an humble adoration and submission, as to an order of superior beings. . . . We believed . . . that man was a rational animal, endowed by nature with rights, and with an innate sense of justice; and that he could be restrained from wrong and protected in right, by moderate powers, confided to persons of his own choice, and held to their duties by dependence on his own will. . . . We believed that men, enjoying in ease and security the full fruits of their own industry, enlisted by all their interests on the side of law and order, habituated to think for themselves, and to follow their reason as their guide, would be more easily and safely governed, than with minds nourished in error, and vitiated and debased, as in Europe, by ignorance, indigence, and oppression.[30]

Regarding freedom of the seas, he declared that "nothing but a general concert of nations can effect it, but from the selfish politics and crooked course of the European governments no such concert in what is right is to be expected." Hence that task would "remain for the two Americas."[31] Peace would be preserved, he

---

[30] To Wm. Johnson, Monticello, June 12, 1823 (Lipscomb and Bergh, *Writings*, XV, 442). Jefferson believed "that government to be the strongest of which every man feels himself a part."—To Governor Edward Tiffin, Washington, February 2, 1807 (*ibid.*, XI, 147). Regarding popular participation in the process of government, see also Ford, *Writings*, I, 113; to Samuel Kercheval, Monticello, July 12, 1816, in *ibid.*, X, 37; to Du Pont, Poplar Forest, April 24, 1816, in *ibid.*, X, 22; to Abbé Arnond, Paris, July 19, 1789, in *ibid.*, V, 102; *ibid.*, VIII, 3.

[31] To Charles Le Brun, Monticello, January 13, 1822 (Mo. Hist. Soc., Bixby Collection). Cf. to William Short, Monticello, August 4, 1820, in Lipscomb and Bergh, *Writings*, XV, 263; to David B. Warden, Monticello, October 30, 1822, in *Mississippi Valley Historical Review*, Vol. XXVIII, No. 2 (September, 1941), 241.

wrote on another occasion, "until the men of Europe shall have recovered breath and strength enough to recommence their sanguinary conflicts which they seem to consider as the object for which they were brought into the world."[32] Of the European countries he said: "They are nations of eternal war. All their energies are expended in the destruction of the labor, property, and lives of their peoples. On our part, never had a people so favorable a chance of trying the opposite system, of peace and fraternity with mankind, and the direction of our means and faculties to the purpose of improvement instead of destruction."[33]

Jefferson's observations as a tourist thus contributed to his effectiveness as a statesman. Wisely shaping important domestic and foreign policies for the United States, he established traditions of freedom which have never lost their vitality. They become especially significant during periods in the nation's history when "the blessed shores of liberty" are menaced anew by tyranny. At such times, Jefferson again stands forth as the champion of mankind's indubitable rights, and speaks to his countrymen no less compellingly than in the era when the infant American republic was struggling to achieve its independence.

[32] To James Workman, Monticello, December 4, 1801 (Mo. Hist. Soc., Bixby Collection).

[33] To James Monroe, Monticello, June 11, 1823 (Lipscomb and Bergh, *Writings*, XV, 436). Cf. Adams, *History of U. S. during Administration of Jefferson*, I, 146–47, 157–61; and to James Madison, Monticello, March 23, 1815, in Ford, *Writings*, IX, 511; to James Monroe, Monticello, October 24, 1823, in *ibid.*, X, 277; to George Ticknor, Monticello, July 4, 1815, in *Mississippi Valley Historical Review*, Vol. XXVIII, No. 2 (September, 1941), 236; to David B. Warden, Monticello, February 27, 1815, June 6, 1817, in *ibid.*, 234, 239.

APPENDICES

TRANSLATION OF JEFFERSON'S PASSPORT

(L. C. 8863. Italicized portions written in ink, on printed form.)

No. 175
PASSPORT

HÔTEL-DE-VILLE
DE PARIS.

Free.   T HE Presidents and Commanders of the Districts of this City & Roads are requested to let pass freely, and without trouble or hindrance, Mr. *Jefferson and his daughters,* accompanied by *their servants,* he having declared to us that *he* wish*es* to go *to America with his carriages and effects,* without other arms than those customary for personal defense.

We request you to aid him with your succour and assistance, if he should be in a situation to have need of it. In faith of which we have delivered the present, in the Hotel-de-Ville.

At Paris, this *twenty fifth of September* one thousand seven hundred eighty *nine.*

Manozils   *J. Lariziere*

Ravaud

Representatives of the Commune.

The officers of the National Guards and in general all Citizens are requested to let pass Mr. Jefferson, minister plenipotentiary of the United States of America and to give him all the assistance of which he might have need. At Paris this 26th Sept. 1789.

Lafayette

JEFFERSON'S RESIDENCE IN RICHMOND

It is not probable that Jefferson was ever an occupant of the old "Palace." However, the inscription on the present Governor's Mansion lists Jefferson among the governors having lived on that spot.[1] In any event, according to Richard Young's map, of 1809 or 1810,[2] the "Palace" was located a little below Grace Street, and thus farther toward Main Street than the present Governor's Mansion. A plot dated 1812 in the Virginia State Archives shows that the house stood close to Capitol Street, and that Twelfth Street, if prolonged through the Capitol Square, would have cut off part of the east end of the house.

Mordecai says: "The Governor's House preceding the present one, was a very plain wooden building of two stories, with only two moderate sized rooms on the first floor. It was for many years unconscious of paint, and the furniture was in keeping with the republican simplicity of the edifice and of its occupants, from Henry and Jefferson down to Monroe and Page. The palings around the yard were usually in a dilapidated condition, and the goats that sported on the steep hillsides of the Capitol Square, claimed and exercised the liberty of grazing on his Excellency's grounds."[3]

This is not a direct statement that Jefferson occupied the "Palace"; and in any event would be of questionable authority, since Monroe refused to occupy the ruinous dwelling and lived in a house at Ninth and Marshall Streets, while Henry occupied the palace in Williamsburg during his first term as governor.

It seems impossible to determine when the old "Palace" was built. Probably it was during Governor Harrison's administration. The house was apparently situated on lot 358. The tax book of September, 1782, shows that the commonwealth owned by purchase James Marsden's four lots with improvements, being numbers 358, 368, 369, and 380. I have not been able to determine when or how this title was acquired; there is no mention of these lots in the photostats of Capitol Square Inquisitions

---

[1] Edward Griffith Dodson, *The Capitol of the Commonwealth of Virginia at Richmond*, 299.

[2] Weddell, *Richmond in Old Prints*, 32.

[3] Mordecai, *Richmond in By-Gone Days*, 59.

in the Virginia State Archives. The original papers relating to those inquisitions are said to have been recorded on November 14, 1876, in Henrico
County Court. Apparently they had already been recorded in 1822, after
having been mislaid for some years in the city court.[4]

On June 27, 1783 it was stated "that the commonwealth is further
entitled to, and have actually paid for, the tenement and four lots now occupied by the Governor, of the probable value of 2000 £."[5] Thus it may
be inferred that at that date the governor was living in a house on lot 358,
acquired from James Marsden. (Apparently an ordinance of October 11,
1782, indicates that there was a small house on lot 369.)[6] At that time the
site of the permanent capitol had not yet been definitely determined and
it may be that the "Palace" was not constructed until after the location
of the capitol had been fixed.

Of a visit paid to Governor Harrison in Richmond on April 26, 1782,
the Marquis de Chastellux wrote: "Je le trouvai établi dans une maison
fort simple, mais assez spacieuse, qu'on venait d'accomoder pour lui."[7]

Several indications pointing to an earlier date are found in the Journal
of the Executive Council. On December 1, 1781, Governor Harrison
took his place on the Council.[8] On December 3, 1781, it was resolved:
"The State Quarter Master is directed to have the Governors Garden immediately paled in, and such repairs done to the houses as may be wanting."[9] On September 27, 1782, it was voted: "The Quarter Master is
directed to have the Windows in the Governors house immediately repaired, and a house built on the public Lott, of sixteen feet square according to the directions of his Excellency for his office."[10] On February 18,
1782, and other days following, the Governor being indisposed, the
Board met at the Governor's house.[11] On September 24, 1782, it was
voted to pay Colonel Turpin for the house Jefferson had occupied.[12]

[4] *Journal of the House of Delegates* for 1821–22, 207.

[5] *Ibid.* for 1783, 92.

[6] Richmond City Hall, Records, No. 1, July 3, 1782, to December 22, 1792,
372.

[7] *Voyages de M. le Marquis de Chastellux dans l'Amérique septentrionale*, II,
121.

[8] Council Journal, 1781–82 (No. 13), 1.

[9] *Ibid.*, 4.

[10] *Ibid.*, 254.

[11] *Ibid.*, 79.

[12] *Ibid.*, 249.

There is no evidence that Turpin's house was ever occupied by Harrison. Jefferson obtained possession of Turpin's house on April 17, 1780, and rented it for one year. At the end of that time, because of the British invasion, the Governor and the legislature fled to Charlottesville. Jefferson's successor, Governor Nelson, was a military man, in the field during most of his short term, and probably did not occupy an official residence in Richmond.

When Governor Harrison took office late in 1781 and it became necessary to provide a house for him and his family, perhaps the Quarter Master hastily improvised one. (Governor Tyler, it will be remembered, said the "Palace" had been "originally badly built.") Or perhaps there was a house standing on Marsden's lot, which was replaced or supplemented, after the location of the capitol was determined, by the structure of which Governor Tyler complained.

On the other hand, Turpin in his letter of December 22, 1780, to Jefferson, after inquiring "when you think a jury will be on my land" in Richmond and when payment for it would likely be made, wished also "to be informed when my Right to that part of the tenement you occupy will cease."[13] This would indicate that Jefferson lived on part of the tract belonging to Turpin which was appropriated by the Directors of Public Buildings. But that land was part of Watson's tenement, which lay east of the road down Shockoe Hill. That road was probably where Governor Street is now situated. In the map of April 18, 1785, by Joseph Watkins the road is east of lot 358.

It is possible, however, that the road passed west of lot 358, in which case Turpin's house might have stood on the site of the governor's dwelling. "A road beginning at Tenth and Broad streets passed through the square between the Palace of Virginia (the Governor's house) and the Capitol, and continued down to Main street."[14]

Governor (or Thirteenth) Street may not follow the original course of the road down Shockoe Hill. On July 17, 1780, the Directors of Public Buildings resolved that Thirteenth Street "be made up of so much of the present road down Shockoe hill and of the Lots and grounds on each side as shall be necessary which street shall be extended from H [Broad] street

---

[13] Robert Armistead Stewart, "Jefferson and his Landlord," *The Researcher*, Vol. I, No. 1 (October, 1926), 6–7.

[14] Weddell, *Richmond in Old Prints*, 102.

to the river in such direction as shall afford the easiest way down or up Shockoe hill." This street was to constitute the eastern boundary of the Capitol Square, and the boundary of the town from Broad Street to Franklin Street. Franklin Street ended at lots 356 and 357. When prolonged to Shockoe Creek, it was to constitute the boundary of the town.[15]

Turpin's property, known as Watson's tenement, lay north and east of the main road down Shockoe Hill. The thirty-acre tract acquired by the commonwealth under the inquisition of January 8, 1783, was not included within the city limits when Richmond was incorporated in 1782, although it was part of the town of Richmond.[16]

Watson's tenement was acquired by Thomas Turpin by deed dated May 2, 1771, from the trustees of William Byrd III. It was lot 340 in Byrd's lottery. In 1783 Thomas Turpin deeded to his son Dr. Philip Turpin all of Watson's tenement except lots already conveyed or covenanted to others.[17]

On May 30, 1782, Thomas Turpin presented a petition to the legislature stating "that several valuable Lots of land and some houses the property of your petitioner have been appropriated for the use of the publick by the Directors of the Publick Buildings and that no valuation has been made of the said Lands and houses nor have any proceedings been had thereon to determine whether or not the publick mean to retain the whole of such property nor has any compensation ever been made to petitioner for the rent of the houses." The petitioner requested that the land not needed be returned to him and that he receive compensation for the part retained.[18]

On January 8, 1783 inquisition proceedings were held, and a jury valued thirty acres of Dr. Philip Turpin's land at 5,000 £. On the same day two gentlemen "chosen by the directors of the Public Buildings & Dr. Turpin, to ascertain the rent of the Brick House & Garden" reported that: "We are of Opinion that the public should pay Col¹ Turpin for his House at the Rate of one hundred Pounds specie pr annum."[19]

[15] Richmond City Hall, Ordinances, October 20, 1806, to March 30, 1816, 29.
[16] Legal opinions of John Marshall and Andrew Ronald, July 15, 1793 (Richmond City Hall, Records, No. 2, January 2, 1793, to May 18, 1795, 20–27).
[17] See deeds dated May 30, 1783, Colo. Thomas Turpin of Powhatan Co. & Mary his wife to William Hay; Thomas Turpin Sr. of the County of Powhatan to Philip Turpin his son (Henrico County Deeds, I, 203, 261).
[18] Virginia State Archives.
[19] Virginia State Archives. Cf. *Calendar of Virginia State Papers*, III, 418.

This brick house was used by the Executive Council, and the hill where it stood came to be known as Council Chamber Hill. A plot in the Valentine Museum shows that in 1798, when it was insured by John Mayo, it was a one story dwelling, 32 by 30 feet, built of brick. There was an "office," 12 by 16 feet, separate from the house, in addition to the kitchen, ice house, smoke house, carriage house, and stable. (It will be remembered that in 1782 an office sixteen feet square for Governor Harrison was authorized by the council.)

Turpin offered to donate two acres of land adjacent to the Council Chamber, "for the express purpose of having Buildings erected thereon for the Residence of the Governor."[20]

On December 14, 1787, a law was passed authorizing the Directors to return to Turpin that part of his land which was not needed by the public.[21] On April 9, 1788, the Directors resolved to reconvey to Turpin all his land, except two acres which were "to be laid off so as to include the garden used at present by the Governor, as annexed to his house."[22] The garden was a valuable piece of land which Turpin had not included in his donation of two acres.[23]

In view of Turpin's long-standing grievance (that land donated by him to be used as a residence for the governor was not applied to that purpose, whereas land not donated was retained as a garden for the governor but all the rest of Turpin's land was returned to him), it seems unlikely that the governor's house could have been situated on Turpin's land. But the dwelling occupied by Jefferson was undoubtedly located somewhere on Turpin's property. Hence it is hardly probable that Jefferson ever lived on the site later used as the governor's residence.[24]

In writing the Governor, Jefferson says: "The enclosed letters from Colo Turpin will in some measure explain to you the reason of my trou-

[20] Virginia State Archives, Philip Turpin's petition of November 11, 1791; *Journal of the House of Delegates* for 1783, 92.

[21] Hening, *Statutes*, XII, 617.

[22] *Journal of the House of Delegates* for 1788, 70.

[23] *Ibid.* for 1795, 96. See also *ibid.* for 1791, 50–51; and *ibid.* for 1792, 125.

[24] Regarding the Turpin house occupied by Jefferson, see Stewart, "Jefferson and his Landlord," *The Researcher*, Vol. I, No. 1 (October, 1926), 5–8, containing the following correspondence: Turpin to Jefferson, December 22, 1780; extract by Jefferson from his reply of December 23, 1780; Turpin to Jefferson, December 30, 1780; Turpin to Jefferson, undated, asking for payment; Jefferson to Governor Benjamin Harrison, Monticello, August 7, 1782.

bling you with the present application. On the removal of the seat of government I engaged his house on the hill. A house having always been found for the Governor I took for granted that the rent of that would be considered as a public charge. Tho' from the nature of my application to Colo Turpin I became personally liable to him, I flatter myself it will still be the opinion that it should be paid by the public. I therefore take the liberty of asking your interposition so far as to have a determination of the point by the Executive if you think it properly within their determination, or a reference to the Auditors if you judge that more proper. But what I most particularly sollicit your favor in is that it might be paid immediately if possible, as I shall otherwise think myself bound to pay it, which I really cannot do without much inconvenience. My tobaccoes of the last year having been destroyed by the enemy, I with great difficulty contrive the paiment of my taxes & can provide the additional sum of this rent, if I am to pay it, by no other means than a sale of some part of my estate. You will observe what Colo Turpin sais in his last letter as to the quantum of the rent, as also in the former letters every thing which had passed on that subject. I thought the first letter left it in my power to fix it at 8000 lb of tobo, & after advising with Mr Buchanon I closed it at that. It is one year's rent for which I stand answerable. I have written to Colo Turpin that I would apply to you on this subject & taken the liberty of desiring him to ask from you the results."[25] The Executive Council on September 24, 1782 authorized payment.

Photostats of Capitol Square Inquisitions in the Virginia State Archives show that on January 8, 1783, a jury valued fifteen acres of Dr. Philip Turpin's land (including improvements) at 4,000 £. and fifteen acres of unimproved land at 1,000 £. These tracts are indicated on a plat by Thomas Prosser dated December 20, 1782. The plat shows a rectangular lot marked "Jefferson" and described as "Jeffersons Lott." The upper end of this lot lies along a street marked "Down the main street"; the lower end is adjacent to lots bearing the names of William Hay and Gulleer, which lie above the "Garden." The long side of the "Jefferson" lot fronts on a "cross street" which intersects the "main road down Shockoe Hill." This road curves across the "cross street," towards the street marked "Down the main street."

The hypothesis that the Turpin house was situated at Broad and

[25] *Ibid.*, 8.

Governor Streets assumes, first, that Jefferson lived in a house on the lot marked "Jefferson," and furthermore that on a correct interpretation of the plat that lot is situated at the location mentioned.

The intersection of a curving road down the hill with a straight street at a point just a short distance below a street at right angles to the straight street strongly suggests the intersection of Governor Street, near where it curves around the present Governor's Mansion into Capitol Street, with Twelfth Street.

The corner lot would be numbered 349. In the tax book for September, 1782, that lot was occupied by Hunter, Banks & Co. who had been there for a period of two years. That would roughly correspond with the dates of Jefferson's occupation of the Turpin house.

That lot is probably included in the land conveyed by the deed of November 8, 1791, from Philip Turpin and Caroline his wife to John Amminett.[26]

It might be possible to locate the Jefferson lot from a survey of some of the other landmarks shown in Prosser's plat, for example, the lots of Hay, "Gulleer," and the Garden. It is believed those lots are conveyed in the following deeds, the descriptions in which might serve to orient the search: William Hay and Elizabeth his wife to Benjamin Harrison, Jr., December 6, 1784 (Henrico County Deeds, I, 309); same to Nicholas Gauteer, December 6, 1784 (Henrico County Deeds, I, 310); T. M. Randolph, Governor, to William Moncure, October 14, 1820 (Richmond Deeds, XVIII, 72, 76 [plot of Governor's Garden]).[27]

It should be noted that an ordinance of December 9, 1835, permitted Gustavus A. Myers, then the owner of the corner lot, in recompense for land taken to widen Broad Street, to extend his property line on Governor Street for a distance varying from ten feet at Broad Street to six and one-half feet at the lower end of the lot. Also an ordinance of May 20, 1816, reduced the width of Capitol Street to sixty-six feet and ordered grading of streets. Particular attention should be given to the extract from the proceedings of the Directors of Public Buildings on July 17, 1780. Jefferson, Archibald Cary, Edmund Randolph, Turner

[26] Henrico County Deeds, III, 522. See Lancaster, *Historic Virginia Homes and Churches*, 129.

[27] See *Journal of the House of Delegates* for 1810–11, 91, regarding sale of Governor's Garden.

Southall, Robert Goode, James Buchanan, and Samuel Duvall were present at that meeting of the Directors. That extract,[28] obtained from William Hay in 1808, preserves the names and locations of streets in Richmond laid out by the Directors in the vicinity of the Capitol Square.[29]

[28] Recorded, pursuant to an ordinance passed July 18, 1808, in Ordinances, October 20, 1806, to March 30, 1816, 27–32, in the Richmond City Hall.

[29] Richmond City Hall, Records, No. 3, January 18, 1808, to December 20, 1813, 21, 24 (under date of June 20, 1808, and July 18, 1808).

CHRONOLOGICAL ITINERARY OF JEFFERSON'S TRAVELS

Compiled chiefly from Jefferson's account books, his autobiography, his travel notes in Lipscomb and Bergh, Writings, XVII, 153–290, and the itinerary and chronology contained in each volume of Ford, Writings. In parentheses, following the place where they are located, are given the names of hostelries patronized by Jefferson.

Attending Continental Congress

1775.

June 11. "Set out from Wms.burgh for Philadelphia." At Ruffin's Ferry.

June 12. At King William Court House and "Aylett's."

June 13. At Fredericksburg.

June 14. At Howe's Ferry.

June 16. At Port Tobacco (Mrs. Halkinson's).

June 17. At Upper Marlboro (Mrs. Gibson's), London Town, Annapolis.

June 18. At Rockhall (Greentree's).

June 19. At "Downs's."

June 20. At Middletown (Witherspoon's), Wilmington, Chester (Mrs. Withey's), "arrived in Philadelphia."

Aug. 1. Left Philadelphia. At Chester (Mrs. Withey's), Christiana Ferry.

Aug. 2. At Newcastle (Mrs. Clay's), Warwick (McCullough's), "Downs's."

Aug. 3. At "Worrall's, in Newtown upon Chester," Rockhall (Hodges's), Annapolis (Middleton's).

Aug. 4. At London Town, Marlborough (Mrs. Gibson's), Piscataway.

Aug. 5. At Young's Ferry, Howe's.

Aug. 6. At Portroyal (Buckner's), Bowling Green.

Aug. 9. At Richmond, attending Virginia Convention.

1775.

Aug. 11. Re-elected member of Continental Congress.

Sep. 25. "set out from Monticello for Philadelphia." At Orange Court House (Bell's).

Sep. 26. At "Porter's on the Rappidan," "Bradley's in Culpepper," "Elk-run church."

Oct. 1. Arrives at Philadelphia.

Dec. 28. Left Philadelphia.

Dec. 29. At Wilmington, "Marshall's," Head of Elk.

Dec. 31. At "Stephenson's on Susquehanna."

1776.

Jan. 1. At "Ewens's."

Jan. 2. At Bushtown.

Jan. 3. At Baltimore.

Jan. 4. At "Rawlings's," and Upper Marlbro', and Piscataway.

Jan. 5. At Port Tobacco.

Jan. 6. At Young's Ferry.

Jan. 7. At Fredericksburgh.

Jan. 9. At Monticello.

May 7. Leaves Monticello.

May 8. At Orange Court House and Culpepper Court House.

May 9. At Fauquier Court House and Red House.

May 10. At "Lacy's," Leesburgh (McIntyre's), and "Knowland's on Patowmack."

May 11. At Fredericktown and Tawneytown (Caleb's).

May 12. At McAlister's Town (Rhenegher's), York (White's), and Wright's Ferry.

May 13. At "Ryckhart's in Lancaster," "at the bull," at "Black-horse."

May 14. At Chester (Mrs. Withey's). Arrives at Philadelphia.

Sep. 3. "Left Philadelphia."

Sep. 4. At "the White horse," "the Three crowns," and Lancaster ("Ryckhart's").

Sep. 5. At Wright's Ferry and York (White's).

1776.

Sep. 6. At "Rheneger's in Mc Alister's town," Tawneytown (Caleb's), and Frederick (Crush's).

Sep. 7. At "Knowland's on Patowmack," Leesburgh (Mc Entire's).

Sep. 8. At "Tyler's at the Red house."

Sep. 9. At "Porter's" and Monticello.

1783.

Oct. 16. "Left Monticello for Congress."

Oct. 17. At "Hayes's."

Oct. 20. At Savage's in Woodstock.

Oct. 24. At Winchester (McGuire's).

Oct. 25. At Harper's Ferry.

Oct. 26. At Fredericktown (Morris's [Catauba King]) and Tawneytown.

Oct. 27. At McAlister's Town.

Oct. 28. At Susquehanna (Jeffery's) and Lancaster (Rykhart's [Bear]).

Oct. 29. At Philadelphia (Thompson's Indn. Queen).

Nov. 3. At Trenton.

Nov. 4. At Princeton, takes seat in Congress.

Nov. 5. Leaves Princeton. At Trenton.

Nov. 6. At "McElroy's," Cross Keys, Bristol, and the "Red Lion."

Nov. 7. At Philadelphia.

Nov. 22. Leaves Philadelphia. At Chester.

Nov. 23. At Newport.

Nov. 25. At Baltimore and Annapolis.

Tour Through New England In 1784

1784.

May 7. Appointed on mission to negotiate treaties of commerce.

May 11. Leaves Annapolis.

May 12. At Rockhall (Spencer's).

May 13. At "Worral's," Chester.

May 14. At Newcastle ("Bail's"). At Chester (Mrs. Withey's). Arrives at Philadelphia.

1784.

May 28.	Leaves Philadelphia. At Bristol (Cross Keys), and Trenton.
May 29.	At Princeton and Brunswick.
May 30.	At Woodbridge, Elizabethtown. Arrives at New York (Mrs. Elsworth's).
June 1.	To Long Island and back.
June 5.	Leaves New York.
June 6.	At Fort Washington (Wilson's) and Rye (Mrs. Haviland's).
June 7.	At Stamford (Mrs. Wells's), Fairfield (Buckley's), and Stratford.
June 8.	At New Haven (the coffee house).
June 9.	At Middletown.
June 10.	At Hartford (Bull's).
June 11.	At Bolton, Lebanon, Norwich.
June 12.	At New London.
June 13.	At Pokatuck bridge and South Kingston.
June 14.	At Newport (Almy's).
June 16.	Left Newport. At Burr's, Warren.
June 17.	At Providence (Chace's).
June 18.	At "Mann's," Dedham ("Ames's"), and Boston.
June 21.	At Charlestown and Winnisimet.
June 22.	At Salem, ferriage Parker River, Ipswich, Newberry, ferriage Merrimac River, and Hampton (Sandburn's).
June 23.	At Portsmouth, N. H.
June 24.	At Exeter (Folsom's), Hampton (Sandburn's), and Newberry.
June 25.	At Beverley, Salem, and Marblehead.
June 26.	At Boston (Col. Ingersol's).

Travels In Europe

July 5.	Sails from Boston on the *Ceres*.
July 26.	Landed at West Cowes. To Portsmouth.
July 29.	At Farnham, Titchfield, Gosport, Portsmouth.
July 31.	Crossed to Havre de Grace (Mahon's l'aigle d'or).
Aug. 1.	At LaBotte, Bolbec, Aliquerville, Yvetot, Barentin, Rouen (Harp's Pomme de Pin).

1784.

Aug. 5.   Leaves Rouen. At Pont Saint-Ouen, Vaudreuil, Gaillon, Vernon, Bonnieres, Mantes, Meulan, Triel.

Aug. 6.   At St. Germain, Marly, Nanterre, Paris.

Aug. 10.   At Passy to see Franklin.

Sep. 15.   At Versailles with Franklin and Adams to see Vergennes.

1785.

June 20.   At St. Denis.

July 7.   At Vincennes.

Oct. 23.   At Sanois.

1786.

Mch. 6.   "Set out for London." At Chantilly and Breteuil.

Mch. 7.   At Abbeville.

Mch. 8.   At Montreuil and Calais.

Mch. 11. At London.

Mch. 22. Seeing castle at Windsor.

Apr. 2.   At Chiswick, Richmond, Twickenham, Hampton Court, Esherplace, Cobham, Weybridge.

Apr. 3.   At Weybridge, Woburn, Twickenham, and London.

Apr. 4.   At Twickenham, Woburn, Sunning Hill, Caversham, and Reading.

Apr. 5.   At Wallingford, Thame, Wotton, Buckingham.

Apr. 6.   At Banbury, Bicester, Stowe, Buckingham, Banbury, Kineton, Stratford-on-Avon.

Apr. 7.   At Hockley, Birmingham, Leasowes, Stourbridge.

Apr. 8.   At Bromsgrove, Hagley, Bromsgrove, Worcester, Winch-castle, Moreton, Lynston, Woodstock.

Apr. 9.   At Blenheim, Woodstock, Oxford, Tatsworth, High Wy-combe, Uxbridge.

Apr. 14. At Kew.

Apr. 17. At Ranelagh.

Apr. 18. At Buckingham House.

Apr. 20. Through Hyde Park and Kensington to Brentford to see Osterly and Sion House.

Apr. 26. "Set out from London for Paris." At Greenwich, Dart-ford, Rochester, Sittingbourne, Canterbury, Dover.

Apr. 27. Seeing castle at Dover.

Apr. 28. At Calais.

1786.

Apr. 29.	At St. Omer, Royes.
Apr. 30.	At Le Bourget. Arrived at Paris.
Aug. 10.	At Suresne.

1787.

Feb. 28.	"Set out from Paris." At Villeneuve, St. Lieu, Melun, Fontainebleau.
Mch. 2.	At Moret, Faussard, Villeneuve, Pont sur Yonne, Sens.
Mch. 3.	At Villevallar, Joigny, Basson, Auxerre, St. Bris, Vermenton, Lucy le Bois.
Mch. 4.	At Cussy les Forges, Rouvray, Maisonneuve, Vitteaux, La Chaleure, Pont de Pany, la Cude, Dijon (Hotel de Conde).
Mch. 7.	At Dijon, La Baraque, Nuits, Beaune, Pommard, Volnay, Meursault.
Mch. 8.	At Aussy, Chagny, Chalon-sur-Saone, Sennecey, Tournus.
Mch. 9.	At St. Albin, Macon, Maison Blanche, St. George de Renan, Chateau de Laye-Epinaye.
Mch. 11.	At Ville franche, Les Echelles, Puits d'or, Lyons (Hotel du Palais royal).
Mch. 15.	At St. Fond, St. Symphorin, Vienne.
Mch. 16.	At Auberive, le Péage, St. Rambert, St. Vallier, Tain.
Mch. 17.	Ferry over Isere. At Valence, La Paillasse, L'Oriol, Laine, Montelimar.
Mch. 18.	At Donserre, Pierrelatte, la Palus, Mornas, Orange, Mornas, Pont St. Esprit.
Mch. 19.	At Bagnols, Connault, Valliguières, Remoulins, St. Gervasy, Nismes.
Mch. 24.	At Arles, Tarascon, St. Remy (Cheval blanc).
Mch. 25.	At Orgon, Pontroyal, St. Cannat, Aix (Hotel St. Jaques).
Mch. 29.	At Aix, Le Pin, Marseilles (Hotel des Princes).
Apr. 2.	At Chateau d'If.
Apr. 5.	At Chateau de Borelli.
Apr. 6.	At Aubagne, Cuges, le Beausset, Toulon.
Apr. 7.	At Toulon.
Apr. 8.	At Toulon, Hyères, Cuers, Pignans, le Luc (Hotel St. Anne).

1787.

Apr. 9.	At Vidauban, le Muy, Fréjus, Lestrelles, Napoule, Antibes.
Apr. 10.	At Nice (Hotel de York).
Apr. 13.	At Scarena.
Apr. 14.	At Sospello, Breglio, Saorgio, Fontan, and Ciandola.
Apr. 15.	At Tende, Limone, Coni (à la Croix blanche).
Apr. 16.	At Centallo, Savigliano, Racconigi, Poirino, and Turin.
Apr. 17.	At Turin (Hotel d'Angleterre).
Apr. 18.	At Moncaglieri, Stupinigi, and Superga.
Apr. 19.	At Settimo, Chivasso, Ciliano, St. Germano, and Vercelli.
Apr. 20.	At Vercelli, Novara, Buffalora, Sedriano, and Milan (Albergo reale).
Apr. 23.	Leaves Milan. At Casino, Rozzano, Binasco, and Pavia (al Croce bianco).
Apr. 24.	At Voghere and Tortona.
Apr. 25.	At Novi (à la Poste), Voltaggio, Campomorone (a la rosa rossa), and Genoa (St. Marthe, Cerf).
Apr. 27.	At Sestri, Pegli, and Nervi.
Apr. 28.	At Noli.
Apr. 29.	At Albenga.
Apr. 30.	At Oneglia and St. Remo (Auberge de la poste).
May 1.	At Ventimiglia, Menton, Monaco, Nice (Hotel de York).
May 2.	At Antibes, Napoules, Lestrelle.
May 3.	At Fréjus, Muy, Vidauban, Luc, Brignoles, Tourves, Pourcieux, La Galiniere, Aix (Hotel St. Jaques).
May 4.	At Le Grand Pin, Marseilles (Hotel des Princes).
May 7.	At Aix, St. Cannat, Pontroyal, Orgon.
May 8.	At St. Andiol, Avignon (Hotel de St. Omer), and Vaucluse.
May 9.	At Ville Neuve d'Avignon, Remoulins, St. Gervasy, Nismes (Hotel de Luxemburg).
May 10.	At Nismes, Uchaud, Colombieres, Lunel, Montpellier.
May 11.	At Montpellier.
May 12.	At Frontignan and Cette (Au grand Gaillon).
May 13.	At Agde.
May 15.	At Beziers, Argilies, and Saumal.
May 16.	At Marseillette.

234

1787.

May 17.   At Carcassonne (Hotel de St. Jean baptiste).

May 18.   At Castelnaudary (Hotel de Notredame).

May 19.   At St. Feriol, Escarmare, Lampy.

May 20.   At Narouze, Villefranche, Baziège.

May 21.   At Toulouse (Hotel du Griffon d'or).

May 22.   At St. Gerry, Grisolles, Montauban, Moissac, Malause, Magistere, Croquelaudy.

May 23.   At Agen (Hotel petit St. Jean), St. Hilaire, Port Ste. Marie, Aiguillon, Tonneins, Marmaude, Mottelandron, La Preole, Cauderat, Langon, Barlade, Castres.

May 24.   At Prade, Bouscaut, Bordeaux (Hotel de Richelieu).

May 28.   At Blaye.

May 29.   At Etauliers, St. Aubin, Mirambeau, St. Genis, Pons, Lajart, Saintes, St. Porchaire, St. Hyppolite, Rochefort.

May 30.   At Bacha, Le Rocher, Rochelle, Usseau, Marans, Moreilles, Ste. Hermine.

May 31.   At Chantenay, St. Fulgent, Montaigu, Aigrefeuille, Nantes (A la Croix verte).

June 1.   At Le Temple, Moere, Pontchateau, Rochebernard, Massillac.

June 2.   At Thex, Vannes, Auray, Landevant, Hennebont, L'Orient (Hotel de l'Épée royale).

June 3.   At Hennebont, Baud, Locminé, Josselin.

June 4.   At Ploermel, Campenéac, Plélan, Mordelles, Rennes.

June 5.   At Bout des Landes, Roudun, Brecharaye, Derval, Nozay, Bout de Bois, Gesvres, Nantes (St. Julien).

June 6.   Manves, le Plessis, Ancenis (Hotel de Bretagne).

June 7.   At Varades, Loriottiere, St. George, Angers, Daguiniere, La Menitré, Roziers, La Croix Verte, La Rivière, Les Trois Volées.

June 8.   At Langeais, Tours, La Frilliere, Amboise, Chanteloupe, Veuve.

June 9.   At Chousy, Blois, Chateau Menars, Menars la ville, Beaugency, Meung, Fourneau, Orleans (À la poste).

June 10.   At Chavilly, Artenay, Toury, Angerville, Montdesir, Etampes, Estrechy, Arpajon, Longjumeau, Croix de Bernis, Paris.

1788.

Mch. 4.	"Set out for Amsterdam." At le Bourget, Louvres, Chapelle, Senlis, Le Pont St. Maxence, Bois le Duc, Gournay, Le Cuvilley, Couchy, Roye, Fonches, Peronne (Grand Cerf).
Mch. 5.	At Fins, Bonair, Cambray, Bouchain, Valenciennes, Quiévran, Quaregnon, Mons, Casteau, Braine le Compte.
Mch. 6.	At Hal, Bruxelles, Malines, Antwerp.
Mch. 7.	At Agtenbroek, Kruystraet, Moerdyk.
Mch. 8.	At Rotterdam.
Mch. 9.	At The Hague.
Mch. 10.	At Amsterdam (Waping van Amsterdam).
Mch. 20.	Excursion to Haarlem.
Mch. 22.	At Saerdam.
Mch. 30.	Leaves Amsterdam.
Mch. 31.	At Utrecht (Aublette's) and Nimuegen.
Apr. 1.	At Cranenburg, Cleves, Santen, Reynberg, Hoogstraat.
Apr. 2.	At Essenberg, Duysberg and Düsseldorf (Zimmerman's).
Apr. 3.	At Langveld, Cologne (Holy Ghost, Ingels), Bonn, Remagen, Andernach, Coblentz (The Wild Man).
Apr. 5.	At Nassau.
Apr. 6.	At Nasteden, Schwalbach, Wiesbaden, Hadersheim, Frankfort (Rothen House).
Apr. 8.	At Hanau.
Apr. 10.	At Hadersheim, Mayence, Hocheim, Mayence.
Apr. 11.	At Rudesheim, Johansberg, Markebronn, Mayence (Hotel de Mayence).
Apr. 12.	At Oppenheim, Worms, Mannheim (Cour du Palatin).
Apr. 14.	At Dossenheim, Heidelberg, Schwetzingen, Kaeferthall.
Apr. 15.	At Spire, Graben, Karlsruh (Au Prince héréditaire).
Apr. 16.	At Rastadt, Scholhofen, Bischofheim, Kehl, Strasbourg (À l'Esprit).
Apr. 18.	At Stutzheim, Wiltenheim, Saverne, Phalsbourg.
Apr. 19.	At Fénestrange, Dieuze, Moyenvic, Champenous, Nancy.
Apr. 20.	At Velaine, Toul, Laye, Void, St. Aubin, Ligny en Barrois, Bar le Duc, St. Dizier.

1788.

Apr. 21.   At Longchamp, Vitry, La Chaussée, Châlons sur Marne, Épernay.

Apr. 22.   Aij, Auvillaij, Cumieres, Pierry.

Apr. 23.   At Port á Bainson, Dormans, Parois, Chateau Thierry, la Ferme de Paris, La Ferté, Meaux, Claye, Bordy, Vergalant, Paris.

1789.

Sep. 26.   "Left Paris." At Vernon.

Sep. 27.   At Bolbec.

Sep. 28.   At Havre (Aigle d'or).

Oct. 8.   Left Havre.

Oct. 9.   Arrived at Cowes (Fountain Inn).

Oct. 11.   At Newport and Carybrook Castle.

Oct. 22.   Embarked on the *Clermont*.

Oct. 23.   Weighed anchor off Yarmouth.

Nov. 23.   Landed at Norfolk.

Tour Through New England In 1791

1791.

May 17.   Leaves Philadelphia.

May 18.   At Bristol, Trenton, and Princeton.

May 19.   At Brunswick, Elizabethtown Point. Reaches New York (Elsworth's).

May 21.   Leaves New York.

May 22.   At "Conklin's."

May 23.   At Poughkeepsie (Hendrickson's).

May 24.   At Lasher's, Swartz's, Katchum's.

May 25.   At Pulvar's, Claverack, Hudson, Kinderhook.

May 26.   At Albany.

May 27.   At Troy, Lansingburg, Waterford. "Visited the falls at Cohoes," lodged at Benjamin's.

May 28.   At Stillwater (Ensign's), Saratoga, McNeel's Ferry, Fort Edwards (Baldwin's).

May 29.   At Sandy Hill Falls, Wing's Falls, Fort George, Fort William Henry.

May 30.   On Lake George. At Ticonderoga (Hay's), Crown Point.

1791.

May 31.	On Lake Champlain. "Sailed half way to Split Rock." Returned to Ticonderoga.
June 1.	"Repassed Lake George." "Back to Fort George."
June 2.	"Visited Wing's Falls and Sandy Hill Falls."
June 3.	"Crossed the Hudson at Saratoga." At Cambridge (Colvin's).
June 4.	Visited the battle field at Bennington.
June 5.	At Bennington (Dewy's), detained by Blue Laws.
June 6.	At Williamstown (Killock's), New Ashfield, Lanesboro (Wheeler's), Pittsfield, Dalton (Mrs. Marsh's).
June 7.	At Worthington (Smith's) and Northampton (Pomeroy's).
June 8.	At West Springfield (Stebbins's), East Springfield, Suffield (Hitchcock's), Windsor, Hartford (Frederick Bull's).
June 10.	At Weathersfield, Sidon Hill, Middletown (Mrs. Bigelow's), "Strandford's."
June 11.	At Guilford (Medab Stone's). "Sailed for Long Island and was on the Sound all night."
June 12.	At Oysterpond Point (Tupple's) and Southhold (Mrs. Peck's).
June 13.	At Riverhead (Griffin's) and Morichies (Downs's).
June 14.	At "Genl. Floyd's," "Hart's," and "Terry's." "Visited the Unquachog Indians."
June 15.	At Hamstead, Flushing (Prince's), and Jamaica.
June 16.	At Brooklyn and New York.
June 17.	At Pauler's Hook, Bergen Point, Staten Island, Richmond, Billing's Point, Perth Amboy.
June 18.	At South Amboy, Spotswood, "Williamson's," Cranberry, Allentown (Francis's).
June 19.	At Bordentown, Burlington, Dun's Ferry. Arrives at Philadelphia.

Table of Jefferson's Trips to the Capital, as Secretary of State, Vice President, and President

Lv. Monticello	Arr. Capital	Lv. Capital	Arr. Monticello
1790–Mch. 1	(N.Y.) Mch. 21	(N.Y.) Sep. 1	Sep. 19
Nov. 8	(Phila.) Nov. 21	- - - - -	- - - - -
1791–Oct. 12	Oct. 22	(Phila.) Sep. 2	Sep. 12
1792–Sep. 27	Oct. 5	July 13	July 22
1793–Oct. 25	Nov. 1	Sep. 17	Sep. 25
1794 - - - - -	- - - - -	Jan. 5	Jan. 16
1797–Feb. 20	Mch. 2	Mch. 13	Mch. 20
May 5	May 11	July 6	July 11
Dec. 4	Dec. 12	- - - - -	- - - - -
1798–Dec. 18	Dec. 25	June 27	July 4
1799–Dec. 21	Dec. 28	Mch. 1	Mch. 8
1800–Nov. 24	(Wash.) Nov. 27	(Phila.) May 15	May 29
1801–Apr. 26	(Wash.) Apr. 29	(Wash.) Apr. 1	Apr. 4
Sep. 27	Sep. 30	July 30	Aug. 2
1802–May 27	May 30	May 5	May 8
Oct. 1	Oct. 4	July 21	July 25
1803–Mch. 31	Apr. 3	Mch. 7	Mch. 11
Sep. 22	Sep. 25	July 19	July 22
1804–May 11	May 13	Apr. 1	Apr. 4
Sep. 27	Sept. 30	July 23	July 26
1805–Apr. 14	Apr. 17	Mch. 14	Mch. 17
Sep. 29	Oct. 3	July 15	July 18
1806–June 4	June 7	May 6	May 9
Oct. 1	Oct. 4	July 21	July 24
1807–May 13	May 16	Apr. 7	Apr. 11
Sep. 30	Oct. 3	Aug. 1	Aug. 4
1808–June 8	June 10	May 6	May 11
Sep. 28	Oct. 2	July 20	July 23
1809 - - - - -	- - - - -	Mch. 11	Mch. 15

Bibliography

❁

BIBLIOGRAPHICAL MATERIAL

Several useful bibliographies on Jefferson are available:

Johnston, Richard H. *A Contribution to a Bibliography of Thomas Jefferson*. Washington, 1905. (Contained in the Memorial Edition of Jefferson's Writings, Vol. XX.)

Tompkins, Hamilton B. *Bibliotheca Jeffersoniana, a List of Books Written by or Relating to Thomas Jefferson*. New York, 1887. (Particularly valuable for earlier writings, especially political pamphlets attacking or defending Jefferson.)

Wise, W. Harvey, and John W. Cronin. *Bibliography of Thomas Jefferson*. Washington, 1935. (A comprehensive recent bibliography.)

Interesting comments on the difficulty of preparing an adequate Jefferson bibliography are found in:

Peden, William H. *Some Aspects of Jefferson Bibliography*. Lexington, Va., 1941. (See also Randolph G. Adams in *The Colophon*, n. s. Vol. III, No. 1 [Winter, 1938], 134–36).

The following three volumes are a helpful guide to an important collection of Jefferson manuscripts now in the Library of Congress:

Calendar of the Correspondence of Thomas Jefferson. Bulletin of the Bureau of Rolls and Library of the Department of State: No. 6, July, 1894 (Letters from Jefferson); No. 8, November, 1894 (Letters to Jefferson); No. 10, June, 1903 (Supplementary). (Synopses of the letters are arranged under the names of the correspondents, by date.)

Information regarding the principal collections of Jefferson manuscripts is given in:

Bullock, Helen D. "The Papers of Thomas Jefferson," *The American Archivist*, Vol. IV, No. 4 (October, 1941), 238–49.

241

MANUSCRIPT COLLECTIONS

Alderman Library, University of Virginia, Manuscript Collections.
Henry E. Huntington Library, San Marino, California, Manuscript Collections.
Historical Society of Pennsylvania, Manuscript Collections.
Library of Congress, Manuscripts Division, Jefferson Papers.
Library of Congress, Manuscripts Division, Madison Papers.
Library of Congress, Manuscripts Division, Shippen Papers.
Library of Congress, Manuscripts Division, William Short Papers.
Massachusetts Historical Society, Jefferson Papers.
Missouri Historical Society, Bixby Collection.
New York Public Library, Manuscripts Division.
Pierpont Morgan Library, Manuscript Collections.

ACCOUNT BOOKS

Jefferson's expenditures, and other memoranda, were recorded by him in notebooks (for some of the earlier years, in the blank pages of almanacs), the location of the originals of which is indicated below:

1767–70 Library of Congress (deposited by General Jefferson Randolph Kean).
1771–72 Massachusetts Historical Society.
1773   Library of Congress.
1774   Massachusetts Historical Society.
1775   Henry E. Huntington Library.
1776–78 Massachusetts Historical Society.
1779–82 Library of Congress.
1783–90 Massachusetts Historical Society.
1791–1803 New York Public Library.
1804–26 Massachusetts Historical Society.

JEFFERSON'S PUBLISHED WRITINGS

Adams, Elizabeth L. (ed.). "The Jefferson Bicentenary: Unpublished Letters by Thomas Jefferson," *More Books, The Bulletin of the Boston Public Library*, Vol. XVIII, No. 4 (April, 1943), 151–62.

Betts, Edwin Morris (ed.). *Thomas Jefferson's Garden Book, 1766–1824.* Philadelphia, 1944.

Brydon, G. MacLaren (ed.). "Letters from Old Trunks," *Virginia Magazine of History and Biography*, Vol. XLVIII, No. 2 (April, 1940), 97–103.

[Cabell, Nathaniel F.] *Early History of the University of Virginia as*

Contained in the Letters of Thomas Jefferson and Joseph C. Cabell. Richmond, 1856.

Cary, Wilson Miles (ed.). "Some Family Letters of Thomas Jefferson," *Scribner's Magazine,* Vol. XXXVI, No. 5 (November, 1904), 573–86.

Chinard, Gilbert. *Les Amitiés américaines de Madame d'Houdetot, d'après sa correspondance inédite avec Benjamin Franklin et Thomas Jefferson.* Paris, 1924.

————. "La Correspondance de Madame de Stael avec Jefferson." *Revue de Littérature comparée,* Vol. II, No. 4 (October, 1922), 621–40.

————. *The Correspondence of Jefferson and Du Pont de Nemours.* Baltimore and Paris, 1931.

————. *Jefferson et les Idéologues.* Baltimore and Paris, 1925.

————. *The Letters of Lafayette and Jefferson.* Baltimore and Paris, 1929.

————. *Trois Amitiés françaises de Jefferson.* Paris, 1927.

Cuthbert, Norma B. "Poplar Forest: Jefferson's Legacy to His Grandson," *The Huntington Library Quarterly,* Vol. VI, No. 3 (May, 1943), 333–56.

Diamond, Sigmund (ed.). "Some Jefferson Letters," *Mississippi Valley Historical Review,* XXVIII, No. 2 (September, 1941), 225–42.

Dickore, Marie (ed.). *Two Letters From Thomas Jefferson to his Relatives the Turpins who Settled in The Little Miami Valley in 1797.* Oxford, Ohio, 1941.

Foley, John P. (ed.). *The Jeffersonian Cyclopedia.* New York, 1900. (A convenient compilation.)

Ford, Paul Leicester (ed.). *Autobiography of Thomas Jefferson.* New York, 1914.

————. *The Works of Thomas Jefferson.* New York, 1904. Federal Edition. 12 vols.

————. *The Writings of Thomas Jefferson.* New York, 1892–99. 10 vols.

Ford, Worthington Chauncey (ed.). *Thomas Jefferson Correspondence Printed from the Originals in the Collections of William K. Bixby.* Boston, 1916.

Jenkins, Charles Francis. *Jefferson's Germantown Letters.* Philadelphia, 1906.

"Letters of Thomas Jefferson to William Short," *William and Mary College Quarterly* (2d series), Vol. XI, No. 3 (July, 1931), 242–

50; No. 4 (October, 1931), 336–42; Vol. XII, No. 2 (April, 1932), 145–56; No. 4 (October, 1932), 287–304; Vol. XIII, No. 2 (April, 1933), 98–116.

Lipscomb, Andrew A., and A. Ellery Bergh (eds.). *The Writings of Thomas Jefferson.* Washington, 1903. Memorial Edition. 20 vols.

Malone, Dumas. *Correspondence between Thomas Jefferson and Pierre Samuel du Pont de Nemours, 1798–1817.* Boston, 1930.

Massachusetts Historical Society (*Collections,* Seventh Series, Vol. I). *The Jefferson Papers.* Boston, 1890.

Missouri Historical Society, "Correspondence of Thomas Jefferson, 1788–1826," *Glimpses of the Past,* Vol. III, Nos. 4–6 (April–June, 1936), 77–133.

Randall, Henry S. *The Life of Thomas Jefferson.* New York, 1858. 3 vols. (The standard biography of Jefferson, containing many of his letters.)

Randolph, Sarah N. *The Domestic Life of Thomas Jefferson.* New York, 1871. (Contains many of Jefferson's family letters.)

Randolph, Thomas J. (ed.). *Memoir, Correspondence and Miscellanies, from the Papers of Thomas Jefferson.* Charlottesville, Va., 1829. 4 vols.

Severance, Frank H. (ed.). "A Bundle of Thomas Jefferson's Letters, Now First Published," *Publications of the Buffalo Historical Society,* Vol. VII (1904), 1–32.

Washington, Henry A. (ed.). *The Writings of Thomas Jefferson.* Washington, D. C., 1853–54. 9 vols.

WRITINGS OF JEFFERSON'S CONTEMPORARIES

Adams, Charles Francis (ed.). *The Works of John Adams, Second President of the United States.* Boston, 1850–56. 10 vols.

———. *Letters of Mrs. Adams, Wife of John Adams.* Boston, 1848. Fourth Edition.

Bulfinch, Ellen Susan. *The Life and Letters of Charles Bulfinch.* Boston, 1896.

Davenport, Beatrix Cary (ed.). *A Diary of the French Revolution by Gouverneur Morris.* Boston, 1939. 2 vols.

Fitzpatrick, John C. (ed.). *The Writings of George Washington.* Washington, 1931–44. 39 vols.

Hunt, Gaillard (ed.). *The Writings of James Madison.* New York, 1900–10. 9 vols.

Johnston, Henry P. (ed.). *Correspondence and Public Papers of John Jay.* New York, 1890–93. 4 vols.

Logan, Deborah Norris. *Memoir of Dr. George Logan of Stenton*. Philadelphia, 1899.

Long, Orie W. *Thomas Jefferson and George Ticknor, a Chapter in American Scholarship*. Williamstown, Mass., 1933.

Marraro, Howard R. (ed.). *Memoirs of the Life and Peregrinations of the Florentine Philip Mazzei 1730–1816*. New York, 1942.

Trumbull, John. *Autobiography, Reminiscences and Letters of John Trumbull, from 1756 to 1841*. New York and London, 1841.

PUBLIC RECORDS

Commonwealth of Virginia. *Acts of the General Assembly.*

———. *Calendar of Virginia State Papers.*

———. *Journal of the Executive Council.*

———. *Journal of the House of Delegates.*

———. *Official Letters of the Governors of the State of Virginia.*

———. *The Statutes at Large.* (Edited by William Waller Hening).

Continental Congress. *Journals.*

ARCHIVES

Albemarle County Deeds (Charlottesville, Va.).

Anne Arundel County Deeds (Annapolis, Md.).

Hall of Records (Annapolis, Md.).

Henrico County Deeds (Richmond, Va.).

Lawyers Title Insurance Company (Richmond, Va.).

Richmond City Hall, Ordinances (Richmond, Va.).

Richmond City Hall, Records (Richmond, Va.).

Richmond Deeds (Richmond, Va.).

Richmond Tax Books (Richmond, Va.).

Valentine Museum (Richmond, Va.).

Virginia State Archives (Richmond, Va.).

NEWSPAPERS

Maryland Journal and Baltimore Advertiser.
Porcupine's Gazette.
Richmond Enquirer.
Richmond Standard.
Virginia Gazette.
Virginia Gazette and General Advertiser.
Williamsburg Gazette.

ARTICLES

Allen, Edward A. "Thomas Jefferson and the Study of English," *Academy*, Vol. IV, No. 1 (February, 1889), 1–10.

Anderson, D. R. "Jefferson and the Virginia Constitution," *American Historical Review*, Vol. XXI, No. 4 (July, 1916), 750–54.

Barnwell, James G. "Some of the Alleys, Courts and Inns of Philadelphia, 1767–1790," *Pennsylvania Magazine of History and Biography*, Vol. XXXVII, No. 145 (January, 1913), 107–16.

Bolton, Theodore, and Harry L. Binsse. "Trumbull, 'Historiographer' of the Revolution," *Antiquarian*, Vol. XVII, No. 1 (July, 1931), 13–18, 50, 52, 54, 56, 58.

Branchi, Dr. E. C. (trans.). "Memoirs of the Life and Voyages of Doctor Philip Mazzei," *William and Mary College Quarterly* (2d series), Vol. X, No. 1 (January, 1930), 1–18.

Brasch, Frederick E. "Thomas Jefferson, the Scientist," *Science*, Vol. XCVII, No. 2518 (April 2, 1943), 300–301.

Brock, Robert A. "The Adams Family," in the *Richmond Standard*, December 11, 1880.

Brown, Ralph H. "Jefferson's Notes on Virginia," *Geographical Review*, Vol. XXXIII, No. 3 (July, 1943), 467–73.

Bryan, William J. "Jeffersonian Principles," *North American Review*, Vol. CLXVIII, No. 6 (June, 1899), 670–78.

[Bulfinch, Thomas.] "Jefferson's Private Character," *North American Review*, Vol. XCI, No. 188 (July, 1860), 107–18.

Caldwell, Lynton K. "The Jurisprudence of Thomas Jefferson," *Indiana Law Journal*, Vol. XVIII, No. 3 (April, 1943), 193–213.

Chamberlain, Alexander F. "Thomas Jefferson's Ethnological Opinions and Activities," *American Anthropologist*, Vol. IX, No. 3 (July–September, 1907), 499–509.

Chandler, Julian A. C. "Jefferson and William and Mary," *William and Mary College Quarterly* (2d series), Vol. XIV, No. 4 (October, 1934), 304–307.

Chinard, Gilbert. "Jefferson and the American Philosophical Society," *Proceedings* of the American Philosophical Society, Vol. LXXXVII, No. 3 (July, 1943), 263–76.

———. "Jefferson and the Physiocrats," *University of California Chronicle*, Vol. XXXIII, No. 1 (January, 1931), 18–31.

———. "Thomas Jefferson as a Classical Scholar," *The American Scholar*, Vol. I, No. 2 (March, 1932), 133–43.

Davis, John W. "Thomas Jefferson, Attorney-at-Law," *Proceedings* of the Virginia State Bar Association, Vol. XXXVIII (1926), 361–77.

Didier, Eugene L. "Thomas Jefferson as a Lawyer," *Green Bag*, Vol. XV, No. 4 (April, 1903), 153–59.

Dorfman, Joseph. "The Economic Philosophy of Thomas Jefferson," *Political Science Quarterly*, Vol. LV, No. 1 (March, 1940), 98–121.

Dumbauld, Edward. "Thomas Jefferson and Pennsylvania," *Pennsylvania History*, Vol. V, No. 3 (July, 1938), 157–65.

———. "Thomas Jefferson in Princeton," *Princeton Alumni Weekly*, Vol. XLIII, No. 26 (April 9, 1943), 5–6.

———. "Where Did Jefferson Live in Paris?," *William and Mary College Quarterly* (2d series), Vol. XXIII, No. 1 (January, 1943), 64–68.

Dunning, E. O. "Private Character of Thomas Jefferson," *New Englander*, Vol. XIX, No. 70 (July, 1861), 648–73.

Finkelnburg, Gustavus A. "Thomas Jefferson as a Lawyer," *American Law Review*, Vol. XXXIX (May–June, 1905), 321–29.

Fitzhugh, Thomas. "Letters of Thomas Jefferson Concerning Philology and the Classics," *University of Virginia Alumni Bulletin*, (3rd series), Vol. XI, No. 2 (April, 1918), 168–87; Nos. 4–5 (August–October, 1918), 377–95; Vol. XII, No. 1 (January, 1919), 66–78; No. 2 (April, 1919), 155–77.

Ford, Paul L. "Thomas Jefferson in Undress," *Scribner's Magazine*, Vol. XII, No. 4 (October, 1892), 509–16.

Foster, Sir Augustus J. "Notes on the United States," *Quarterly Review*, Vol. LXVIII, No. 135 (June, 1841), 20–57.

Fowler, Samuel. "The Political Opinions of Jefferson," *North American Review*, Vol. CI, No. 209 (October, 1865), 313–35.

Galbreath, C. B. "Thomas Jefferson's Views on Slavery," *Ohio Archaeological and Historical Quarterly*, Vol. XXXIV, No. 2 (April, 1925), 184–202.

Garbett, Arthur S. "Thomas Jefferson's Life-Long Love of Music," *Etude*, Vol. LIX, No. 8 (August, 1941), 510, 568.

Gauss, Charles E. "Thomas Jefferson's Musical Interests," *Etude*, Vol. LI, No. 6 (June, 1933), 367–68, 419.

Gould, William D. "The Religious Opinions of Thomas Jefferson," *Mississippi Valley Historical Review*, Vol. XX, No. 2 (September, 1933), 191–208.

Greely, Arthur W. "Jefferson as a Geographer," *National Geographic Magazine*, Vol. VII, No. 8 (August, 1896), 269–71.

Guernsey, A. H. "Thomas Jefferson and His Family," *Harper's New Monthly Magazine*, Vol. XLIII, No. 255 (August, 1871), 366–80.

Hall, J. Lesslie. "The Religious Opinions of Thomas Jefferson," *Sewanee Review*, Vol. XXI, No. 2 (April, 1913), 164–76.

Hamilton, J. G. de Roulhac. "Jefferson and Religion," *The Reviewer*, Vol. V, No. 4 (October, 1925), 5–15.

Hart, Andrew deJarnette, Jr. "Thomas Jefferson's Influence on the Foundation of Medical Instruction at the University of Virginia," *Annals of Medical History*, n. s. Vol. X, No. 1 (January, 1938), 47–60.

Hart, Charles H. "Life Portraits of Thomas Jefferson," *McClure's Magazine*, Vol. XI, No. 1 (May, 1898), 47–55.

[Hawks, Francis L.] "Character of Mr. Jefferson; review of the Life of Mr. Jefferson by George Tucker," *The New York Review*, Vol. I, No. 1 (March, 1837), 5–58.

Hellman, C. Doris. "Jefferson's Efforts towards the Decimalization of United States Weights and Measures," *Isis*, Vol. XVI, No. 49 (November, 1931), 266–314.

Herzberg, Max J. "Thomas Jefferson as a Man of Letters," *South Atlantic Quarterly*, Vol. XIII, No. 4 (October, 1914), 310–27.

Hipkiss, Edwin J. "Portrait Sculpture by Houdon," *Bulletin of the Museum of Fine Arts* [Boston], Vol. XXXII, No. 193 (October, 1934), 70–74.

Honeywell, Roy J. "President Jefferson and His Successor," *American Historical Review*, Vol. XLVI, No. 1 (October, 1940), 64–75.

Hyde, Henry M. "Baltimore Inn, 100 Years Old, Still Is in Use," *Baltimore Evening Sun*, January 24, 1927.

Jackson, Joseph F. A. "Washington in Philadelphia," *Pennsylvania Magazine of History and Biography*, Vol. LVI, No. 222 (April, 1932), 110–55.

Jones, Edgar D. "Thomas Jefferson and Religion," *Christian Century*, Vol. XLIII, No. 24 (June 17, 1926), 774–75.

Kean, Robert G. "Thomas Jefferson as a Legislator," *Virginia Law Journal*, Vol. XI, (December, 1887), 705–24.

Kilgo, John C. "A Study of Thomas Jefferson's Religious Belief," *Trinity Archive*, Vol. XIII, No. 6 (March, 1900), 331–46. (Hostile to Jefferson. The author was sued for libel by a clergyman. See Josephus Daniels, *Editor in Politics* [Chapel Hill], 1941, 116–19.)

Kimball, Fiske. "Jefferson and the Arts," *Proceedings* of the American Philosophical Society, Vol. LXXXVII, No. 3 (July, 1943), 238–45.

———. "In Search of Jefferson's Birthplace," *Virginia Magazine of History and Biography*, Vol. LI, No. 4 (October, 1943), 313–25.

———. "The Life Portraits of Jefferson and Their Replicas," *Proceed-*

ings of the American Philosophical Society, LXXXVIII, No. 6 (December, 1944), 497–534.

————. "Thomas Jefferson as Architect: Monticello and Shadwell," *The Architectural Quarterly of Harvard University*, Vol. II, No. 4 (June, 1914), 89–137.

Kimball, Marie G. "The Epicure of the White House," *Virginia Quarterly Review*, Vol. IX, No. 1 (January, 1933), 71–81.

————. "The Furnishing of Monticello," *Antiques*, Vol. XII, No. 5 (November, 1927), 380–85; No. 6 (December, 1927), 482–86.

————. "Jefferson in Paris," *North American Review*, Vol. CCXLVIII, No. 1 (Autumn, 1939), 73–86.

————. "Jefferson's Farewell to Romance," *Virginia Quarterly Review*, Vol. IV, No. 3 (July, 1928), 402–19.

————. "Jefferson's Furniture Comes Home to Monticello," *The House Beautiful*, Vol. LXVI, No. 2 (August, 1929), 164–65, 186, 188, 190.

————. "The Original Furnishings of the White House," *Antiques*, Vol. XV, No. 6 (June, 1929), 481–86; Vol. XVI, No. 1 (July, 1929), 33–37.

————. "A Playmate of Thomas Jefferson," *North American Review*, Vol. CCXIII, No. 2 (February, 1921), 145–56.

————. "Thomas Jefferson, Patron of the Arts," *Antiques*, Vol. XLIII, No. 4 (April, 1943), 164–67.

————. "Thomas Jefferson's French Furniture," *Antiques*, Vol. XV, No. 2 (February, 1929), 123–28.

————. "William Short, Jefferson's Only 'Son'," *North American Review*, Vol. CCXXIII, No. 3 (Sept.–Oct.–Nov., 1926), 471–86.

Knoles, George H. "The Religious Ideas of Thomas Jefferson," *Mississippi Valley Historical Review*, Vol. XXX, No. 2 (September, 1943), 187–204.

Latané, John H. "Jefferson's Influence on American Foreign Policy," *University of Virginia Alumni Bulletin* (3rd series), Vol. XVII, No. 3 (July–August, 1924), 245–69.

Lossing, Benson J. "Monticello," *Harper's Monthly Magazine*, Vol. VII, No. 38 (July, 1853), 145–60.

Lucas, Frederic A. "Thomas Jefferson—Palaeontologist," *Natural History*, Vol. XXVI, No. 3 (May–June, 1926), 328–30.

Luther, Frederic N. "Jefferson as a Naturalist," *Magazine of American History*, Vol. XIII, No. 4 (April, 1885), 379–90.

McAdie, Alexander. "A Colonial Weather Service," *Popular Science Monthly*, Vol. XLV, No. 3 (July, 1894), 331–37.

————. "Thomas Jefferson at Home," *Proceedings* of the American Antiquarian Society, n. s. Vol. XL, Part I (April, 1930), 27–46.

Malone, Dumas. "Polly Jefferson and Her Father," *Virginia Quarterly Review*, Vol. VII, No. 1 (January, 1931), 81–95.

Martin, Henry A. "Jefferson as a Vaccinator," *North Carolina Medical Journal*, Vol. VII, No. 1 (January, 1881), 1–34.

Matthews, Albert (ed.). "Journal of William Loughton Smith," Massachusetts Historical Society *Proceedings*, LI (1918), 20–88.

Mayo, Barbara. "Twilight at Monticello," *Virginia Quarterly Review*, Vol. XVII, No. 4 (Autumn, 1941), 502–16.

Merriam, Charles E. "The Political Theory of Jefferson," *Political Science Quarterly*, Vol. XVII, No. 1 (March, 1902), 24–45.

————., and Frank P. Bourgin. "Jefferson as a Planner of Natural Resources," *Ethics*, Vol. LIII, No. 4 (July, 1943), 284–92.

Miller, August C., Jr. "Jefferson as an Agriculturist," *Agricultural History*, Vol. XVI, No. 2 (April, 1942), 65–78.

Morris, Roland S. "Jefferson as a Lawyer," *Proceedings* of the American Philosophical Society, Vol. LXXXVII, No. 3 (July, 1943), 211–15.

Mott, Royden J. "Sources of Jefferson's Ecclesiastical Views," *Church History*, Vol. III, No. 4 (December, 1934), 267–84.

Nicolay, John G. "Thomas Jefferson's Home," *Century Magazine*, Vol. XXXIV, No. 5 (September, 1887), 643–53.

Oliver, John W. "Thomas Jefferson—Scientist," *Scientific Monthly*, Vol. LVI, No. 5 (May, 1943), 460–67.

Osborn, Henry Fairfield. "Thomas Jefferson, the Pioneer of American Palaeontology," *Science*, Vol. LXIX, No. 1790 (April 19, 1929), 410–13.

Parkes, Henry Bamford. "Jeffersonian Democracy," *Symposium*, Vol. IV, No. 3 (July, 1933), 302–23.

Parmelee, Mary P. "Jefferson and His Political Philosophy," *Arena*, Vol. XVIII, No. 95 (October, 1897), 505–16.

Powell, E. P. "Jefferson and Religion," *Open Court*, Vol. X, No. 24 (June 11, 1896), 4943–4945.

Preston, Howard W. "Washington's Visits to Providence," Rhode Island Historical Society *Collections*, Vol. XIX, No. 4 (October, 1926), 97–115.

Proctor, Lucien B. "Jefferson and Marshall," *Albany Law Journal*, Vol. LIX (March 25, 1899), 289–93.

Randolph, Fred J., and Fred L. Francis. "Thomas Jefferson as Meteorologist," *Monthly Weather Review*, Vol. XXIII, No. 12 (December, 1895), 456–58.

Schachner, Nathan. "Jefferson: A Slippery Politician," *American Mercury*, Vol. XLVI, No. 181 (January, 1939), 49–55.

Shapley, Harlow. "Notes on Thomas Jefferson as a Natural Philosopher," *Proceedings* of the American Philosophical Society, Vol. LXXXVII, No. 3 (July, 1943), 234–37.

Smith, Margaret Bayard. "Washington in Jefferson's Time," *Scribner's Magazine*, Vol. XL, No. 3 (September, 1906), 292–310.

Stapley, M. "Thomas Jefferson, the Architect," *Architectural Record*, Vol. XXIX, No. 2 (February, 1911), 177–85.

Stevens, Maud L. "Washington and Newport," *Bulletin of the Newport Historical Society*, No. 84 (July, 1932), 12–16.

Stewart, Robert A. "Jefferson and His Landlord," *The Researcher*, Vol. I, No. 1 (October, 1926), 5–8.

Surface, George T. "Thomas Jefferson: A Pioneer Student of American Geography," *Bulletin* of the American Geographical Society, Vol. XLI, No. 12 (December, 1909), 743–50.

Thomas, Charles S. "Jefferson and the Judiciary," *The Constitutional Review*, Vol. X, No. 2 (April, 1926), 67–76.

Torrence, William Clayton. "Thomas and William Branch of Henrico and Some of Their Descendants," *William and Mary College Quarterly* (1st series), Vol. XXV, No. 2 (October, 1916), 107–16.

True, Katharine M. "The Romantic Voyage of Polly Jefferson," *Harper's Magazine*, Vol. CXXIX, No. 757 (September, 1914), 489–97.

True, Rodney H. "Thomas Jefferson in Relation to Botany," *Scientific Monthly*, Vol. III, No. 4 (October, 1916), 344–60.

———. "Thomas Jefferson's Garden Book," *Proceedings* of the American Philosophical Society, Vol. LXXVI, No. 6 (1936), 939–45.

Ward, James E. "Thomas Jefferson's Contributions to Agriculture," *University of Virginia News Letter*, Vol. XIX, No. 14 (April 15, 1943).

Warren, Charles. "Why Jefferson Abandoned the Presidential Speech in Congress," Massachusetts Historical Society *Proceedings*, Vol. LVII (1924), 123–72.

Wayland, John W. "The Poetical Tastes of Thomas Jefferson," *Sewanee Review*, Vol. XVIII, No. 3 (July, 1910), 283–99.

Whiting, Margaret A. "The Father of Gadgets," *Stone & Webster Journal*, Vol. XLIX, No. 5 (May, 1932), 302–15.

Wilson, Milburn L. "Jefferson, Father of Agricultural Science," United States Department of Agriculture, *Extension Service Review*, Vol. XIV, No. 5 (May, 1943), 74.

———. "Thomas Jefferson—Farmer," *Proceedings* of the American

Philosophical Society, Vol. LXXXVII, No. 3 (July, 1943), 216–22.

Wilson, Woodrow. "Jefferson Day Address," *Princeton Alumni Weekly*, Vol. VI, No. 29 (April 28, 1906), 551–54.

Wilstach, Paul. "Jefferson's Little Mountain," *National Geographic Magazine*, Vol. LV, No. 4 (April, 1929), 481–503.

————. "Thomas Jefferson's Secret Home," *Country Life*, Vol. LIII, No. 6 (April, 1928), 41–43.

Wright, Louis B. "Thomas Jefferson and the Classics," *Proceedings* of the American Philosophical Society, Vol. LXXXVII, No. 3 (July, 1943), 223–33.

Wyman, William I. "Thomas Jefferson and the Patent System," *Journal of the Patent Office Society*, Vol. I, No. 1 (September, 1918), 5–8.

BOOKS

Adams, Henry. *A History of the United States during the Administration of Thomas Jefferson.* New York, 1889–90. 4 vols.

Adams, Herbert. *Thomas Jefferson and the University of Virginia.* Washington, 1888.

Adams, James Truslow. *The Living Jefferson.* New York, 1936.

Adams, Randolph G. "Thomas Jefferson, Librarian," in *Three Americanists*. Philadelphia, 1939. (An excellent account of the sale of Jefferson's library to the government, to form the nucleus of the Library of Congress.)

Ailly, Antoine E. d'. *Historische Gids van Amsterdam.* Amsterdam, 1929.

Almanach Parisien en faveur des étrangers et des personnes curieuses. Paris, 1777.

Ames, Seth. *Works of Fisher Ames.* Boston, 1854. 2 vols.

Arrowood, Charles F. *Thomas Jefferson and Education in a Republic.* New York, 1930.

Austin, James T. *The Life of Elbridge Gerry.* Boston, 1828. 2 vols.

Baker, William S. *Washington after the Revolution.* Philadelphia, 1898.

Baring-Gould, Sabine. *In Troubadour Land: A Ramble in Provence and Languedoc.* London, 1891.

Barry, Joseph. *The Strange Story of Harper's Ferry.* Martinsburg, W. Va., 1903.

————. [Josephus Junior]. *Annals of Harper's Ferry.* Martinsburg, W. Va., 1872. Second Edition.

Bassett, John S. *The Life of Andrew Jackson.* New York, 1911. 2 vols.

Bayles, Richard M. *History of Providence County.* New York, 1891. 2 vols.

Beard, Charles A. *Economic Origins of Jeffersonian Democracy.* New York, 1915.

Bemis, Samuel F. *The American Secretaries of State and Their Diplomacy.* New York, 1927–29. 10 vols.

———. *Jay's Treaty: A Study in Commerce and Diplomacy.* New York, 1923.

Betts, Edwin M., and Hazlehurst B. Perkins. *Thomas Jefferson's Flower Garden at Monticello.* Richmond, 1941.

Biddle, Nicholas. *Eulogium on Thomas Jefferson.* Philadelphia, 1827.

Boutell, Lewis H. *Thomas Jefferson, the Man of Letters.* Chicago, 1891.

Bowen, Clarence W. *The History of the Centennial Celebration of the Inauguration of George Washington as First President of the United States.* New York, 1892.

Bowers, Claude G. *Jefferson and Hamilton.* Boston, 1925.

———. *Jefferson in Power.* Boston, 1936.

———. *The Young Jefferson, 1743–1789.* Boston, 1945.

Brock, Robert A. *The Vestry Book of Henrico Parish.* Richmond, 1874.

Brock, Robert K. *Archibald Cary of Ampthill.* Richmond, 1937.

Brugmans, Hajo. *Opkomst en Bloei van Amsterdam.* Amsterdam, 1911.

Bullock, Helen D. *My Head and My Heart.* New York, 1945.

Caldwell, Lynton K. *The Administrative Theories of Hamilton and Jefferson.* Chicago, 1944.

[Carpenter, Stephen C.] *Memoirs of the Hon. Thomas Jefferson, Secretary of State, Vice-President, and President of the United States; Containing a Concise History of those States, from the Acknowledgement of their Independence. With a View of the Rise and Progress of French Influence and French Principles in that Country. Printed for the purchasers.* [New York], 1809. 2 vols. (This book was withdrawn as libelous. It charges Jefferson with subserviency to France. It even treats the Louisiana Purchase as merely an opportunity to contribute money to the coffers of Bonaparte.)

Carr, Sir John. *A Tour through Holland.* London, 1807.

Chafee, Zechariah, Jr. *Free Speech in the United States.* Cambridge, Mass., 1941.

Chancellor, Edwin Beresford. *The History of the Squares of London.* London, 1907.

Chastellux, François Jean, Marquis de. *Voyages de M. le Marquis de Chastellux dans l'Amérique septentrionale.* Paris, 1786. 2 vols.

Chinard, Gilbert (ed.). *The Commonplace Book of Thomas Jefferson.* Baltimore and Paris, 1926.

————. *The Literary Bible of Thomas Jefferson*. Baltimore and Paris, 1928.

————. *Thomas Jefferson: the Apostle of Americanism*. Boston, 1929.

Christian, W. Asbury. *Richmond, Her Past and Present*. Richmond, 1912.

[Clinton, de Witt.] *A Vindication of Thomas Jefferson; against the Charges Contained in a Pamphlet, Entitled, "Serious Considerations," &c*. By Grotius. New York, 1800.

Collins, V. Lansing. *Princeton Past and Present*. Princeton, 1931.

Coolidge, Harold J. *Thoughts on Thomas Jefferson*. Boston, 1936.

Crofut, Florence S. *Guide to the History and the Historic Sites of Connecticut*. New Haven, 1937. 2 vols.

Crothers, Samuel McChord. *The Religion of Thomas Jefferson*. [Boston, 1926.]

Curtis, William E. *The True Thomas Jefferson*. Philadelphia, 1901.

Danvers, John T. *A Picture of a Republican Magistrate of the New School; Being a Full Length Likeness of His Excellency Thomas Jefferson, President of the United States*. New York, 1808. (A clever political diatribe against Jefferson.)

Davis, John. *Travels of Four Years and a Half in the United States of America*. London, 1803.

Davis, Richard B. *Francis Walker Gilmer: Life and Learning in Jefferson's Virginia*. Richmond, 1939.

Decatur, Stephen. *The Private Affairs of George Washington*. Boston, 1933.

Dexter, Franklin B. *Literary Diary of Ezra Stiles*. New York, 1901. 3 vols.

[Dickins, Asbury.] *The Claims of Thomas Jefferson to the Presidency Examined at the Bar of Christianity*. By a Layman. Philadelphia, 1800.

Dodd, William E. *Thomas Jeffersons Rückkehr zur Politik*. [Leipzig, 1899.]

Dodson, Edward Griffith. *The Capitol of the Commonwealth of Virginia at Richmond*. Richmond, 1937.

Donaldson, Thomas. *The House in Which Thomas Jefferson Wrote the Declaration of Independence*. Philadelphia, 1898.

Dwight, Theodore. *The Character of Thomas Jefferson, as Exhibited in His Own Writings*. Boston, 1839.

Edwards, Everett E. *Jefferson and Agriculture*. Washington, 1943. (U. S. Department of Agriculture, *Agricultural History Series*, No. 7.)

[Evans, Thomas.] *A Series of Letters, Addressed to Thomas Jefferson, Esq. President of the United States, Concerning His Official Conduct and Principles.* Philadelphia, 1802.

Everett, Alexander H. *A Defense of the Character and Principles of Mr. Jefferson.* Boston, 1836.

Frary, Ihna T. *They Built the Capitol.* Richmond, 1940.

———. *Thomas Jefferson, Architect and Builder.* Richmond, 1931.

Freeman, Douglas Southall. *R. E. Lee, A Biography.* New York, 1934–35. 4 vols.

Garlick, Richard C., Jr. *Philip Mazzei, Friend of Jefferson: His Life and Letters.* Baltimore, 1933.

Giacometti, Georges. *Le Statuaire Jean-Antoine Houdon et son Époque.* Paris, 1918–19. 3 vols.

Gilpatrick, Delbert H. *Jeffersonian Democracy in North Carolina.* New York, 1931.

Goldring, Douglas. *The French Riviera and the Valley of the Rhone from Avignon to Marseilles.* New York, 1932.

Gray, Francis Calley. *Thomas Jefferson in 1814.* Boston, 1924.

Griswold, Rufus W. *The Republican Court.* New York, 1856.

Hale, Edward E. *Franklin in France.* Boston, 1888. 2 vols.

Hall, Courtney R. *A Scientist in the Early Republic, Samuel Latham Mitchill, 1764–1831.* New York, 1934.

Halsey, Robert H. *How the President, Thomas Jefferson, and Doctor Benjamin Waterhouse Established Vaccination as a Public Health Procedure.* New York, 1936.

Hamilton, John C. *History of the Republic of the United States of America as Traced in the Writings of Alexander Hamilton and His Contemporaries.* New York, 1857–64. 7 vols.

Harley, Lewis R. *The Life of Charles Thomson.* Philadelphia, 1900.

Hart, Charles Henry, and Edward Biddle. *Memoirs of the Life and Works of Jean Antoine Houdon.* Philadelphia, 1911.

Harvey, Alexander M. *Jefferson and the American Constitution.* [Topeka, Kan., 1926.]

Hassell, John. *Tour of the Isle of Wight.* London, 1790. 2 vols.

Hazelton, John H. *The Declaration of Independence: Its History.* New York, 1906.

Hazen, Charles D. *Contemporary American Opinion of the French Revolution* ("Jefferson in France," 1–53). Baltimore, 1897.

Henderson, John C. *Thomas Jefferson's Views on Public Education.* New York, 1890.

Henkels, Stan[islaus] V. (ed.). [*Catalogue of Hampton L. Carson*]

Collection of Engraved Portraits of Thomas Jefferson, Benjamin Franklin, and Gilbert Motier de La Fayette. [Philadelphia, 1904.]

Honeywell, Roy J. *The Educational Work of Thomas Jefferson.* Cambridge, Mass., 1931. (A comprehensive study of this phase of Jefferson's activities.)

Humphreys, Frank L. *Life and Times of David Humphreys.* New York, 1917. 2 vols.

Isham, Samuel. *The History of American Painting.* New York, 1927. Second Edition.

Jackson, Joseph F. A. *Encyclopedia of Philadelphia.* Harrisburg, Pa., 1931–33. 4 vols.

———. *Literary Landmarks of Philadelphia.* Philadelphia, 1939.

———. *Market Street Philadelphia.* Philadelphia, 1918.

James, Marquis. *Andrew Jackson: Portrait of a President.* Indianapolis, 1937.

Jenkins, Charles Francis. *Washington in Germantown.* Philadelphia, 1905.

Johnson, Allen. *Jefferson and His Colleagues: a Chronicle of the Virginia Dynasty.* New Haven, 1921.

Journals of the Continental Congress. Washington, 1904–37. 34 vols.

Kimball, Fiske. *Thomas Jefferson and the First Monument of the Classical Revival in America.* Harrisburg, Pa., 1915.

———. *Thomas Jefferson, Architect.* Boston, 1916.

Kimball, Marie G. *The Furnishings of Monticello.* [Philadelphia, (?), 1940.]

———. *Jefferson: The Road to Glory.* New York, 1943.

———. *Thomas Jefferson's Cook Book.* Richmond, 1938.

Kite, Elizabeth S. *L'Enfant and Washington.* Baltimore, 1929.

Kleffens, E. N. van. *Juggernaut over Holland.* New York, 1941.

[Knox, Samuel.] *A Vindication of the Religion of Mr. Jefferson, and a Statement of His Services in the Cause of Religious Liberty.* By a friend to Real Religion. Baltimore, [1800.]

Koch, Adrienne. *The Philosophy of Thomas Jefferson.* New York, 1943.

Lambeth, William A. *Thomas Jefferson as an Architect.* Boston, 1913.

Lancaster, Robert A., Jr. *Historic Virginia Homes and Churches.* Philadelphia, 1915.

Lee, Edmund Jennings. *Lee of Virginia.* Philadelphia, 1895.

Lee, Henry. *Observations on the Writings of Thomas Jefferson, with Particular Reference to the Attack They Contain on the Memory of the Late Gen. Henry Lee.* New York, 1832.

Lichtenstein, Gaston. *Thomas Jefferson as War Governor*. Richmond, 1925.

[Linn, William.] *Serious Considerations on the Election of a President: Addressed to the Citizens of the United States*. New York, 1800.

Little, John P. *History of Richmond*. Richmond, 1933. (First published 1851.)

Lossing, Benson J. *The Pictorial Field-Book of the Revolution*. New York, 1851–52. 2 vols.

[Lowell, John.] *The New England Patriot, Being a Candid Comparison of the Principles and Conduct of the Washington and Jefferson Administrations*. Boston, 1810.

Lutz, Earle. *A Richmond Album*. Richmond, 1937.

McKee, George H. *Th. Jefferson Ami de la Révolution française*. Lorient, 1928.

Manning, Warren H. *Thomas Jefferson as a Designer of Landscapes*. Boston, 1913.

Marraro, Howard R. (trans.). *Memoirs of the Life and Peregrinations of the Florentine Philip Mazzei, 1730–1816*. New York, 1942.

[Mason, John Mitchell.] *The Voice of Warning, to Christians, on the Ensuing Election of a President of the United States*. New York, 1800.

Massie, Susanne W., and Frances A. Christian (eds.). *Homes and Gardens in Old Virginia*. Richmond, 1930.

Mayo, Bernard. *Jefferson Himself*. Boston, 1942. (A good life of Jefferson, consisting chiefly of neatly dovetailed extracts from his own writings.)

————. *Thomas Jefferson and His Unknown Brother Randolph*. Charlottesville, Va., 1942.

Merriam, Charles E. *History of American Political Theories*. New York, 1903.

Minnigerode, Meade. *Jefferson, Friend of France*. New York, 1928.

Mitchill, Samuel L. *A Discourse on the Character and Services of Thomas Jefferson, More Especially as a Promoter of Natural and Physical Science*. New York, 1826.

Mordecai, Samuel. *Richmond in By-Gone Days*. Richmond, 1856.

Mott, Frank Luther. *Jefferson and the Press*. Baton Rouge, La., 1943.

New York Historical Society, *Revolutionary Papers*, I (1879).

Nock, Albert J. *Jefferson*. New York, 1926.

Olivier, W. J. *Manuel des Étrangers à Amsterdam*. Amsterdam, 1838.

Padover, Saul. *Jefferson*. New York, 1942.

Parton, James. *Life of Andrew Jackson*. New York, 1860. 3 vols.

————. *Life of Thomas Jefferson*. Boston, 1874.

Patton, John S., and Sallie J. Doswell. *Monticello and Its Master*. Charlottesville, Va., 1925.

Pierson, Hamilton W. *Jefferson at Monticello: the Private Life of Thomas Jefferson*. New York, 1862.

Réception de la statue de Thomas Jefferson troisième Président des États-unis Oeuvre de David d'Angers offerte à la ville d'Angers par Hon. Jefferson M. Levy citoyen américain le samedi 16 septembre 1905. Mesnil, 1905.

Rhodes, Thomas. *The Story of Monticello*. Washington, 1928.

Robinson, William A. *Jeffersonian Democracy in New England*. New Haven, 1916.

Rowland, Kate Mason. *The Life of George Mason*. New York, 1892. 2 vols.

Sadler, Elizabeth H. *The Bloom of Monticello*. Richmond, 1926.

Sale, Edith Tunis (ed.). *Historic Gardens of Virginia*. Richmond, 1923.

————. *Interiors of Virginia Houses of Colonial Times*. Richmond, 1927.

Scharf, John T. *The Chronicles of Baltimore*. Baltimore, 1874.

————. *History of Baltimore City and County*. Philadelphia, 1881.

————, and Thompson Westcott. *History of Philadelphia*. Philadelphia, 1884. 3 vols.

Sears, Louis M. *Jefferson and the Embargo*. Durham, N. C., 1927.

Serious Facts, Opposed to "Serious Considerations," or, the Voice of Warning to Religious Republicans. By Marcus Brutus. October, 1800.

Shepperson, Archibald B. *John Paradise and Lucy Ludwell of London and Williamsburg*. Richmond, 1942. (Jefferson and William Short, as well as Shippen and Rutledge, play a prominent part in this interesting story of the domestic and financial difficulties in which the Paradises were continually involved.)

[Simpson, Lloyd D.] *Notes on Thomas Jefferson by a Citizen of Maryland*. Philadelphia, 1885.

Slicer, Thomas R. "Thomas Jefferson and the Influence of Democracy upon Religion," in *Pioneers of Religious Liberty in America* (161–84), edited by Samuel A. Eliot. Boston, 1903.

Smith, David E. *The Poetry of Mathematics* ("Thomas Jefferson and Mathematics," 49–70). New York, 1934.

Smith, Margaret Bayard. *The First Forty Years of Washington Society*. New York, 1906.

[Smith, William Loughton.] *The Politicks and Views of a Certain Party*,

Displayed. Printed in the year M,DCC,XCII. (Also attributed to Alexander Hamilton.)

———. *The Pretensions of Thomas Jefferson to the Presidency Examined; and the Charges against John Adams Refuted. Addressed to the Citizens of America in General; in Particular to the Electors of the President.* United States [Philadelphia?], October, 1796.

———. *The Pretensions of Thomas Jefferson to the Presidency Examined; and the Charges against John Adams Refuted.* Part the second. United States [Philadelphia?], November, 1796.

Smyth, Clifford. *Thomas Jefferson the Father of American Democracy.* New York, 1931.

Sparks, Jared. *Memoirs of the Life and Travels of John Ledyard.* London, 1828.

Stanard, Mary Newton. *Richmond, Its People and Its Story.* Philadelphia, 1923.

Staples, William R. *Annals of the Town of Providence.* Providence, 1843.

Stokes, Isaac Newton Phelps. *The Iconography of Manhattan Island.* New York, 1915–28. 6 vols.

Thomas, Elbert D. *Thomas Jefferson: World Citizen.* New York, 1942.

Tompkins, Edmund P., and J. Lee Davis. *The Natural Bridge and Its Historical Surroundings.* Natural Bridge, Va., 1939.

Townsend, George A. *Monticello and Its Preservation Since Jefferson's Death.* Washington, 1902.

Tucker, George. *The Life of Thomas Jefferson.* Philadelphia, 1837. 2 vols.

Tyler, Lyon G. *The Letters and Times of the Tylers.* Richmond, 1884. 2 vols.

———. *Williamsburg, The Old Colonial Capital.* Richmond, 1907.

Tyler, Moses C. *The Literary History of the American Revolution.* New York, 1897–98. 2 vols.

Ulmann, Albert. *A Landmark History of New York.* New York, 1939.

United States Constitution Sesquicentennial Commission, *Loan Exhibition of Portraits.* Washington, 1937.

Warren, Charles. *Odd Byways in American History.* Cambridge, Mass., 1942.

———. *The Supreme Court in United States History.* Boston, 1922.

Watson, John F. *Annals of Philadelphia and Pennsylvania in the Olden Time.* Philadelphia, 1844. 2 vols.

Weddell, Alexander W. *Richmond, Virginia, in Old Prints.* Richmond, 1932.

Wehle, Harry B. *American Miniatures 1730–1850*. Garden City, 1927.

Wells, William V. *The Life and Public Services of Samuel Adams*. Boston, 1865. 3 vols.

Westcott, Thompson. *The Historic Mansions and Buildings of Philadelphia*. Philadelphia, 1877.

——. *A History of Philadelphia*. Philadelphia, 1867–84. 5 vols. (Scrapbooks of articles from the Philadelphia *Sunday Dispatch* in Hist. Soc. of Pa. library.)

Whately, Thomas. *Observations on Modern Gardening*. London, 1777. Fourth Edition.

Williams, John Sharp. *Thomas Jefferson: His Permanent Influence on American Institutions*. New York, 1913.

Williamson, George C. *Richard Cosway, R. A.* London, 1905.

Wilson, Charles M. *Meriwether Lewis*. New York, 1934.

Wilson, Woodrow. *Mere Literature* ("A Calendar of Great Americans," 187–212). Boston, 1896.

Wilstach, Paul. *Jefferson and Monticello*. New York, 1925.

Wiltse, Charles M. *The Jeffersonian Tradition in American Democracy*. Chapel Hill, N. C., 1935.

Winter, Pieter Jan van. *Het aandeel van den Amsterdamschen handel aan den opbouw van het Amerikaansche gemeenebest*. The Hague, 1927–33. 2 vols.

Wolfe, John H. *Jeffersonian Democracy in South Carolina*. Chapel Hill, N. C., 1940.

Woodfin, Maude H. "Contemporary Opinion in Virginia of Thomas Jefferson," in *Essays in Honor of William E. Dodd,* edited by Avery Craven, 30–83. Chicago, 1935.

Woolery, William K. *The Relation of Thomas Jefferson to American Foreign Policy 1783–1793*. Baltimore, 1927.

[Wortman, Tunis.] *A Solemn Address to the Christians and Patriots upon the Approaching Election of a President of the United States, in Answer to a Pamphlet entitled "Serious Considerations"* etc. New York [1800.]

Writers' Project, Virginia. *Virginia, A Guide to the Old Dominion*. New York, 1940.

Young, Arthur. *Travels in France*. London, 1892. Fourth Edition.

Index

✿

THOMAS JEFFERSON
AMERICAN TOURIST

HAS BEEN SET ON THE LINOTYPE IN

THE CASLON OLD FACE TYPES

AND PRINTED ON WOVE

ANTIQUE PAPER

UNIVERSITY OF

OKLAHOMA PRESS

NORMAN